FIFTH EDITION

RECORDS
MANAGEMENT

Norman F. Kallaus

Professor of Business Administration
The University of Iowa
Iowa City, Iowa

Mina M. Johnson

Professor of Business Emeritus
San Francisco State University

CONTRIBUTING AUTHORS:

Judith Read Smith

Instructor of Business and
Office Administration
Portland Community College
Cascade Campus

Karen Van Dyke

Assistant Professor of
Business Education
St. Louis Community College
St. Louis, Missouri

KG40EA
PUBLISHED BY
SOUTH-WESTERN PUBLISHING CO.
CINCINNATI, OH   DALLAS, TX

Acquisitions Editor:	Karen Schneiter
Developmental Editor:	Penny Shank
Consulting Editor:	Mary Lea Ginn
Production Editor:	Alan Biondi
Associate Editors:	Laurie Winget
	Tom Lewis
Designer:	Elaine St. John-Lagenaur
Production Artists:	Steve McMahon
	Rick Moore
Associate Photo Editor/Stylist:	Mike O'Donnell

Copyright © 1992

by South-Western Publishing Co.
Cincinnati, Ohio

ISBN: 0-538-70335-0

Library of Congress Catalog Card Number: 90-62768

2 3 4 5 6 7 8 9 Ki 9 8 7 6 5 4 3 2

Printed in the United States of America

Cover Photo: © DIGITAL ART/Westlight

PREFACE

RECORDS MANAGEMENT, Fifth Edition, continues the strong tradition of serving as a basic introduction to the increasingly comprehensive field of records management. As such, the fifth edition emphasizes principles and practices of effective records management for manual and automated records systems. This approach offers practical information to students as well as to professionals at managerial, supervisory, and operating levels.

The experiences and basic philosophies of the authors are clearly presented in this latest revision. Emphasis is placed on the need to understand the record life cycle within which information functions in the organization. Because the operations of all records systems—manual and automated—rely on basic storage and retrieval rules, the authors stress the overall importance of understanding how paper records systems function before undertaking the more complex task of studying automated records systems.

As a text for students in postsecondary institutions, RECORDS MANAGEMENT, Fifth Edition, may be used for short courses or seminars emphasizing filing systems or longer courses, such as quarter or semester plans. Basic manual systems concepts are discussed, and database concepts needed for understanding automated records storage and retrieval methods are introduced. In addition, this edition updates other aspects of information technology, such as computer and word processing systems, microimage systems, and optical disks, which are having an increased impact on the records management field.

As a reference book, this latest edition of RECORDS MANAGEMENT serves several purposes. It presents sound principles of records management that include the entire range of records—paper, microimage records, and magnetic and optical disk media used in automated systems. While the key management functions as they relate to records management are introduced, emphasis is placed upon control for ensuring that the records system achieves its stated goals. Professionals who direct the operation of records systems will find this fifth edition to be especially valuable because it includes new alphabetic indexing rules that agree with the simplified filing rules of the Association for Records Managers and Administrators, Inc.

Organization of Text

The text consists of 5 parts organized into 12 chapters and 2 Appendixes. Part l introduces the student to the expanding area of records management. Following this overview, Part 2 centers on alphabetic storage and retrieval methods for manual and computer database systems. Part 3 presents a detailed description of adaptations of the alphabetic storage and retrieval method; namely, subject, numeric, and geographic storage methods.

Part 4 covers information technology, which includes a thorough update of microimage systems and the emerging technology that integrates the computer with other automated records systems. This part also stresses the continuing need to understand basic records management principles before delving into the complexities of automated systems. To complete the textbook from a management perspective, Part 5 offers a comprehensive view of the role of control in records systems. In addition, it reviews many practical procedures for controlling paperwork problems in both large and small offices. New features of the fifth edition are the appendixes that cover career opportunities and job descriptions in records management (Appendix A) and card and special records commonly used in the office (Appendix B).

Goals for the student are included at the beginning of each chapter in the new fifth edition. Important terms are printed in bold type throughout each chapter and are listed alphabetically at the end of each chapter for easy review. In the Glossary at the back of the textbook, these same terms are defined. New questions for review and discussion and a new Applications section, which presents short practical cases for solution, are also provided at the end of each chapter.

Manual/Computer Practice Set

The filing practice set that accompanies RECORDS MANAGEMENT, entitled RECORDS MANAGEMENT PROJECTS, Fifth Edition, is substantially revised and includes computer applications. This set of practical learning materials consists of 12 manual filing jobs in which students practice card filing and correspondence filing in alphabetic, subject, consecutive numeric, terminal-digit numeric, and geographic filing systems. In addition, students will practice requisition/charge-out and transfer procedures.

Computer applications using PC-File+, Version 3.0, are an important addition to RECORDS MANAGEMENT PROJECTS, Fifth Edition. Students will apply the alphabetic indexing rules to a computer records database after achieving a thorough understanding of manual filing. Ten optional computer filing jobs are provided.

Study Guide

Another new feature of the fifth edition learning materials package is the study guide, which is designed to reinforce the material covered in the textbook. In the study guide we include reviews of important terms, sample test questions, and a host of practical activities to supplement the textbook exercises assigned by the instructor.

Videotape

With the fifth edition, a videotape covering active filing and special records equipment, image technology, and inactive records centers is available to bring the real-world office setting into the classroom.

Transparencies

An important new feature of this fifth edition is the set of two-color acetate transparencies. These transparencies will provide additional teaching tools for classroom use. Suggestions for their use are included in the manual.

Testing Package

The testing package that accompanies RECORDS MANAGEMENT, Fifth Edition, includes a Placement Test, four Achievement Tests, and a Final Examination. Both paper and computerized forms of the tests are available for class use.

Instructor's Manual

The instructor's manual that accompanies RECORDS MANAGE-MENT, Fifth Edition, provides instructors with suggested methods of instruction, teaching aids, suggested readings, a listing of professional associations, and time schedules that apply to different teaching situations. Teaching suggestions are also provided for each chapter as well as the answers to the review and discussion questions, solutions to the end-of-chapter Applications, and the Checking Your

Knowledge of the Rules activities that appear in Chapters 2 and 3. Detailed solutions for all of the practice set jobs are also included in the instructor's manual, in addition to the finding tests to be used with the practice set and their solutions. Answers to the Placement, Achievement, and Final tests are also provided.

The authors are grateful to many firms and individuals who assisted in completing this extensive revision of RECORDS MANAGEMENT. Further, we appreciate the help of the filing equipment and supplies manufacturers and vendors who gave time and information to the authors in their efforts to update this edition effectively.

The authors are especially grateful to the following individuals who served as contributing authors on this edition: Judy Read Smith—Portland Community College, Cascade Campus, Portland, Oregon; and Karen Van Dyke—St. Louis Community College at Forest Park, St. Louis, Missouri.

Special thanks are given to the following people whose critical reviews provided helpful guidance to the authors: Liz Dickerman—Eastern New Mexico University, Portales, New Mexico; Jeanette Dostourian—Cypress College, Cypress, California; Melba Herrick—Chesapeake College, Wye Mills, Maryland; Terry Horn—Chemeketa Community College, Salem, Oregon; Ken Howey—York Technical College, Rock Hill, South Carolina; and Janet Miller—Rend Lake College, Ina, Illinois.

In addition, special appreciation is extended to our families, friends, and each other whose encouragement and direction have been invaluable in completing this revision. The result, we believe, is an easily understandable, instructive, up-to-date introduction to the field of records management.

Norman F. Kallaus
Mina M. Johnson

CONTENTS

1

The Field of Records Management

1 ■ An Overview of Records Management

Part 1 introduces you to the field of records management and to the nature and purpose of records. Also, this first Part includes a concise treatment of records management history and key legislation important to the effective operation of modern business firms. A highlight of the Part is the discussion of records management as a key organizational function and the growing career opportunities available in the field.

1 AN OVERVIEW OF RECORDS MANAGEMENT

GOALS

After completing this chapter, you will be able to:

1. Define *record, records management,* and other related terms.
2. Describe the classifications of records found in an office.
3. State why records are used and give examples of records commonly used.
4. Name two laws important to your role as a citizen and office worker in today's society and state why they are important.
5. Describe the management functions necessary to operate a records management program effectively.
6. List the stages in the life cycle of a record and describe the activities in each stage.
7. Describe common problems found in records systems.
8. State why paper records continue to be used widely in records systems.
9. Identify three levels of records management positions and common job titles associated with each level.

In most jobs today we make increasing use of information. We frequently refer to this time in our history as the *Information Age;* we often call this generation the *Information Society.* Computers, so much a part of today's world, are called *information-processing machines* because of their key role in information systems. In order to survive, businesses and organizations must have up-to-date *information* in the *right form,* at the *right time,* in the *right place* to make management decisions. Finally, all of us use information minute by minute to manage our lives and perform our jobs.

Generally, we store information on records of various types; and, in turn, we organize records into complex systems. As we rely more

Information is a valuable business resource.

and more on information, we need greater numbers of records. Like all other office "products," records must be properly managed. In this overview chapter, you are introduced to important records management terms and concepts and to a brief history of records and legislation to control them. You will also learn about the content of records management programs and a wide range of career opportunities in this growing field. Keep in mind that in this textbook we will deal with records in business firms; however, the principles you learn should also help you understand how to use records efficiently in other types of organizations, including your home.

RECORDS: CLASSIFICATION AND USE

As you begin a study of records management, several basic concepts need to be understood. These concepts include definitions of key terms, classifications of records, and reasons why records are used and will continue to be used by all of us throughout our lives. As you study each of these concepts, relate them to your own personal situation as well as to your job, if you are now employed. By doing so, you will learn more quickly and retain better what you will need for future work in the office.

Let's define a **record** as recorded information, regardless of media or characteristics, made or received by, and used in the operation of, an organization. All of us easily recognize the most common records such as correspondence (letters and memorandums), reports, forms, and books, all of which are written and usually appear on paper. But also consider *oral records* that capture the human voice and appear on cassettes and other magnetic media. Less obvious are records that appear on film, such as movies, videotapes, photographs, and microfilm. Even less obvious are the records produced by the computer and on optical disk, which are discussed in Chapter 10. Figure 1-1 on the next page shows three record forms familiar to most of us.

Records appear in many forms.

Records are valuable property, or resources, of a firm; and, like all other resources, they must be properly managed. **Records management** is the systematic control of all records from the time they are created, or received, through their processing, distribution, organization, storage, and retrieval to their ultimate disposition.

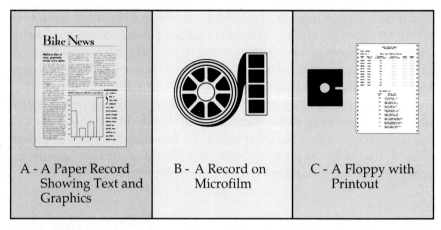

| A - A Paper Record Showing Text and Graphics | B - A Record on Microfilm | C - A Floppy with Printout |

Figure 1-1 ■ Common Record Forms

How Records Are Classified

We classify records in many ways.

Usually we classify records in three basic ways: (1) by the type of *use*, (2) by the *place where they are used*, and (3) by the *value* of the records to the firm. We discuss briefly each of these classifications in this section.

Classification by Use. Classification according to records use includes transaction documents and reference documents. **Transaction documents** are records of a firm's day-to-day operations. These documents consist primarily of business forms. Examples are invoices, requisitions, purchase and sales orders, bank checks, statements, contracts, shipping documents, and personnel records such as employment applications and attendance reports. **Reference documents**, on the other hand, contain information needed to carry on the operations of the firm over long periods of time. We refer to such records for information about previous decisions, quotations on items to purchase, statements of administrative policy, and plans for running the firm. Common reference documents, the most common and largest category of records maintained in an office, are business letters, reports, and interoffice memorandums. Other examples include catalogs, price lists, brochures, and pamphlets.

Classification by Place of Use. Classification by *place of use* of the records refers to external and internal records. We create an **external**

record for use outside the firm. Examples of such records are letters sent to a customer or client, to an organization's suppliers, or to the various branches of the government. The larger group of records classified by their place of use is that of internal records. We use an **internal record** to store information needed to operate the firm. Such a record may be created inside or outside the business. Examples are communications between the firm and its employees (payroll records, bulletins, and government regulations) and communications among a firm's departments (inventory control records, interoffice memorandums, purchase requisitions, and reports). Very important internal records are maintained by the accounting department regarding the presence and use of assets and liabilities owed and local, state, and federal tax information.

Classification by Value of the Record to the Firm. From an inventory and analysis of the use of each major record, a manager determines the *value of the record* to the firm. Then, on the basis of this evaluation, a program is developed for retaining (keeping on file) all key records in the firm. The retention of records is an important part of a records management program and is discussed in Chapters 7 and 12.

Each record maintained by a firm falls into one of the four categories that tell us *how long the records should be retained*. These categories are (1) vital, (2) important, (3) useful, and (4) nonessential.

Vital records must be kept permanently because they are needed for continuing the operations of the firm and are usually not replaceable. Legal papers, such as articles of incorporation, reports to shareholders, titles to property owned by the firm, and minutes of important meetings are vital records. **Important records** assist in performing the firm's business operations and if destroyed are replaceable only at great cost. Accounts receivable and sales records, financial and tax records, and selected correspondence and reports are important records. **Useful records** are helpful in conducting business operations and may, if destroyed, be replaced at slight cost. General correspondence (letters and memorandums) and bank statements are useful records that may be destroyed after their value has passed. The least valuable records are the **nonessential records** that should be destroyed after use. Examples of nonessential records are announcements and bulletins to employees, acknowledgments, and

Keep records that have value.

notices of routine telephone messages that are later confirmed by letter.

Why Records Are Used

Records serve as the "memory" of a business. They "remember" the information needed for operating the firm. For example, we develop and record management policies in order to furnish broad guidelines for operating a business. Each department (for example, finance, marketing, accounting, and human resources) bases its entire method of operations upon records. Usually we find that records are used because they have one or more of the following values to the firm:

1. *Administrative value*, in that they help employees perform office operations within the firm. Examples of such records include policy and procedures manuals and handbooks, organization charts, and major contracts.
2. *Fiscal value*, because records can document operating funds or serve tax audit purposes. Examples of this type of record include tax returns, records of financial transactions such as purchase and sales orders, invoices, balance sheets, and income statements.
3. *Legal value*, because they provide evidence of business transactions. Examples of such records include contracts, financial agreements, and deeds to property owned.
4. *Historical value*, because they furnish a record of the organization's operations and major shifts of direction over the years. Minutes of meetings, the corporate charter, public relations documents, and information on corporate officers all fall into this records category. In addition, the value of many records increases with the passage of time. Original copies of the Declaration of Independence and the Gettysburg Address are well-known examples, as is the original drawing of Ford's first Model T automobile.

Aren't your personal records similar to those used in business?

From a personal standpoint, why do you keep a copy of your diploma, your birth certificate, the title of ownership to your automobile, or the promissory note that provided you with the money to attend college? And why do we protect our prescriptions for drugs, our latest blood pressure and cholesterol readings, and social security information? The answer is simple: *In today's complex world, we cannot get along without them! We need them for the information they contain.*

RECORDS MANAGEMENT HISTORY AND LEGISLATION

When we visit museums in our country or in ancient civilizations, such as those in Greece and Turkey, we find many examples of early records. Examples are religious scrolls, documents proclaiming control over conquered people, and hieroglyphics describing early life-styles. Carvings on the walls of caves in Latin America tell us about the lives of early inhabitants and how they conducted their business affairs. Tours of early Native American dwellings in the western states give us similar examples or records of early life in their tribes. In our own age, computerized records provide information about our population and the way businesses operate. In comparing the records of earlier periods in history with those of the present age, we find that records and attitudes toward records have changed.

Early Records

Most of the business records before 1600 were based upon simple transactions and provided evidence of moneys received and spent, lists of articles bought and sold, and simple contracts. Such records were created by hand (that is, *manually*) until the printing press and later the typewriter were invented. These machines increased the speed by which records are created and processed.

Until the 1950s, when computers were first used in business, records were almost entirely paper documents. The most important emphasis during this stage in history was getting the records properly placed in the files. Emphasis on retrieval surfaced later (see Figure 1-2 on the next page).

Early offices stressed orderly filing of records.

Before World War II, management directed its main effort toward the factory or plant. Usually the plant work force was large compared with the office staff. Thus, managers generally gave their main attention to the factory because the factory produced the tangible products from which profits came and against which expenses were charged. In such a setting, management assumed that records should be the sole responsibility of the office staff. Little importance or status was granted to the records function in early business firms.

Figure 1-2 ■ Retrieving Records Stored in a Computer

Modern Records

World War II caused many changes in society and in the economies of the world. During this time a highly productive industrial system was in operation with new government regulations that required large volumes of records. The federal government recognized the need for controlling the volume of records created both during and after the war. In 1946, President Truman appointed the first Hoover Commission to study the policies and records needs of the federal government. The Commission's work was responsible for establishing the General Services Administration (GSA) to improve government practices and controls in records management.

The federal government began the first records management program.

Later, a second Hoover Commission found that many reports required of business and industry were already available in other government agencies. Also, large numbers of records were submitted to government by industry, but (surprisingly) many were never used. As a result, the second Hoover Commission in 1955 concluded that there was a critical, continuing need for the management of governmental records. A government-wide records management program was then created under the direction of the GSA to oversee the reduction of paperwork in each government agency.

The federal government's pioneer studies in records management were widely acclaimed. They provided the example and motivation needed by business, industry, and lower levels of government to study the need for records and for setting up programs for their management. Since the earlier studies, the federal government's concern for properly using and controlling information has continued with the passage of important records legislation. Significant examples of federal legislation affecting records are presented in the next section.

Federal Laws for Controlling Records

As information and records systems increase by leaps and bounds, so too does legislation to protect information and records. In the aftermath of the Watergate problems of the early 1970s, which stemmed in part from the lack of control of records, new federal legislation was passed by Congress. Two laws have special meaning to you as you prepare for a career in office and records management. Both laws aim to protect individuals against the misuse of filed information.

Federal laws help us manage records.

The Freedom of Information Act of 1966 gives you the right to see information about yourself. Thus, you may request records kept by private and public organizations, such as medical offices, hospitals, dental clinics, law offices, government agencies, counseling clinics, banks, and the human resources (personnel) departments in business firms. You may have access to such records after obtaining permission from the organization that has this information on file.

The Privacy Act of 1974 (with later amendments) gives you the right to exclude others from seeing your files without your consent, as well as the right to know who has had access to your records. Many states have passed additional legislation aimed at protecting the files of individuals. The magnitude of this privacy problem is illustrated by these facts about yourself, a typical United States citizen:

1. The federal government has about 18 separate files on you. Your own state government has an additional dozen files.
2. The Internal Revenue Service knows how much money you make and where it comes from.

It's difficult to maintain privacy with automation.

3. The Social Security Administration knows more than you do about your earnings.
4. At least one credit bureau keeps files on you.[1]

As you continue your studies in records management, you need to understand other legislation affecting the control of records.

Of special relevance to this field are: (1) the Federal Records Act of 1950 and its later amendments, (2) the Copyright Act of 1976, (3) the Right to Financial Privacy Act of 1978, (4) the Paperwork Reduction Act of l980, (5) the Video Privacy Act of 1988, and (6) the Computer Matching and Privacy Protection Act of l988. Also, the Fair Credit Reporting Act allows bureau members controlled access to credit- and tenant-bureau files.

As an office worker responsible for company files, you need to know the rights of people asking to see the files. You also need to maintain control over the files, such as by recording the names of persons who have read the files. Some firms maintain much confidential information and develop lists of individuals who may see such files. For all other persons, such files are off limits.

RECORDS MANAGEMENT: A KEY ORGANIZATIONAL FUNCTION

Many people think that they know what management is. To them, it's simply *what managers do!* However, if we look carefully at the process of management, we see a basic set of activities that **all of us— managers and nonmanagers alike**—*do.* This means that *all of us use the management process and thus are managers to some degree.* The question we must answer, then, is What is management?

The Process of Management

Management is the process of using an organization's resources to achieve specific goals through the functions of planning, organizing, leading, and controlling.

Management consists of four basic functions.

Planning involves establishing goals or objectives and the methods required to achieve them. With the firm's goals in mind, *organizing* takes place, a step that calls for arranging the tasks, people,

---

[1]Morton C. Paulson, "Someone's Got a File on You," *Changing Times*, July, 1989, pp. 41-42.

and other resources needed to meet the goals set in the planning stage. *Leading* refers to managerial behavior (such as training, supervising, and motivating) that supports the achievement of an organization's goals. Finally, *controlling* means measuring how well the goals have been met.

Keep these four functions in mind when you study the management of records. Also, observe how you are a manager because you, too, perform these steps when you manage your study time, your money, and your social and professional life. Now, can't you see why we made the claim earlier that all people are managers?

The Life Cycle of Records

As a manager, you must see the whole picture, which involves understanding the four managerial functions discussed earlier and how each relates to the other. In the same way, the person responsible for managing records must clearly understand the stages making up the life cycle of a record.

Each record has a life span. As Figure 1-3 shows, the **record life cycle** involves five functional phases that occur from the creation of a record to its final disposition. Note how this cycle is carried out when

Like people, records have a life cycle.

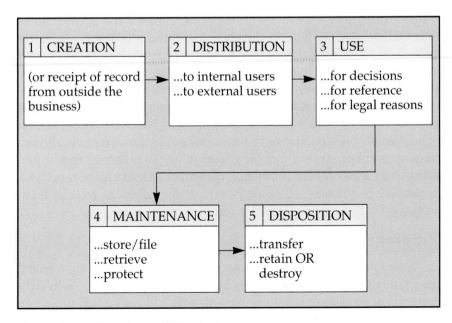

Figure 1-3 ■ The Record Life Cycle

we examine common records. Whenever a letter is typed, a form filled out, a cassette tape dictated, or a pamphlet printed, a record is *created*. This record is then *distributed* (sent) to the person responsible for its *use*. Records are commonly used in decision making, for documentation or reference, in answering inquiries, or in satisfying legal requirements.

When a decision is made to keep the record for use at a later date, records must be stored, retrieved, and protected—three key steps in the *maintenance* of records. During this phase, the records must be *stored* (filed), which involves preparing and placing records into their proper storage places. After a record is stored, a request is made to *retrieve* (find and remove) the record from storage for *use*. And once the retrieved record is no longer needed for active use, it may be *re-stored* and *protected* using appropriate equipment and environmental and human controls to ensure the security of the record. Also involved in the maintenance phase are such activities as updating stored information and purging or throwing away obsolete records that are no longer useful or that have been replaced by more current ones.

The last phase in the record life cycle is *disposition*. After a predetermined period of time has elapsed, records to be kept are *transferred* to less expensive storage sites within the firm or to an external storage center. At the end of a stated number of years, the records are *disposed of*, either by destruction or transfer to a permanent storage place, called the **archives**. The basis for disposition of records is the records retention schedule discussed in Chapter 12.

Filing is *not* records management.

The record life cycle is an important concept for you to understand. It shows, for example, that *filing is but one phase of records management*. Thus, there is much more to an effective records management program than filing. Knowing the meaning and importance of the *entire* record life cycle, you will be able to understand what is needed to manage all records—those on paper as well as those stored on other media such as microfilm or magnetic media.

Programs for Managing Records

As mentioned earlier, to manage records we must set up a record program that includes all stages in the record life cycle. While the contents of records management programs will vary, such programs generally have these features:

1. *Well-defined goals that are understood by all workers.* Figure 1-4 outlines six common goals of successful records management programs.

GOALS OF THE RECORDS MANAGEMENT PROGRAM AT THE XYZ COMPANY

1. To provide *accurate, timely information* whenever and wherever it is needed.

2. To provide information at the *lowest possible cost.*

3. To provide the *most efficient records systems*, including space, equipment, and procedures for creating, storing, retrieving, retaining, transferring, and disposing of records.

4. To *protect information* by designing and implementing effective measures for records control.

5. To determine *methods for evaluating* all phases of the records management program.

6. To *train company personnel* in the most effective methods of controlling and using records.

Figure 1-4 ■ Goals of a Records Management Program

2. *A simple, sound organizational plan.* Sometimes, the program is *centralized* (physically located and controlled in one area); in other cases, it is *decentralized* (with the physical location of storage in departments where records are created and used). Each plan offers advantages and disadvantages that managers should consider carefully before deciding on an organizational plan (see Figure 1-5 on the next page). In large firms where work can be specialized, records management is closely tied in with computers, word processing, and other information systems, as shown in Figure 1-6 on the next page.

3. *Efficient procedures for managing each of the five stages in the record life cycle* that were shown in Figure 1-3. We will study these procedures in detail in Chapter 12.

4. *A well-trained staff* as discussed later in this chapter.

Figure 1-5 ■ Choosing an Organizational Plan

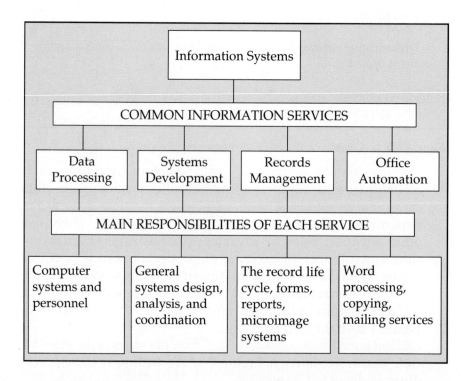

Figure 1-6 ■ Location of Records Management in a Large Organization

Problems in Records Systems

The programs for managing records discussed earlier achieve their goals through the operation of an organization's records system. In this sense, a **records system** is a group of interrelated resources — people, equipment and supplies, space, procedures, and information — acting together according to a plan to accomplish the goals of the records management program. Anything that interferes with the operation of one or more of these resources either individually or in combination creates a problem in the records system and hence hinders the effectiveness of the records management program.

A records system is a group of interrelated resources.

Common problems in records systems and typical symptoms of such problems include:

1. Management problems	No overall plan for managing records
	No plan for retaining or destroying records
	No standards for evaluating workers
2. Human problems	Lack of concern about the importance of records
	Hoarding of records
	Assuming that people know how to operate the files
3. Inefficient filing procedures	Overloaded and poorly labeled drawers and folders
	Failure to protect records
	Misfiles resulting in lost records or slow retrieval
	Records taken from and placed in files without proper authorization
4. Poor use of equipment	No equipment standards
	No use of fire-resistant equipment
	Wrong type of cabinets for records being used
	Poor, or no, use of automated systems

5. Inefficient use of space   Crowded working conditions
                                      Poor layout of storage area
                                      Inadequate use, or absence, of
                                      microfilmed records

6. Excessive records costs   Created because of all the above
                                      problems

To resolve such problems, managers turn to various forms of information technology. Microfilm use is increasing in offices throughout the world, and computers are being used more and more in all settings including the home, office, and factory. From the constant publicity about the so-called "computer takeover," we might assume that paper records—along with file cabinets, folders, and other aspects of traditional records systems and procedures—are out of date.

The "paperless" office, however, is far more fiction than fact. What is true, on the other hand, is that the number of noncomputer records (largely paper records) is growing. Look at the findings of two recent studies regarding two highly important problem areas for the office that affect the *volume* and *cost* of records:

Paper remains the most common records storage medium.

1. *About 95 percent of all office data is stored on paper, 4 percent on microfilm, and the remaining 1 percent on other storage media (largely in computer systems)*. By 1996, paper storage may decrease to 85 percent.[2] (A key point to remember, then, is that we work in offices that are, and will contiinue to be, mainly paper-based.)

2. *About 35 percent of all files are never used, and 95 percent are never used after the first year*. Also, studies show that 1-5 percent of all records are misfiled, and that the average cost of a misfiled record is between $80 and $100.[3]

3. One records specialist estimates that, on a typical workday, United States businesses generate 600 million pages of computer output, 235 million photocopies, and 76 million letters. These documents are multiplying at an annual rate of between 20 and 22 percent. At this rate the amount of stored information could double every four years. During this same typical workday, the

[2]Whitney S. Minkler, "An Objective Overview of Digital Imaging (Optical Disk) Systems Procurements," *Records Management Quarterly*, October, 1988, p. 7.

[3]David Barcomb, *Office Automation: A Survey of Tools and Technology*, Digital Press, Bedford, MA, 1989, p. 142.

file cabinets across the country store an estimated 21 trillion pages, or about one carton of paper for every person on earth.[4]   At present, we have doubtless exceeded that rate.

The computer is not currently capable of automating all typing, sorting, storing, and retrieving tasks. In fact, experts estimate that nearly two-thirds of all business information used in the nation's offices cannot be read by the computer. This type of information is handwritten on typed forms, or on microfilm; it remains on desks, in storage cabinets, and behind vault doors.

Because the majority of business records systems are paper-based, and also because the computers cannot handle many paper-systems problems, *the paper records system is the place to begin a study of records management*. The tangible nature of such records, the fact that paper records are familiar to each of you, and that such records can be easily located make the study of paper records the logical introduction to the records management field. From such study, you need to understand alphabetic storage and retrieval systems discussed in Part Two along with subject, numeric, and geographic storage and retrieval systems explained in Part Three.

Because our world depends more and more on the use of computers and microimage records, you should find the chapters in Part Four of special interest. And the concept of control—control of all aspects of a records management program—is explained in detail in Part Five. Additional information—on career opportunities and job descriptions as well as on card and special records—is available in the Appendixes.

CAREER OPPORTUNITIES IN RECORDS MANAGEMENT

Opportunities to work with records exist in every type and size of office. In the smallest office with one secretary and an owner/manager, working with records occupies much of the time of both people. In this setting, opportunities for records work are unlimited. Check the classified ads section of all daily newspapers for lists of many positions of this type.

---

[4]Barcomb, p. 5.

In larger offices with a more specialized staff, firms often employ records supervisors who direct the work of several records clerks. And in major corporations or other large administrative headquarters, such as the City Hall in major cities, you can find the following three levels of records workers as shown in Figure 1-7:

1. *Managerial level*, where the top position is the records manager who is responsible for directing the entire program discussed in Chapter 12.

Many opportunities for careers await you in records management.

2. *Supervisory level*, which includes specialists responsible for operating the records center, supervising the use of business forms, and directing the use of microfilm records.

3. *Operating level*, which includes those workers responsible for routine filing and retrieving tasks, and assisting with vital records and records retention work. Because this is the level of work emphasized in this textbook, we shall concentrate on the basic principles involved in storing and retrieving paper records.

See Appendix A for more detailed information on career paths in records management as well as job descriptions for positions in this field.

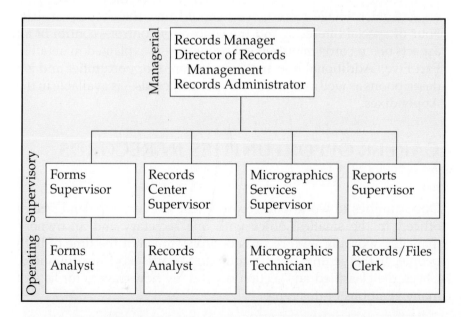

Figure 1-7 ■ Typical Job Levels and Job Titles in Records Management

You can easily locate information on this rapidly growing profession by checking the regular publications of the various professional associations specializing in administrative work. The Association of Records Managers and Administrators, Inc. (ARMA) is the most important professional group interested in improving educational programs in schools and industry and providing on-the-job knowledge about records management.

Information on career opportunities can be found regularly in ARMA's *Records Management Quarterly*, in the *Dictionary of Occupational Titles*, and in the *Occupational Outlook Handbook*. Other professional associations, such as the Administrative Management Society (AMS), the Association of Information and Image Management (AIIM), and the American Medical Records Association (AMRA), publish periodicals that contain information about career trends in records management. You can find copies of such publications in college, university, and city libraries.

As our country moves to a service economy based on information technology, many opportunities will appear for careers including management positions in information systems. Records management, which is a subspecialty of information systems, is growing in size and importance and offers a challenging future in the world of work.

IMPORTANT TERMS

archives	record life cycle
external record	records management
important records	records system
internal record	reference documents
management	transaction documents
nonessential records	useful records
record	vital records

REVIEW AND DISCUSSION

1. In your own words, define the terms *record* and *records management*. Discuss what you would have to do with your personal copies of course grade records if you wanted such records to be properly managed. (Goal 1)
2. What are the main classifications for records? What types of records are commonly found in each classification? (Goal 2)

3. Bring to class five examples of business records. Classify them in as many ways as possible. How can you fit your classification of records into those of other students in your class? (Goal 2)

4. Using the records you identified for Question 3 above, outline the uses of each record. If such information is not available for each record, how can it be found? (Goal 3)

5. Compare the records operations of early offices with those found in modern offices and show the role of legislation in such offices. (Goal 3)

6. Locate one office worker who has been employed for 25-30 years and a second worker who has been employed for 5-10 years. Discuss with them the nature of their office settings for the first five years of their jobs. What information would you expect to find? (Goal 3)

7. Compare the Privacy Act with the Freedom of Information Act. What values do these acts have for records management? (Goal 4)

8. In this textbook, a claim was made that all of us are managers to some degree since all of us use the steps in the management process. How does this apply to your instructor? to you as a student? (Goal 5)

9. List the stages in the record life cycle and describe the activities that occur during each stage. What stages, if any, do you eliminate in your own personal records cycle? Why? (Goal 6)

10. What are some common problems found in records systems? (Goal 7)

11. Why is the paper record so commonly created, used, and stored in offices, despite the increasing use of automation and computers? (Goal 8)

12. Explain what kind of career path records management offers and how you can best prepare yourself for work and advancement in this field. (Goal 9)

APPLICATIONS (APP)

APP 1-1. Identifying Records Needed for a New After-Hours Business

At the end of this school term, Jerry Lane and Rita Ortega plan to graduate and marry. Jerry has long been an accomplished woodworker and has sold many of his products; Rita is just as skilled in sewing crafts and excels in making items that reflect her heritage. She, too, has sold some of her wares. Both plan to keep their present part-time jobs, "just in case," and set about to organize an after-hours business selling their products.

In planning their business, this conversation occurred:

Jerry: You take care of the records. For our small operation, you can keep them in a notebook as you do where you work.

Rita: No, I can't. There's much more to small business records than meets the eye.

Jerry: (remaining unconvinced) If our business "clicks," we'll get a computer to solve all our records problems anyway.

1. Compare the basic attitudes of Jerry and Rita toward records.
2. What's your impression of the management style (democratic, dictatorial, authoritative, etc.) that seems to be developing in this conversation about their new business?
3. What can Rita do to convince Jerry of the importance of a sound records system?
4. List the basic records that Rita should create if she is to be in charge of the records as Jerry states.
5. Where can the couple get sound information to help them start their new records system? (Goals 3, 5, 6, 7, 9)

APP 1-2. Comparing the "Haves" with the "Have-Nots": A Group Exercise in Information Gathering

In your class there are two types of students: (1) the "Haves" (those who have had office and records experience), and (2) the "Have-Nots" (those who have not had such experience). In order that the entire class can better apply what they are learning in class; and in order that each group can better understand where the other group is "coming from," your instructor asks you to align yourself with the appropriate group and then to follow the instructions given below.

In order to organize this group exercise, your instructor has asked each of you to develop a set of questions about office records for the other group and bring the questions to class. (Note: In some cases, the same set of questions may be asked each group.) During class, you are to organize the exercise properly so that a record (such as meeting minutes) is kept of questions, answers, and related discussion during the exercise.

After completing the exercise, each student should summarize any related discussion that does not fit into the question-answer sequence. Finally, each student should show how Application 1-2 did (and did not) help you to learn more about applying the contents of this chapter. The information gathered during the exercise should be condensed in a short report, as directed by your instructor. (Goals 3-8)

2

Alphabetic Storage and Retrieval

Part 1 introduced you to the expanding area of records management and the increasing number of career opportunities in this field. With this background, Part 2 highlights the rules for alphabetic storage and retrieval systems as well as the equipment and supplies used in manual and computer systems. Special coverage is given to computer alphabetic indexing and the operation of computer databases in the modern office. Principles and procedures for retrieval and transfer of records conclude this Part.

ALPHABETIC INDEXING RULES 1-5

GOALS

After completing this chapter, you will be able to:

1. Explain the necessity for indexing rules in alphabetic storage of names, and the importance of following these rules consistently.
2. Index, code, and arrange personal and business names in indexing order of units.
3. Index, code, and arrange minor words and symbols in business names.
4. Index, code, and arrange personal and business names with punctuation and possessives.
5. Index, code, and arrange personal and business names with single letters and abbreviations.
6. Index, code, and arrange personal and business names with titles and suffixes.
7. Define *card record* and list the advantages and disadvantages of using card records.
8. Describe and explain the need for cross-referencing procedures.
9. Describe coding procedures for original and cross-reference card records.

NEED FOR ALPHABETIC ORDER

Records help a business do business.

Records help a business *do* business. Without some type of organized way of storing records, the primary purpose of keeping records would not be met. Business records help the decision maker have the right information at the right time at the lowest possible cost. In order to store the records in the most efficient way possible, some type of filing or storing method must be used. A **filing method** is the way records are stored in a container. This text will present alphabetic, subject, numeric, and geographic methods of storage. Alphabetic storage is discussed in Chapters 2 - 6, subject storage in Chapter 7, numeric storage in Chapter 8, and geographic storage in Chapter 9. The most common method of storage is alphabetic.

In alphabetic filing, items are arranged according to the letters of the alphabet. Sounds simple, right? Everyone knows the alphabet! Unfortunately, consistent alphabetic filing isn't that simple. Look in the telephone books of two major cities, and you will find major discrepancies in the order of the listings. Another example is filing under the letters "Mc." *Mc* is not one of the 26 letters of the alphabet; however, it is included in some alphabetic filing systems and not in others.

ARMA Filing Rules

The most important concept to remember is: *All filing is done to retrieve information.* To retrieve information efficiently, a set of rules must be followed. Different businesses have different needs for information retrieval. No one universal set of rules for alphabetic filing is followed by every business because the goals and needs of each business vary. The Association of Records Managers and Administrators, Inc. (ARMA) has published *Alphabetic Filing Rules*, containing rules for storing records alphabetically. **ARMA** is an organization designed to help professionals in records management perform their jobs easier and better. As you learned in Chapter 1, there seems to be no end to the amount of paper records generated. With the simplified rules recommended by ARMA, businesses have a place to start in setting up an efficient alphabetic storage system.

ARMA's Simplified Filing Standard Rules are shown in Figure 2-1 on the next page. The rules in this chapter and in Chapter 3 are written to agree with the ARMA Simplified Filing Standard Rules and Specific Filing Guidelines.

Variations exist in the procedures for storing records alphabetically. Therefore, the procedures to be used in any one office must be determined, recorded, approved, and followed with no deviation. Without written rules for storing records alphabetically, procedures will vary with time, changes in personnel, and oral explanations. Unless those who maintain the records are consistent in following storage procedures, locating records will not be possible. *The real test of an efficient storage system is being able to find records once they have been stored.*

Why do we need written rules for filing?

If you thoroughly understand the rules in this textbook, you will be able to adjust to any exceptions encountered in the specific office where you may work. Records managers who adopt these rules for their offices will find them understandable, logical, workable, and comprehensive enough to provide answers to the majority of storage questions that arise.

The Association of Records Managers and Administrators, Inc. (ARMA International), the professional organization for the records management field, recommends the following Simplified Filing Standard Rules for consistency in filing.

1. Alphabetize by arranging files in unit-by-unit order and letter-by-letter within each unit.

2. Each filing unit in a filing segment is to be considered. This includes prepositions, conjunctions, and articles. The only exception is when the word *the* is the first filing unit in a filing segment. In this case, *the* is the last filing unit. Spell out all symbols; e.g., &, $, #, and file alphabetically.

3. File "nothing before something." File single unit filing segments before multiple unit filing segments.

4. Ignore all punctuation when alphabetizing. This includes periods, commas, dashes, hyphens, apostrophes, etc. Hyphenated words are considered one unit.

5. Arabic and Roman numbers are filed sequentially before alphabetic characters. All Arabic numerals precede all Roman numerals.

6. Acronyms, abbreviations, and radio and television station call letters are filed as one unit.

7. File under the most commonly used name or title. Cross-reference under other names or titles that might be used in an information request.

Figure 2-1 ■ ARMA Simplified Filing Standard Rules

In this chapter, you will be using three of the six steps for storing alphabetically: Indexing, Coding, and Cross-Referencing. Chapter 5 explains all six of the alphabetic storing procedures.

Indexing

Mentally determining the filing segment of the record is *indexing*.

Indexing is the mental process of determining the filing segment (or name) by which the record is to be stored. The **filing segment** is the name by which the record is stored and requested. In alphabetic storage, indexing means determining the name that is to be used in filing.

The indexing step is more difficult when correspondence is being stored than it is when cards are being put in alphabetic order. On a card, the name is easily recognized; on correspondence, the name may appear in various places on the record. Because accurate indexing is necessary for quick retrieval, the indexing step is extremely important. *Careful, accurate indexing is perhaps the most exacting step in the storage procedure.* In an alphabetic arrangement, the selection of the right name (the filing segment) by which to store means that the record will be found quickly when it is needed. If the wrong name is selected, much time will be wasted trying to locate the record when it is eventually requested.

In order to select the filing segment, keep the following in mind: *The name most likely to be used in calling for the record, usually the most important one, is the one to be used for storage.*

Take a look at the examples in Figure 2-2. Several new terms are introduced in this figure: **Key Unit, Unit 2, Unit 3,** and **Unit 4.** These

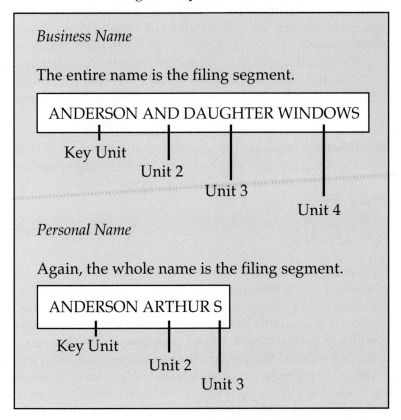

Business Name

The entire name is the filing segment.

ANDERSON AND DAUGHTER WINDOWS

Key Unit

Unit 2

Unit 3

Unit 4

Personal Name

Again, the whole name is the filing segment.

ANDERSON ARTHUR S

Key Unit

Unit 2

Unit 3

Figure 2-2 ■ Coded Filing Segments, Key Unit, and Succeeding Units

identified units combine to form **indexing units** of the filing segment; in other words, the indexing units are the various words that make up the filing segment. The **key unit** is the first unit of the filing segment and the one by which the record is stored. Units 2, 3, 4, and so on, are the next units by which the placement of the record is further determined. The use of these terms is helpful when deciding how an item is to be filed. By mentally identifying the key and succeeding units, you are making a complex process a little simpler and easier to handle.

Coding

Coding is the physical marking of the record to indicate by what name, number, or subject it is to be stored. Coding is a physical act, as contrasted with indexing, which is a mental determination. The coding procedure for this book is to underline the key unit, then number each succeeding unit (2, 3, 4, etc.) that has been mentally identified in the indexing process. When the records are coded, the indexing order of the filing segment is marked. The **indexing order** is the order in which units of the filing segment are considered when the record is stored.

In order to code properly, a set of rules for alphabetic storage must be faithfully followed. **Indexing rules** are the written procedures that describe how the filing segments are ordered. The indexing rules that follow give you a good start in following appropriate alphabetic storage procedures.

Actually marking the record is *coding*.

Cross-Referencing

While indexing a record, the filer may determine that the record could be requested by a name other than the one selected for coding. Because that record may be requested by the *other* name or names that were not coded, it is desirable to prepare a cross-reference. A **cross-reference** is an aid used to find a record stored by a filing segment other than the one selected for storing. The record is stored under the name the filer assumes to be the most important (key unit). Cross-referencing is used so that records can be retrieved quickly, even if they are requested by a name other than the one originally coded. This chapter presents the first five alphabetic indexing rules and the cross-references that go with them. Cross-referencing is mentioned here and will be discussed in detail after the rules have been presented.

Indexing Rules

The rules for alphabetic storage are presented here with examples to help you understand how to apply the rules. Study each rule and the examples of its application carefully; above all, be sure you understand the rule.

Here is an effective way to study: First, read the rule carefully. Make sure you understand the meaning of the words used to state the rule. Then, look at the examples. Note that the complete name is given at the left. Then the name is separated into indexing units at the right according to the rule you are studying. Be sure you understand why the name has been separated as it has.

| Read the rules carefully.

In determining alphabetic order, compare the units in the filing segments for differences. If the key units are alike, move to the second units, the third units, and succeeding units until a difference occurs. It is at that point of difference that correct alphabetic order is determined. Marks that appear over or under some letters in foreign names are disregarded (such as Señora, Marçal, René, Valhallavägen). In this text, you will find an underline in each example except the first one; this underline indicates the letter of the unit that determines alphabetic order. Examples are numbered for ease in referring to them. Be sure you understand each rule before going to the next.

RULE 1: INDEXING ORDER OF UNITS

A. Personal Names

A personal name is indexed in this manner: (1) the surname (last name) is the key unit, (2) the given name (first name) or initial is the second unit, and (3) the middle name or initial is the third unit. If determining the surname is difficult, consider the last name as the surname.

| Nothing before something!

A unit consisting of just an initial precedes a unit that consists of a complete name beginning with the same letter—*nothing before something*. Punctuation is omitted.

Examples of Rule 1A:
Index Order of Units in Names

Name	Key Unit	Unit 2	Unit 3
1. Alice T. Dale	DALE	ALICE	T
2. Steven K. Dallas	DAL_L_AS	STEVEN	K
3. Sylvia N. Daly	DAL_Y_	SYLVIA	N
4. Doug E. Dillon	D_I_LLON	DOUG	E
5. Dreana Lee Dillon	DILLON	DR_E_ANA	LEE
6. E. Matthew Dillon	DILLON	_E_	MATTHEW
7. Edith Ann Dillon	DILLON	E_D_ITH	ANN
8. Matt E. Dillon	DILLON	MA_T_T	E
9. Julia E. Dillow	DILLO_W_	JULIA	E
10. Phyllis S. Dillow	DILLOW	_P_HYLLIS	S

B. Business Names

Business names are indexed *as written* using letterheads or trademarks as guides. Each word in a business name is a separate unit. Business names containing personal names are indexed as written.

Examples of Rule 1B:
Index Order of Units in Names

Name	Key Unit	Unit 2	Unit 3	Unit 4
1. Bill Dale Forwarding Company	BILL	DALE	FORWARDING	COMPANY
2. Dale Die Casting Company	_D_ALE	DIE	CASTING	COMPANY
3. Dale Machinery Company	DALE	_M_ACHINERY	COMPANY	
4. Dallas Wholesale Company	DAL_L_AS	WHOLESALE	COMPANY	
5. Dally Awhile Books	DALL_Y_	AWHILE	BOOKS	
6. Dillon Bookstore	D_I_LLON	BOOKSTORE		
7. Dillon Family Steakhouse	DILLON	_F_AMILY	STEAKHOUSE	
8. Dillon National Bank	DILLON	_N_ATIONAL	BANK	
9. Dilly Dally Nursery	DILL_Y_	DALLY	NURSERY	
10. Edith Ann Fabrics	_E_DITH	ANN	FABRICS	

Check Your Knowledge of the Rules

1. On a separate sheet of paper, code items a - j by underlining the key unit and numbering second, third, and fourth units.

   a. Suzy Wong   d. Li Wu Wong
   b. Albert Brown Hosiery   e. Elspeth Gregory
   c. Edward Albert   f. Bill Green Car Company

g. T. F. Sommers

h. E. William Smith

i Glen Scott Cleaners

j. R. A. Sheridan Aviation

2. Are the two names in each of the following pairs in correct alphabetic order? Explain.

a. Ross Clothing Store
   Charlene Ross

b. Angela Rose
   Rose Garden Nursery

c. Bill Dale
   Bill Dale Custom Painting

d. Linda Lindsay Natural Foods
   Roy A. Lindsay

e. Allen Todd
   Todd Allen Furniture Company

f. Dorothy Johnson
   Dorothy Johnsen

g. Martin Ulbert
   Josephine Urroz

h. Red Robin Restaurant
   Red Robin Bait Shop

i. Pioneer Museum
   Pioneer Cemetary

j. L. G. Baker
   Lila G. Baker

RULE 2: MINOR WORDS AND SYMBOLS IN BUSINESS NAMES

Articles, prepositions, conjunctions, and symbols are considered separate indexing units. Symbols are considered as spelled in full. When the word "The" appears as the first word of a business name, it is considered the last indexing unit.

Articles: A, AN, THE
Prepositions: AT, IN, OUT, ON, OFF, BY, TO, WITH, FOR, OF, OVER
Conjunctions: AND, BUT, OR, NOR
Symbols: &, ¢, $, #, % (AND, CENT or CENTS, DOLLAR or DOLLARS, NUMBER or POUND, PERCENT)

Symbols are spelled out.

Examples of Rule 2:

Index Order of Units in Names

Name	Key Unit	Unit 2	Unit 3	Unit 4	Unit 5
1. Barb and Sam Miniature Golf	BARB	AND	SAM	MINIATURE	GOLF
2. Barb the Clown	BARB	THE	CLOWN		
3. The Biltmore Hotel	BILTMORE	HOTEL	THE		
4. By the Shore Motel	BY	THE	SHORE	MOTEL	
5. The ¢ Smart Shop	CENT	SMART	SHOP	THE	
6. Cent Wise Drug	CENT	WISE	DRUG		

Name	Key Unit	Unit 2	Unit 3	Unit 4	Unit 5
7. $ and ¢ Store	DOLLAR	AND	CENT	STORE	
8. Dollar Saver Motel	DOLLAR	SAVER	MOTEL		
9. Pound Drug Store	POUND	DRUG	STORE		
10. Rentals By The #	RENTALS	BY	THE	POUND	

RULE 3: PUNCTUATION AND POSSESSIVES

Punctuation is ignored.

All punctuation is disregarded when indexing personal and business names. Commas, periods, hyphens, apostrophes, dashes, exclamation points, question marks, quotation marks, and slash marks (/) are disregarded, and names are indexed as written.

Examples of Rule 3:

Index Order of Units in Names

Name	Key Unit	Unit 2	Unit 3	Unit 4
1. Alice's Custom Designs	ALICES	CUSTOM	DESIGN	
2. Allen-Miller Law Firm	ALLENMILLER	LAW	FIRM	
3. Rosetta Allen-Troy	ALLENTROY	ROSETTA		
4. All-in-One Store	ALLINONE	STORE		
5. "A-OK" Pilot Shop	AOK	PILOT	SHOP	
6. The On/Off Freeway Hotel	ONOFF	FREEWAY	HOTEL	THE
7. Robin's Bobbins & Such	ROBINS	BOBBINS	AND	SUCH
8. The Robin's Nest	ROBINS	NEST	THE	
9. Robin's Secret Hide-away	ROBINS	SECRET	HIDEAWAY	
10. Whodonit? Mystery Tours	WHODONIT	MYSTERY	TOURS	

Check Your Knowledge of the Rules

1. On a separate sheet of paper, code items a - j by underlining the key unit, and numbering the second, third, or fourth units.

   a. Out-and-About Travel   f. The Beary Good Store
   b. Karen Poppino-Brown   g. $ Off Discount Store
   c. The Spotted Cow Dairy   h. All-Over-Town Delivery
   d. Inside/Outside Framers   i. #s Away Diet Center
   e. Allison Beary-Caldwell   j. Lambert & Wong Law Firm

2. Are the two names in each of the following pairs in correct alphabetic order? Explain.

a. Bertha's $ Saver
   Frank Bertha
b. Rod-N-Reel Store
   Rodriguez & Gonzales
      Associates
c. Do-Rite General Contractors
   Do-Rite Builders
d. George & Son Electric
   George & Sons Alignment
e. Lamb-Western Company
   Lamb Industries

f. Temp-A-Cure Company
   Temp-Control Mechanics
g. Nor-West Growing Company
   Nor'Wester Novelties
h. Larissa M. Swanson
   Larry's Swan Shop
i. Heckman & Perez Law Firm
   David Heckman
j. Chi Kuo
   Ching-yu Kuo

RULE 4: SINGLE LETTERS AND ABBREVIATIONS

A. Personal Names

Initials in personal names are considered separate indexing units. Abbreviations of personal names (Wm., Jos., Thos.) and nicknames (Liz, Bill) are indexed as they are written.

B. Business Names

Single letters in business and organization names are indexed as written. If there is a space between single letters, index each letter as a separate unit. An acronym (a word formed from the first, or first few, letters of several words) is indexed as one unit regardless of punctuation or spacing. Abbreviated words (Mfg., Corp., Inc.) and names (IBM, GE) are indexed as one unit regardless of punctuation or spacing. Radio and television station call letters are indexed as one unit.

Examples of Rule 4:

Index Order of Units in Names

Name	Key Unit	Unit 2	Unit 3	Unit 4
1. I C I Realty	I	C	I	REALTY
2. IBM Corp.	IBM	CORP		
3. K & O Security	K	AND	O	SECURITY
4. KKRS Radio Station	KKRS	RADIO	STATION	

Name	Key Unit	Unit 2	Unit 3	Unit 4
5. K-Nine Klips	KNINE	KLIPS		
6. KOGO Television	KOGO	TELEVISION		
7. Eliz. T. Marsh	MARSH	ELIZ	T	
8. Vic. Ramos	RAMOS	VIC		
9. UARCO, Inc.	UARCO	INC		
10. US Bancorp	US	BANCORP		

RULE 5: TITLES AND SUFFIXES

A. Personal Names

Personal titles are considered the last unit.

A title before a name (Dr., Miss, Mr., Mrs., Ms., Prof.), a seniority suffix (II, III, Jr., Sr.), or a professional suffix (CRM, DDS, Mayor, MD, PhD, Senator) after a name is the last indexing unit. Numeric suffixes (II, III) are filed before alphabetic suffixes (Jr., Mayor, Senator, Sr.,). If a name contains both a title and a suffix, the title is the last unit.

Royal and religious titles followed by either a given name or a surname only (Father Leo) are indexed and filed as written.

Note: If a person's professional title comes after the name, it is referred to as a suffix; e.g., CPA, CRM, CMA, Senator.

Examples of Rule 5A:

Index Order of Units in Names

Name	Key Unit	Unit 2	Unit 3	Unit 4
1. Father John	FATHER	JOHN		
2. Ms. Ada Guzman, CPA	GUZMAN	ADA	CPA	MS
3. Dr. Ada Guzman	GUZMAN	ADA	DR	
4. Mr. Goro Nagai	NAGAI	GORO	MR	
5. Queen Anne	QUEEN	ANNE		
6. Sister Mary	SISTER	MARY		
7. Father John Smith	SMITH	JOHN	FATHER	
8. John Wilson, Jr.	WILSON	JOHN	JR	
9. John P. Wilson	WILSON	JOHN	P	
10. John P. Wilson II	WILSON	JOHN	P	II
11. John P. Wilson III	WILSON	JOHN	P	III
12. John Wilson, Sr.	WILSON	JOHN	SR	
13. Sister Margret Mary Wilson	WILSON	MARGRET	MARY	SISTER
14. Miss Suzi Yuan	YUAN	SUZI	MISS	
15. Mrs. Suzi Yuan	YUAN	SUZI	MRS	
16. Ms. Suzi Yuan	YUAN	SUZI	MS	

B. Business Names

Titles in business names are indexed as written.

Examples of Rule 5B:

Index Order of Units in Names

Name	Key Unit	Unit 2	Unit 3	Unit 4
1. Aunt Sally's Cookie Shop	AUNT	SALLYS	COOKIE	SHOP
2. Captain Bean's Coffee	CAPTAIN	BEANS	COFFEE	
3. Dr. Carla's Chimney Works	DR	CARLAS	CHIMNEY	WORKS
4. Father Time's Antiques	FATHER	TIMES	ANTIQUES	
5. Mister Oscar's Gym	MISTER	OSCARS	GYM	
6. Mr. Video Connection	MR	VIDEO	CONNECTION	
7. Mrs. T's Day Care	MRS	TS	DAY	CARE
8. Ms. Salon of Beauty	MS	SALON	OF	BEAUTY
9. Professor Owl's Pre-School	PROFESSOR	OWLS	PRESCHOOL	
10. Sisters of Charity	SISTERS	OF	CHARITY	

Check Your Knowledge of the Rules

1. On a separate sheet of paper, code items a - j by underlining the key unit and numbering the second and succeeding units.

    a. Father Castile

    b. Ms. Eva Torres, CRM

    c. Miss Char. Campbell, DVM

    d. Call/System Company

    e. COR Construction, Inc.

    f. WKRA Radio Station

    g. A & N Drop Box Service

    h. Friends-of-the-Road Trucking

    i. The Colonial Arms Apts.

    j. SERA Architects PC

2. Are the two names in each of the following pairs arranged in correct alphabetic order? Explain.

    a. Magdalena's Coffee Shop
       Magic $ Saver

    b. James Evans, Sr.
       James Evans, Jr.

    c. Mrs. Carmen Zapata
       Z-Pro Company

    d. XYZ Rentals, Inc.
       X M Chemical Co.

    e. Mrs. C's Chocolates
       MVP Pizza Shop

    f. The Yarn Barn
       Ye Olde Print Shop

    g. L-M Equipment Co.
       L & M Appliance Repair

    h. Sharon's "Of Course"
       Miss Sharon Oest

    i. The Office King
       The Office Doctor

    j. FAX-R-Us, Inc.
       FAX to You Company

3. Are the following names in alphabetic order? If so, indicate by writing "Yes." If not, write "No;" then determine the correct alphabetic order and show it by rearranging the numbers.

Example: 1. A-Z Rentals
            2. AAA Used Cars
            3. A. Wilson Enterprises

Answer: No, 3-2-1

a. 1. In and Out Diner
   2. ITC Truck Company
   3. I Do I Do Catering

f. 1. Dr. Jun Chiba
   2. Jun Chiba, M.D.
   3. Mr. Jun Chiba, CMA

b. 1. Alberta Husk
   2. The Husk Company
   3. David Husk

g. 1. Queen Anne
   2. The Queen's Closet
   3. Margaret F. Queen

c. 1. Brother Alfonso Blanco
   2. Cynthia Blanco-White
   3. Forentino Blanco

h. 1. Professor Rebecca Bartels
   2. The Professor Book Store
   3. Professor T's Academy

d. 1. Ronald Redford III
   2. Ronald Redford
   3. Ronald Redford II

i. 1. The Captain's Surf & Turf
   2. Captain Cynthia S. Wilson
   3. Cap'n Hook's Sea Food

e. 1. AMP Factory
   2. AMPAK, Inc.
   3. AMPCO Parking, Inc.

j. 1. Janice Cooper, CPA
   2. Ms. Janice Cooper
   3. Sister Janice Cooper

ALPHABETIC CARD FILING

Many offices use an alphabetic card file to store information that is frequently referenced. In the next section, card records are defined. The advantages and disadvantages of using card records are discussed as well as instructions for preparing card records. Last, you will be introduced to the basic concepts of cross-referencing using card records.

What Is a Card Record?

In many offices, card record files of the names and addresses of persons and businesses are kept in alphabetic arrangement. A **card record** is a piece of card stock used for storing information that is frequently referenced. The card stock provides the durability to withstand large volume usage. These cards are prepared according to the style selected by the files supervisor or records manager so that the cards can be handled with maximum efficiency and ease.

> Frequently referenced records are sometimes in card form.

To understand the advantages and disadvantages of card records, remember the basic difference between card records and records kept in other forms. One main item or unit of information is stored on each card. For this reason, a card has often been called a **unit record**, which is a record that stores one main item or piece of information on a card. Each card is handled as a single item or record unit. Some examples of unit records are microfiche and aperture cards, which are discussed in detail in Chapter 11.

Advantages of Card Records. Cards as unit records offer many advantages to the records manager. These advantages include the saving of space because of their size and the easy visibility of the record; one employee can work with a great deal of information without changing position. Also, cards are handled more easily than are papers because of the more uniform size and thickness of cards.

Card records offer several other advantages over records that are maintained on sheets of paper as lists of information subject to frequent change. With only one key information item on each card, such as a customer name or the name of a cataloged library book, information is easy to locate. If a change occurs in the address of a customer, or if a new book is added or an old book removed from the library, new information can be quickly inserted and the obsolete information can be deleted, or the card itself can physically be removed from the file.

Because only one main item of information appears on each card, the information on such cards can be easily rearranged in any sequence desired. For example, assume that a sales department's information needs require that customer name cards be arranged alphabetically by customer name. At another time, the cards are rearranged by customer name according to the numeric codes assigned to products purchased. In a third instance, the cards are rearranged geographically by the sales territories in which each customer is located. Cards can also be divided into groups or stacks, which permits several records clerks to use the entire file at once.

Disadvantages of Card Records. Card record systems also have disadvantages. For example, cards that are removed from the file can easily get out of sequence, especially when a stack is dropped. Small-size cards are easily lost, misfiled, or misplaced when removed from the file. Under certain conditions, it may be difficult to add, delete, or change information on a card without removing the card from the file; and in manual systems, it is sometimes difficult to type information on the top or bottom margins of the card. When information is recorded on cards from another document, errors can easily occur if the person posting the information is careless or inattentive to detail. Time is also required to transfer information from one record to another. Preparation and maintenance of card record systems is labor intensive (time-consuming).

Preparation of Cards

Cards need a uniform appearance.

Information that is contained on each card must follow the same pattern. This helps to ensure consistency and ease in finding the information. As you read the following explanation, refer frequently to Figure 2-3, which shows one style of name card preparation that is commonly used in both manual and computer-based systems.

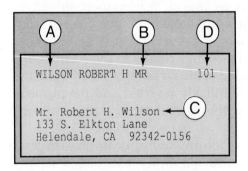

Figure 2-3 ■ Name Card Preparation

1. Key the name of the person or business, in all caps with no punctuation, in indexing order beginning on the third space from the left edge of the card and on the third line from the top edge. The key unit is always the first word typed (see A in Figure 2-3), followed by the second and succeeding units. A person's title should be typed if it is known (See B in Figure 2-3).
2. Rekey the name and address a triple space below the entry on the third line. This time it is keyed as it would be on an envelope, with

upper and lower case letters and with punctuation (note C in Figure 2-3).

3. If the name on the card is to be used with a numeric system, type the code number in the upper right corner of the card (see D in Figure 2-3).

Cross-Referencing

Some records of persons and businesses may be requested by a name that is different from the one by which it was stored. This is particularly true if the key unit is difficult to determine. When a record is likely to be requested by any of several names, an aid called a *cross-reference* is prepared. A cross-reference card shows the name in a form other than that used on the original card, and it indicates the location of the original card. The filer can then find requested records regardless of the name used in the request for those records. A cross-reference card may be identical with all other cards in size and color, or it may be distinctively different in color so that it will stand out clearly from the other cards.

> When a record could be requested by another name, prepare a cross-reference.

Cross-referencing must be done with discretion. Too many cross-references crowd the files and may hinder retrieval rather than help. Each cross-reference requires valuable time, creates at least one additional card that must be stored, and therefore requires additional space in the storage equipment.

Four types of personal names should be cross-referenced:

1. Unusual names.
2. Hyphenated surnames.
3. Alternate names.
4. Similar names.

There are nine types of business names that should be cross-referenced. Four will be covered in this chapter; the remainder, in Chapter 3.

1. Compound names.
2. Abbreviations and acronyms.
3. Popular and coined names.
4. Hyphenated names.

An explanation of the procedure to be followed in cross-referencing each of these kinds of names follows.

Personal Names. Cross-references should be prepared for the following types of personal names.

1. Unusual names. When determining the last name is difficult, index the last name first on the original record. Prepare a cross-reference with the first name indexed first. Examples are: Allen Todd, Ai-lien Feng, and Guillermo Quintero.

On the original card for Allen Todd, Todd is the key unit, and Allen is the second unit. However, a request might come in for Todd Allen. The cross-reference would show Allen as the key unit and Todd as the second unit. Someone looking under Allen would find the cross-reference under T for Todd. Study the examples in Figure 2-4.

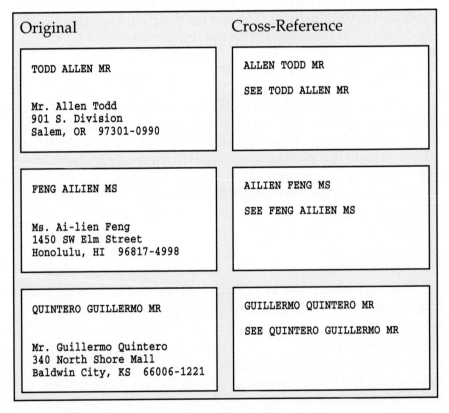

Figure 2-4 ■ Original and Cross-Reference Cards for Unusual Names

2. Hyphenated surnames. With hyphenated surnames, the request could be in either of the two names. The cross-reference enables retrieval in either case. Examples are Roberta A. Nedry-Patterson and Mr. Arturo Barba-Silva.

Original	Cross-Reference
NEDRYPATTERSON ROBERTA A	PATTERSON ROBERTA A NEDRY SEE NEDRYPATTERSON ROBERTA A
BARBASILVA ARTURO MR	SILVA ARTURO BARBA MR SEE BARBASILVA ARTURO MR

3. Alternate names. Examples are Mrs. Roberta Patterson, Mrs. James Patterson, Roberta A. Nedry-Patterson, and Mrs. Roberta A. Patterson; Marcella Gano and Mrs. Marcella Smith; and James Earl Carter and Jimmy Carter.

Original	Cross-Reference
PATTERSON ROBERTA MRS	PATTERSON JAMES MRS SEE PATTERSON ROBERTA MRS SEE ALSO NEDRYPATTERSON ROBERTA A SEE ALSO PATTERSON ROBERTA A MRS
GANO MARCELLA	SMITH MARCELLA MRS SEE GANO MARCELLA
CARTER JAMES EARL	CARTER JIMMY SEE CARTER JAMES EARL

4. Similar names. For some names like Dailey and Munroe, there are a variety of spellings. A SEE ALSO cross-reference is prepared for all possible spellings. If the card isn't found under one spelling, the filer checks the SEE ALSO card for other possible spellings.

Original	Original
DAILEY SEE ALSO DALY DAILY DALEY	DALY SEE ALSO DAILEY DAILY DALEY
DAILY SEE ALSO DAILEY DALY DALEY	DALEY SEE ALSO DAILEY DALY DAILY
MUNROE SEE ALSO MUNRO MONROE	MUNRO SEE ALSO MONROE MUNROE
MONROE SEE ALSO MUNRO MUNROE	

Business Names.   Cross-references should be prepared for the following types of business names. The original name is the name appearing on the letterhead.

1. Compound Names. When a business name includes two or more individual surnames, prepare a cross-reference for each surname other than the first. For example, Norris, Jones & Smith, Attorneys.

Original	Cross-Reference
NORRIS JONES AND SMITH ATTORNEYS	JONES SMITH AND NORRIS ATTORNEYS SEE NORRIS JONES AND SMITH ATTORNEYS
	SMITH NORRIS AND JONES ATTORNEYS SEE NORRIS JONES AND SMITH ATTORNEYS

2. Abbreviations and Acronyms. When a business is commonly known by an abbreviation or an acronym, a cross-reference is prepared for the full name.

Examples are IBM (International Business Machines Corporation), HFC (Household Finance Company), and AT&T (American Telephone and Telegraph Co.).

Original	Cross-Reference
IBM	INTERNATIONAL BUSINESS MACHINES CORP SEE IBM
HFC	HOUSEHOLD FINANCE COMPANY SEE HFC
ATANDT	AMERICAN TELEPHONE AND TELEGRAPH CO SEE ATANDT

3. Popular and Coined Names. Often a business is known by its popular and/or coined name. A cross-reference will assist in retrieval. Examples are Freddy's (Fred Meyer Department Store), Penney's (J. C. Penney Company, Inc.), and Gill's (J. K. Gill Company).

Original	Cross-Reference
FREDDYS	FRED MEYER DEPARTMENT STORE SEE FREDDYS
PENNEYS	J C PENNEY COMPANY INC SEE PENNEYS
GILLS	J K GILL COMPANY SEE GILLS

4. Hyphenated Names. Just as in personal names, business names with hyphens need to be cross-referenced for each surname combination other than the first. Examples are Hastins-Humble Brokerage and Gilbert-Hasenberry Architects.

Original	Cross-Reference
HASTINSHUMBLE BROKERAGE	HUMBLEHASTINS BROKERAGE SEE HASTINSHUMBLE BROKERAGE
GILBERTHASENBERRY ARCHITECTS	HASENBERRYGILBERT ARCHITECTS SEE GILBERTHASENBERRY ARCHITECTS

Check Your Knowledge of Cross-Referencing

Which of the following should have cross-references?

1. WKKP Radio Station
2. IBM Corporation (International Business Machines Corporation)
3. Bartel-Simmons Cattle Company
4. Nelson Allen
5. Mrs. Joanna Paulson-Childer
6. The Riverside Terrace
7. Akeo Saga, M.D.
8. Smitty's (Smith's Cafe & ConcertHall)
9. Barnett, Wall & Wakui Brokerage
10. AT&T (American Telephone and Telegraph)

If the names on cards are coded, the name on the first line of the card is always used to determine placement in the file. This applies to original cards and to cross-reference cards. The key unit is underlined, and the remaining units are numbered 2, 3, etc.

IMPORTANT TERMS

ARMA	indexing
card record	indexing order
coding	indexing rules
cross-reference	indexing units
filing method	key unit
filing segment	unit record

REVIEW AND DISCUSSION

1. Why is consistency in filing important? (Goal 1)
2. Everyone knows the alphabet. Why is it important to have indexing rules? (Goal 1)

3. In personal names, what is the key unit? (Goal 2)
4. How is the key unit of a business name determined? (Goal 2)
5. How do you index an ampersand (&) used in a business name? (Goal 3)
6. How do you index and code a person's hyphenated last name? (Goal 4)
7. Code each name and give reasons for your coding. (Goal 5)
    UPS, Inc.
    U P S Associates
8. How do you index religious titles? (Goal 6)
9. Give one advantage and one disadvantage for using a card record system. (Goal 7)
10. Describe a method for physically coding cards. (Goal 9)
11. Why are cross-references necessary? (Goal 8)
12. Can you have too many cross-references? (Goal 8)
13. Give two examples of personal names that should be cross-referenced. (Goal 8)
14. Give two examples of business names that should be cross-referenced. (Goal 8)

APPLICATIONS (APP)

APP 2-1. Arranging Personal and Business Names in Alphabetic Indexing Order (Goals 2-6, 9)

A. On 3" x 5" cards or on slips of paper of that size, type or print in indexing order the names given below. Also type the number (given on the next two pages) of the name in the top right corner of the card.

B. Prepare cross-reference cards where necessary, according to the suggestions given in this chapter. On the cross-reference card, indicate the number of the item, plus an X.

C. Code each card for alphabetic filing.

D. Arrange all cards, including cross-references, in alphabetic order.

E. In a vertical column on a separate sheet of paper, list the numbers typed or printed on the cards that you have now arranged in alphabetic order.

F. Save the cards for use in Chapter 3.

Names

1. L. D. Mattson, 1351 West Losey, Hartford, CT 06110-6033
2. L & D Enterprises, 742 Pine St., Suite 1201, Galesburg, IL 61401-3425
3. L-D-T Services, 404 Spring Park Blvd., Lansing, MI 48912-6766
4. Lundgren/Larson Associates, 890 Francis Ave., Boston, MA 02174-3682
5. Leland Lundgren, 302 Sitka St., Juneau, AK 99801-6195
6. Mirko Matosin, 888 Bayou Lane, Baton Rouge, LA 70802-2322
7. Lorraine Matsen, 1602 Wade St. SE, Pittsburgh, PA 15217-1123
8. Miller, Lundgren, & Naber Attorneys, 2350 N. Montgomery Ave., Austin, TX 78705-3245
9. N/S Corporation, 455 SE Vineyard Lane, Lincoln, NE 68501-1273
10. Lynda Naber Associates, Inc., 450 NW Lovejoy, San Francisco, CA 94102-6722
11. Miracle Auto Repair, 4845 S. Bellevue Crescent, Chevy Chase, MD 20815-1101
12. Mirror-Image Styling Salon, 100 S. Potter Street, Jackson, MS 39202-1763
13. Mr. & Ms. Hair Design, 414 W. Seventh Street, Andover, NH 03216-2233
14. Nunamaker Storage, Inc., 4700 E. Morningside Dr., Cincinnati, OH 45227-6511
15. Nu-Way Oil Company, 44 Hillcrest, South Burlington, VT 05401-2217
16. NQI, Ltd., 1650 Northern Avenue, Bangor, ME 04401-1014
17. Paul Nutter, 1750 S. Sunnyvale, Providence, RI 02909-1435
18. Walter L. Nutting, 106 S. Elm St., Chicago, IL 60680-1876
19. NuWay Painting Co., 126 W. Grant Lane, Little Rock, AR 72211-5452
20. Miss Muffin Company, 217 S. Douglas Street, Dover, DE 19901-2235
21. Mr. Steven K. Miller, CPA, 1515 S. Adams Ave., Washington, DC 20020-3466
22. Matsumi Luu, CRM, 134 North Luanna Blvd., Boise, ID 83710-2222

23. Luxury Homes, Inc., 34 South Square Mall, Baldwin City, KS 66006-1221
24. Mike Lutz Tire Company, 380 SE 14th St., Lawrenceville, IL 62439-3844
25. Lyle Phillips Typing Service, 31 Spinosa Ave., Concordia, KY 40157-3234

APPLYING THE RULES

Job 1, Card Filing, Rules 1-5. *All supplies necessary for completing Job 1 and all other jobs in* Records Management Projects, *5th ed., are contained in the practice set.*

3 ALPHABETIC
INDEXING RULES 6-10

GOALS
After completing this chapter, you will be able to:

1. Index, code, and arrange personal and business names with articles and particles.
2. Index, code, and arrange business names with numbers.
3. Index, code, and arrange the names of organizations and institutions.
4. Index, code, and arrange personal and business names that are identical.
5. Index, code, and arrange government names.
6. Prepare cross-references for business names that are divisions and subsidiaries, changed names, similar names, foreign business, and foreign government names.
7. Select appropriate subject categories to be used within an alphabetic arrangement.

Here is the second half of the alphabetic indexing rules! The five rules explained in this chapter require the same careful study that you gave to the rules in Chapter 2. Note especially the examples, as they will help you to understand the rules. All of the rules about hyphens, punctuation, single letters, and so forth, apply to these names in the same way that they were used in Chapter 2. After completing these rules, you are well on your way to mastering a standard set of indexing rules for personal and business names.

RULE 6: PREFIXES—FOREIGN ARTICLES AND PARTICLES

A foreign article or particle in a personal or business name is combined with the part of the name following it to form a single indexing

A foreign article or particle is combined to form a single indexing unit.

unit. The indexing order is not affected by a space between a prefix and the rest of the name, and the space is disregarded when indexing.

Examples of foreign articles and particles are a la, D', Da, De, Del, De la, Della, Den, Des, Di, Dos, Du, E', El, Fitz, Il, L', La, Las, Le, Les, Lo, Los, M', Mac, Mc, O', Per, Saint, San, Santa, Santo, St., Ste., Te, Ten, Ter, Van, Van de, Van der, Von, Von der.

Examples of Rule 6:

Index Order of Units in Names

Name	Key Unit	Unit 2	Unit 3	Unit 4
1. Brian DuBry's Pro Shop	BRIAN	DUBRYS	PRO	SHOP
2. Fernanda D'Agostino	DAGOSTINO	FERNANDA		
3. Gary Del Carrpio	DELCARRPIO	GARY		
4. E'Lan Medical Equipment, Inc.	ELAN	MEDICAL	EQUIPMENT	INC
5. El Castor Industries, Ltd.	ELCASTOR	INDUSTRIES	LTD	
6. LaBar, McDonald & VanDyke	LABAR	MCDONALD	AND	VANDYKE
7. LaPaloma Women's Clothing	LAPALOMA	WOMENS	CLOTHING	
8. Antonia L. L'Auberge	LAUBERGE	ANTONIA	L	
9. LaVoy's Wig & Beauty	LAVOYS	WIG	AND	BEAUTY
10. MacEwan Tax Service	MACEWAN	TAX	SERVICE	
11. Saint Claire's Arts & Crafts	SAINTCLAIRES	ARTS	AND	CRAFTS
12. Joseph Ste. Cyr	STECYR	JOSEPH		
13. Sylvia D'Bay's Studio	SYLVIA	DBAYS	STUDIO	
14. Katherine TenClay	TENCLAY	KATHERINE		
15. Van Der Zanden Seed Cleaning	VANDERZANDEN	SEED	CLEANING	

RULE 7: NUMBERS IN BUSINESS NAMES

Numbers in digit form are arranged before letters of the alphabet.

Numbers spelled out (such as *seven*) in business names are filed alphabetically. Numbers written in digits are filed before alphabetic letters or words (B4 Photographers comes before Beleau Building Co.). Names with numbers written in digits in the first units are filed in ascending (lowest to highest number) order before alphabetic names (229 Club, 534 Shop, Bank of Chicago). Arabic numerals are filed before Roman numerals (2, 3, II, III).

Names with inclusive numbers (33-37) are arranged by the first digit(s) only (33). Names with numbers appearing in other than the first position (Pier 36 Cafe) are filed alphabetically and immediately before a similar name without a number (Pier and Port Cafe).

When indexing numbers written in digit form that contain *st, d,* and *th* (1st, 2d, 3d, 4th), ignore the letter endings and consider only the digits (1, 2, 3, 4).

Examples of Rule 7:

Index Order of Units in Names

Name	Key Unit	Unit 2	Unit 3	Unit 4
1. 7 Day Food Market	7	DAY	FOOD	MARKET
2. 21st Century Graphics, Inc.	21	CENTURY	GRAPHICS	INC
3. 24 Carrot Cake Bakery	24	CARROT	CAKE	BAKERY
4. 99 Auto Repairs	99	AUTO	REPAIRS	
5. 100-110 VanMeter Court	100	VANMETER	COURT	
6. The 100 VanMeter Shop	100	VANMETER	SHOP	THE
7. 2001 Hair Styling	2001	HAIR	STYLING	
8. 12500 Commercial Windows	12500	COMMERCIAL	WINDOWS	
9. XXI Club	XXI	CLUB		
10. Fourth Dimension, Inc.	FOURTH	DIMENSION	INC	
11. Highway 26 Cafe	HIGHWAY	26	CAFE	
12. Mall 210	MALL	210		
13. Mark VI Productions	MARK	VI	PRODUCTIONS	
14. One Main Place	ONE	MAIN	PLACE	
15. One-Hundred Grand Avenue Apts.	ONEHUNDRED	GRAND	AVENUE	APTS

Check Your Knowledge of the Rules

On a separate sheet of paper, code the following names by underlining the key unit and numbering second and succeeding units. Write "Yes" if the names are in alphabetic order. Write "No" if the names are not in correct alphabetic order and show the correct order by rearranging the numbers. The first problem has been done for you.

a.
                2
1. <u>EL-CO</u> Enterprises
             2
2. Colleen <u>Eller-McKinstry</u>
               2
3. <u>El Dorado</u> Hotel

Answer: No; 1,3,2

b.
1. 7-9 Shop
2. V Iberian Way
3. 21st Century Investments

c.
1. Labels Unlimited, Inc.
2. LaBelle Beauty Salon
3. Bob LaBelle

d.
1. Darrell J. MacKay
2. MacKay Construction Co.
3. Mack's Cafe & Concert Hall

e.
1. Philip TenEyck
2. 10 Minute Delivery
3. Philip S. TenEyck

f. 1. Cynthia de la Cross
    2. Kelly DeLacey
    3. Kevin DelaCruz

g. 1. # 1 Deliveries
    2. # 1 Auto Sales
    3. 10 # Line Shop

h. 1. William Van Der Hout
    2. Frans. Vander Hout
    3. Michael Vanderhout

i. 1. George LaDu
    2. Ladybug Nursery
    3. Janell LaDuke

j. 1. Elegance In Motion Limos
    2. El Rancho Florists
    3. Ellert, Ann Marie

RULE 8: ORGANIZATIONS AND INSTITUTIONS

Names of organizations and institutions are indexed as written on their letterheads.

Banks and other financial institutions, clubs, colleges, hospitals, hotels, lodges, magazines, motels, museums, newspapers, religious institutions, schools, unions, universities, and other organizations and institutions are indexed and filed according to the names written on their letterheads.

Examples of Rule 8:

Index Order of Units in Names

Name	Key Unit	Unit 2	Unit 3	Unit 4	Unit 5
1. Assembly of God Church	ASSEMBLY	OF	GOD	CHURCH	
2. Assn. of Paper Workers	ASS<u>N</u>	OF	PAPER	WORKERS	
3. Associated General Contractors	ASS<u>O</u>CIATED	GENERAL	CONTRACTORS		
4. The Bank of California	<u>B</u>ANK	OF	CALIFORNIA	THE	
5. The Bank of Nova Scotia	BANK	OF	<u>N</u>OVA	SCOTIA	THE
6. College of the Redwoods	<u>C</u>OLLEGE	OF	THE	REDWOODS	
7. Federated Farm Workers	<u>F</u>EDERATED	FARM	WORKERS		
8. First Christian Church	F<u>I</u>RST	CHRISTIAN	CHURCH		
9. First National Bank	FIRST	<u>N</u>ATIONAL	BANK		
10. Foundation for the Blind	F<u>O</u>UNDATION	FOR	THE	BLIND	

Name	Key Unit	Unit 2	Unit 3	Unit 4	Unit 5
11. The Homeless Foundation	HOMELESS	FOUNDATION	THE		
12. Japanese Karate Association	JAPANESE	KARATE	ASSOCIATION		
13. Jewish Historical Society	JEWISH	HISTORICAL	SOCIETY		
14. John F. Kennedy High School	JOHN	F	KENNEDY	HIGH	SCHOOL
15. John Robert Powers School	JOHN	ROBERT	POWERS	SCHOOL	
16. Journal of Photography	JOURNAL	OF	PHOTOGRAPHY		
17. Kiwanis Club	KIWANIS	CLUB			
18. The Lamplight Hotels	LAMPLIGHT	HOTELS	THE		
19. Pacific University	PACIFIC	UNIVERSITY			
20. Public Employees Retirement	PUBLIC	EMPLOYEES	RETIREMENT		
21. Rotary Club of Detroit	ROTARY	CLUB	OF	DETROIT	
22. Rowe Junior High School	ROWE	JUNIOR	HIGH	SCHOOL	
23. School of Arts and Crafts	SCHOOL	OF	ARTS	AND	CRAFTS
24. Society of Jesus, Oregon Region	SOCIETY	OF	JESUS	OREGON	REGION
25. Spokane Falls Community College	SPOKANE	FALLS	COMMUNITY	COLLEGE	
26. Statesmen News	STATESMEN	NEWS			
27. St. Vincent's Hospital	STVINCENTS	HOSPITAL			
28. University of California at Irvine	UNIVERSITY	OF	CALIFORNIA	AT	IRVINE

Check Your Knowledge of the Rules

1. On a separate sheet of paper, underline the key unit; then number the second and succeeding indexing units in each of the following:

    a. Associated Psychotherapists of Northern California

    b. Association of General Contractors

    c. Church of Religious Science

    d. Milwaukee First Church of The Nazarene

    e. Temple Baptist Church

    f. Temple Beth Israel

    g. Woodlawn Hospital

    h. Union Gospel Missionaries

    i. University Hospital

    j. Gonzaga University

2. Are the following pairs in correct alphabetic order? If not, why not?

    a. International Organization of Masters, Mates & Pilots
        International Pentecostal Church

    b. International Brotherhood of Electrical Workers
        International Brotherhood of Barbers

    c. American Cancer Society of Selma
        American Baptist Churches of Idaho

    d. American Legion Post 52
        American Red Cross, Mississippi Chapter

    e. American Association of Retired Persons, Chapter 78
        American Assn. of University Women

RULE 9: IDENTICAL NAMES

When personal names and names of businesses, institutions, and organizations are identical (including titles as explained in Rule 5), filing order is determined by the addresses. Compare addresses in the following order:

1. City names.
2. State or province names (if city names are identical).
3. Street names, including *Avenue, Boulevard, Drive, Street* (if city and state names are identical).

    a. When the first units of street names are written in digits (18th Street), the names are filed in ascending numeric order (1, 2, 3) and placed together before alphabetic street names (18th Street, 24th Avenue, 36th Drive SW).

    b. Street names with compass directions (North, South, East, and West) are considered as written (South Park Avenue). Numbers after compass directions are considered before alphabetic names (East 8th, East Main, Sandusky, SE Eighth, Southeast Eighth).

4. House or building numbers (if city, state, and street names are identical).

    a. House and building numbers written as figures are filed in ascending numeric order (8 Riverside Terrace, 912 Riverside

Check city, then state, then street if names are identical.

Terrace) and placed together before alphabetic building names (The Riverside Terrace).

b. If a street address *and* a building name are included in an address, disregard the building name.

c. ZIP Codes are not considered in determining filing order.

Examples of Rule 9:

Index Order of Units in Names

(Names of Cities Used to Determine Filing Order)

1. First National Bank Elko, NV	FIRST	NATIONAL	BANK	ELKO	NV
2. First National Bank Reno, NV	FIRST	NATIONAL	BANK	RENO	NV

(Names of States and Provinces Used to Determine Filing Order)

3. LaVerne's Beauty Shop Miami, FL	LAVERNES	BEAUTY	SHOP	MIAMI	FL
4. LaVerne's Beauty Shop Miami, MO	LAVERNES	BEAUTY	SHOP	MIAMI	MO
5. Sandpiper Motel Gladstone, MI	SANDPIPER	MOTEL	GLADSTONE	MI	
6. Sandpiper Motel Gladstone, NJ	SANDPIPER	MOTEL	GLADSTONE	NJ	

(Names of Streets and Building Numbers Used to Determine Filing Order)

7. Fast Eddie's Diner 4350 12th Street Lubbock, TX	FAST	EDDIES	DINER	LUBBOCK	TX	12	STREET	
8. Fast Eddie's Diner 350 36th Street Lubbock, TX	FAST	EDDIES	DINER	LUBBOCK	TX	36	STREET	
9. Fast Eddie's Diner 18650 Grant Avenue Lubbock, TX	FAST	EDDIES	DINER	LUBBOCK	TX	GRANT	AVENUE	
10. Fast Eddie's Diner 12500 Grant Street Lubbock, TX	FAST	EDDIES	DINER	LUBBOCK	TX	GRANT	STREET	12500
11. Fast Eddie's Diner 17000 Grant Street Lubbock, TX	FAST	EDDIES	DINER	LUBBOCK	TX	GRANT	STREET	17000
12. Fast Eddie's Diner 175 NE 13 Street Lubbock, TX	FAST	EDDIES	DINER	LUBBOCK	TX	NE	13	STREET
13. Fast Eddie's Diner 405 NE Ninth Street Lubbock, TX	FAST	EDDIES	DINER	LUBBOCK	TX	NE	NINTH	STREET
14. Fast Eddie's Diner 985 Silver Elm Drive Lubbock, TX	FAST	EDDIES	DINER	LUBBOCK	TX	SILVER	ELM	DRIVE

Check Your Knowledge of the Rules

On a separate sheet of paper, code each of the following by underlining the key unit, then number each succeeding unit. Next, determine if the pairs are in correct alphabetic order, and write "Yes" or "No" to indicate your decision.

a. First Church of Christ
    150 SE Concord
    Dallas, OR

    First Church of Christ
    725 N 48 Street
    Dallas, TX

b. Juliana Nelson
    4550 Elm Street
    Dayton, OH

    Juliana Nelson
    975 Cedar Street
    Dayton, OH

c. The Inquirer
    870 N Main Street
    Granite, OK

    The Inquirer
    370 Main Street
    Granite, OR

d. The Corner Market
    115 SE 8 Street
    Philadelphia, PA

    The Corner Market
    1150 SE 8 Street
    Philadelphia, PA

e. Bi-Rite $ Saver
    8th and Grand Streets
    Auburn, NH

    Bi-Rite $ Saver
    16875 Main Street
    Auburn, WV

f. US National Bank
    210 N Brentwood Blvd.
    Los Angeles, CA

    US National Bank
    150 S Brentwood Avenue
    Los Angeles, CA

RULE 10: GOVERNMENT NAMES

Government names are indexed first by the name of the governmental unit — country, state, county, or city. Next, index the distinctive name of the department, bureau, office, or board. The words "Office of," "Department of," "Bureau of," etc., are separate indexing units if they are part of the official name.

Note: If "of" is not a part of the official name as written, it is not added.

The first three units of the federal government are UNITED STATES GOVERNMENT.

A. Federal

The first three indexing units of a United States (federal) government agency name are *United States Government*.

Examples of Rule 10A:

(Units 1, 2, and 3 are UNITED STATES GOVERNMENT for each example.)

Indexing Order of Units

Names	Unit 4	Unit 5	Unit 6	Unit 7	Unit 8	Unit 9	Unit 10
1. United States Forest Service Department of Agriculture	AGRICULTURE	DEPARTMENT	OF	FOREST	SERVICE		
2. Department of Interior Geological Survey	INTERIOR	DEPARTMENT	OF	GEOLOGICAL	SURVEY		
3. Internal Revenue Service Department of the Treasury	TREASURY	DEPARTMENT	OF	THE	INTERNAL	REVENUE	SERVICE

B. State and Local

The first indexing units are the names of the state, province, county or parish, city, town, township, or village. Next, index the most distinctive name of the department, board, bureau, office, or governments/political division. The words "State of," "County of," "City of," "Department of," etc., are added only *if needed* for clarity and in the official name, and are considered separate indexing units.

Examples of Rule 10B:

Indexing Order of Units

Name	Unit 1	Unit 2	Unit 3	Unit 4	Unit 5	Unit 6
1. Banking Office Department of Commerce Baton Rouge, LA	LOUISIANA	COMMERCE	DEPARTMENT	OF	BANKING	OFFICE
2. Department of Public Safety (State Government) Baton Rouge, LA	LOUISIANA	PUBLIC	SAFETY	DEPARTMENT	OF	
3. Transportation Dept. Marion County Salem, OR	MARION	COUNTY	TRANSPORTATION	DEPT		
4. Bridge Maintenance Engineering Department Seattle, WA	SEATTLE	ENGINEERING	DEPARTMENT	BRIDGE	MAINTENANCE	
5. Planning Commission Starland Municipal District Drumheller, AB	STARLAND	MUNICIPAL	DISTRICT	PLANNING	COMMISSION	

C. Foreign

The distinctive English name is the first indexing unit for foreign government names. This is followed, if needed and if it is in the official name, by the balance of the formal name of the government. Branches, departments, and divisions follow in order by their distinctive names. States, colonies, provinces, cities, and other divisions of foreign governments are followed by their distinctive or official names as spelled in English.

Examples of Rule 10C:

Name	Indexed Order
1. Canada	CANADA DOMINION OF
2. Jumhuriyah Misr al-Arabiya	EGYPT ARAB REPUBLIC OF
3. Republique Francaise	FRENCH REPUBLIC
4. Bundesrepublik Deutschland	GERMANY FEDERAL REPUBLIC OF
5. Bharat	INDIA REPUBLIC OF
6. Nippon	JAPAN

Note: The *United States Government Manual* and the *Congressional Directory*, published annually, report a current list of United States government agencies and offices. *Countries, Dependencies, Areas of Special Sovereignty, and Their Principal Administrative Divisions*, published by the U.S. Department of Commerce, National Bureau of Standards, provides a list of geographic and political entities of the world and associated standard codes. The *State Information Book* by Susan Lukowski provides an up-to-date list of state departments and their addresses. The *World Almanac and Book of Facts*, updated annually, includes facts and statistics on many foreign nations, and is helpful as a source which gives the English spellings of many foreign names. Your local and/or college library should have these reference books.

Check Your Knowledge of the Rules

1. On a separate sheet of paper, underline the key unit. Number succeeding units in each of the following names.

   a. Nat'l Assn. of Broadcasters
   b. Independent Order of Oddfellows
   c. First Methodist Church

    d. The Boise Register Guard

    e. International Dunes Hotel

    f. American Confederation of Bakers

    g. Building Dept., Anaheim, CA (City Government)

    h. Bureau of Tourism, Lyoveldio Island (Iceland)

    i. American Deaf Society

    j. International Association of Diabetics

    k. Association of Retarded Citizens

    l. Sisters of Mercy Hospital

    m. Bureau of Indian Affairs, Department of Interior (Federal Government)

    n. Brotherhood of International Wood Workers

    o. Neighbors of Meadowcraft

2. Arrange items a - o from question 1 in alphabetic order.

3. On a separate sheet of paper, code the following pairs of names by underlining the key unit and numbering succeeding units. Next, indicate if the pairs are in correct alphabetic order by writing *Yes* or *No*.

    a. St. Mary's Academy
       St. Mary's Church

    b. 21 Skidoo Gallery
       The 21 Club

    c. Babe Ruth Elementary
       School
       Babe Ruth Community
       College

    d. Public Works Dept.
       Buxton, ND
       Public Works Dept.
       Buxton, NC

    e. Central Savings Bank
       1430 Plymouth St.
       Providence, RI
       Central Savings Bank
       350 E First Avenue
       Providence, RI

    f. Daily News, Huntsville, UT
       Daily News, Huntsville, ON
       (Ontario, Canada)

    g. Elliniki Dimokratia
       (Greece Democracy)
       Warren S. Greco

    h. School of Arts and Crafts
       School of the Arts

    i. San Carlos Apartments
       Mr. Tatsumi Sanada

    j. Freedom Museum
       Historical & Museum
         Commission
       Harrisburg, PA (State Govt.)
       Archives & Records
       Historical & Museum
         Commission
       Harrisburg, PA (State Govt.)

CROSS-REFERENCES, BUSINESS NAMES

In Chapter 2, you learned that cross-references should be prepared for business names that are (1) compound names, (2) abbreviations and acronyms, (3) popular and coined names, and (4) hyphenated names. In this chapter, you will learn to prepare cross-references for the following types of business names:

5. Divisions and Subsidiaries
6. Changed Names
7. Similar Names
8. Foreign Business Names
9. Foreign Government Names

An explanation of the procedure to be followed in cross-referencing each of these kinds of names follows.

Divisions and Subsidiaries

A division or subsidiary of a business is cross-referenced.

When one company is a subsidiary or a division or branch of another company, the name appearing on the letterhead of the branch or subsidiary is the one indexed on the original record. A cross-reference is made under the name of the parent company. Examples are U.S. Plywood and Drexel-Heritage Furniture, which are subsidiaries of Champion International.

Original	Cross-Reference
US PLYWOOD	CHAMPION INTERNATIONAL SEE DREXELHERITAGE FURNITURE US PLYWOOD
DREXELHERITAGE FURNITURE	CHAMPION INTERNATIONAL SEE DREXELHERITAGE FURNITURE US PLYWOOD

Changed Names

A changed name of a company is cross-referenced.

At times a company may change its name. The records must then be changed to indicate the name change and to ensure that the new name will be used for storage purposes. The records already in storage are usually refiled under the new name, and the former name is put in the records as a cross-reference. Examples are Mobil Oil Company to BP Oil Company and American Eagle Airlines to Amerigo Airlines.

Original	Cross-Reference
BP OIL COMPANY	MOBIL OIL COMPANY SEE BP OIL COMPANY
AMERIGO AIRLINES	AMERICAN EAGLE AIRLINES SEE AMERIGO AIRLINES

Similar Names

Similar names for a business include examples like Northwest or North West, Goodwill or Good Will, and All State or Allstate. If the name could be considered as one unit or two, it is a good candidate for a cross-reference.

Original	Original
NORTHWEST SEE ALSO NORTH WEST	GOODWILL SEE ALSO GOOD WILL
ALLSTATE SEE ALSO ALL STATE	

Foreign Business Names

The spelling of the name of a foreign business is often the original spelling in the foreign language that is then usually translated into English for coding. The English translation should be written on the document to be stored, and the document stored under the English spelling. When a request for records is written in the native language, the filer will find that a cross-reference bearing the original spelling is an aid in finding the records. Special care should be taken to type correct spellings and markings because these may differ greatly from the English form.

Foreign government and business names are cross-referenced.

Original	Cross Reference
K LINE	KAWASAKI KISEN KAISHA LTD SEE K LINE
VENEZUELAN LINE	VENEZOLANA DE NAVEGACIÓN SEE VENEZUELAN LINE

Foreign Government Names

The spelling of the name of a foreign government and its agencies, like foreign businesses, is often spelled in the foreign language. Also, the translation should be written on the document to be stored. The document is stored under the English spelling.

Original	Cross-Reference
ETHIOPIA PEOPLES REPUBLIC	ETYOPIA HEBRETASEBAWIT SEE ETHIOPIA PEOPLES REPUBLIC
POLISH PEOPLES REPUBLIC	POLSKA RZECZPOSPOLITA LUDOWA SEE POLISH PEOPLES REPUBLIC

The original record is stored in one place according to the alphabetic rules being used. A cross-reference is made, if necessary, for any of the reasons just discussed. The cross-reference will, in all probability, be on a label affixed to the tab of a guide or on a sheet of paper inserted into a folder. The guide or the sheet may be a distinctive color so that it is easy to find.

Check Your Knowledge of Cross-References

On a separate sheet of paper, make a cross-reference for each of the items that needs one.

1. John J. LaCroix
2. Dade County Public Works, Miami, Florida
3. St. Germaine Orthodox Church
4. Los Angeles Police Department
5. Stanton & Smith Security Systems
6. Patent Scaffolding Co., A Div. of Hardco Corp.
7. Anchorage Daily News
8. Ministry of Defense, Dominion of Canada
9. Po Chien Die Casting Company
10. Southwest Mfg. Co.

SUBJECTS WITHIN ALPHABETIC ARRANGEMENT

Within an alphabetic arrangement, records may sometimes be stored and retrieved more conveniently by a subject title than by a specific name. Beware, however, of using so many subjects that the arrangement becomes primarily a subject arrangement with alphabetic names as subdivisions! A few typical examples of acceptable subjects to use within an otherwise alphabetic name arrangement are:

1. *Applications.* The job for which applications are being made is more important than are the names of the applicants.
2. *Bids or projects.* Similar records are kept together regardless of the names of the writers, as all records pertain to the same bid or the same project.
3. *Special promotions or celebrations.* All records relating to the event are grouped together by subject instead of being spread throughout storage under the names of the writers or the companies.
4. *Branch office memos and duplicated information sent to many different offices.* Material of this nature is kept together to keep storage containers from becoming filled with duplicate records in many different places.

The procedure for the subject storage method is explained in detail in Chapter 7. Its application in this chapter consists of writing the subject title on the record if it does not already appear there. The main subject is the key unit. Subdivisions of the main subject are considered as successive units. The name of the correspondent is considered last.

For example, on all records pertaining to applications, the word APPLICATIONS is written as the key unit. The specific job applied for is a subdivision of that main subject and is the next unit (AC-COUNTANT in the first example). Further subdivisions may be necessary (See FACTORY CLERK/TYPIST in the third example and OFFICE CLERK/TYPIST in the fourth example). The applicant's name is coded last.

Index Order of Units in Names

Key Unit	Unit 2	Unit 3	Unit 4	Unit 5
1. APPLICATIONS	ACCOUNTANT	JOLLY	BRENDA	
2. APPLICATIONS	ADMINISTRATIVE	FUNG	KAREN	
3. APPLICATIONS	CLERKTYPIST	FACTORY	CHARLSTON	SUE
4. APPLICATIONS	CLERKTYPIST	OFFICE	GEORGE	VICKY
5. APPLICATIONS	DATA	PROCESSING	PACE	CHERYL
6. APPLICATIONS	MAINTENANCE	FACTORY	OWINGS	JERRY
7. APPLICATIONS	MAINTENANCE	HEADQUARTERS	LASELLE	DON
8. APPLICATIONS	WORD	PROCESSING	MCCOLLUM	BILL

REVIEW AND DISCUSSION

1. Arrange the following names in alphabetic order and explain your reasons. (Goal 1)
    a. Dolores LaVee
    b. Le-Ve Tree Surgery
    c. Francis Le Vee
    d. Ardis La Vee
    e. LaVee's Hair Design

2. Arrange the following names in alphabetic order and explain your reasons. (Goal 2)
    a. 3 Rs Day Care
    b. 100 Rays Tanning Salon
    c. 26 Freeway In-and-Out Restaurant
    d. 7 Rs Landscape and Nursery

3. Arrange the following names in alphabetic order and explain your reasons. (Goal 3)
    a. St. Paul's Catholic Church
    b. St. Louis First National Bank
    c. The St. Paul Register
    d. St. Louis Children's Home
    e. St. Louis Chapter of the National Organization for Women

4. School names are often identical in different cities. If you had several identically named schools to arrange in alphabetic order, what would determine the alphabetic arrangement? (Goal 3 and 4)

5. Code, then arrange the following federal government names in alphabetic order. Hint: The first three units are the same on each one. (Goal 5)
    a. Human Nutrition Information Service
        Food and Consumer Services
        Department of Agriculture
    b. National Park Service
        Office of the Assistant-Secretary
        Fish and Wildlife and Parks
        Department of Interior
    c. Center for Veterinary Medicine
        Food and Drug Administration
        Department of Health and Human Services

    d. Bureau of Prisons
       Department of Justice
    e. Federal Aviation Administration
       Department of Transportation
    f. Naval Air Systems Command
       Department of the Navy
    g. Bureau of Engraving and Printing
       Department of the Treasury
    h. Bureau of Public Affairs
       Department of State
    i. Centers for Disease Control
       Office of Assistant
       Secretary for Health
       Department of Health and Human Services
    j. Antitrust Division
       Department of Justice

6. In arranging city, county, province, or state government correspondence alphabetically, what are the key units to be coded? (Goal 5)

7. Which of the following items need cross-references? Explain why cross-references are needed and show what the cross-references would be. (Goal 6)
    a. Transportación Marítima Mexicana (Mexican Line)
    b. McCarthy and LaBarr Consultants
    c. North East Beauty College
    d. Hardwood Floors Co., a div. of Wymax Construction Company, Inc.
    e. Köninkrijk België (Kingdom of Belgium)

8. Why are subject categories ever found in an alphabetically arranged name file? Give at least two examples of subjects that might be found. (Goal 7)

APPLICATIONS (APP)

APP 3-1. Arranging Cards in Alphabetic Order

A. On 3" x 5" cards or on slips of paper of that size, type or print the names listed on the following pages in indexing order. Also type the number of the names on the top right corner of the card.

B. Prepare cross-reference cards where necessary according to the suggestions given in this chapter. Type the original number and an "X" to indicate a cross-reference.
C. Code each card for alphabetic filing.
D. Arrange all cards, including cross-references, in alphabetic order.
E. In a vertical column on a separate sheet of paper, list the numbers on the cards that you have now arranged in alphabetic order.
F. After you have checked your work and corrected any errors, merge these cards with the cards you prepared for App. 2-1 in Chapter 2.
G. In a vertical column on a separate sheet of paper, list the numbers of all the cards from Chapters 2 and 3 that you have arranged in alphabetic order (cross-references included). (Goals 1-6)

Names

26. New London Baptist Church, 330 Beech Ave., New London, CT 06320-0330
27. 9 to 5 Uniform Shop, 1250 S. Mill St., Dutton, VA 23050-5142
28. Hannah LaGrange, 3800 Bowman Rd., Baskett, KY 42402-3801
29. Transportation Dept., Sri Nepala Sarkai (Kingdom of Nepal)
30. LeRose Salon of Beauty, 145 Ross St., Leaf, MS 39456-1089
31. North West Investment Properties, 350 N. Silas St., Tacoma, WA 98408-4521
32. The Monitor, 3560 Main St., McIntosh, MN 56556-1243
33. Mid-Valley Estimators, 6354 N. Vineyard, Marion, NY 14505-6543
34. LaMesilla State Monument, 42 Palamino Way, Las Cruces, NM 88008-5200 (An agency of the state government.)
35. Mt. St. Helen's Souvenir Shop, 9520 Ashton Way, Cougar, WA 98616-5102
36. 57 Street Club, 19450 - 57 Street, Somerton, AZ 85350-5700
37. Laguna Beach Fire Department, 485 Hosedown Way, Laguna, FL 32413-1001
38. Department of Tourism, Estados Unidos Mexicanos (United Mexican States)
39. Mountain View Public Works, 35 Greenway Plaza, Mountain View, AR 72560-3520 (City government)

40. Thelma C. L'Esperance, 442 Lark Avenue, San Antonio, TX 78263-4400

41. Mrs. Q's Bakery, 450 S. Harris Street, Montgomery, IN 47558-4700

42. New London Brotherhood of Iron Workers, 255 Exeter, New London, MN 56273-2550

43. Mid-Valley National Bank, 16750 S. McLoughlin Blvd., Marion, NC 28752-1675

44. Mrs. Q's Bakery, 30250 N. Harris Street, Montgomery, IN 47558-4350

45. LaSalle County Court, 4350 Cedar Street, Alexandria, LA 71301-0032

46. Sikandra Norton, 32 Terrace Ct., Teaticket, MA 02536-0230

47. Joyce L. McIntyre, 1425 S. McKnight St., McAdoo, PA 18237-7466

48. The Monitor, 120 N. Main Street, McIntosh, SD 57641-1205

49. Northwest Tag & Label Company, 791 S. Memory Lane, Lima, OH 45801-7918

50. Museum of Fine Arts, 215 Cimmaron Trail, Santa Fe, NM 87501-2150 (An agency of the state government.)

APPLYING THE RULES

Job 2, Card Filing, Rules 6-10; Job 3, Card Filing, Rules 1-10

4 ALPHABETIC INDEXING RULES FOR COMPUTER DATABASES

GOALS

After completing this chapter, you will be able to:

1. Define the terms *bit*, *byte*, *field*, *computer record*, *file*, and *ASCII* value.
2. Apply the ASCII values when determining the sorting order of indexing units for a computer database.
3. Identify three important points when indexing and coding filing segments for either manual or computer storage.
4. Identify and briefly describe three types of records management computer databases.
5. Describe how a computer database is designed.
6. Describe how the components of a database are interrelated.
7. List and briefly describe the type of operations performed on a computer database.
8. Analyze, compare, and adjust filing segments for input into a computer database.

This chapter concludes the "rules" chapters about alphabetic storage procedures. In Chapters 2 and 3, you were introduced to standard alphabetic indexing rules for personal and business names. In this chapter, you will analyze the difference between computer alphabetic indexing and how *you* process filing segments for use in a manual storage system.

As mentioned in Chapter 1, a manual storage system is the best place to start learning about alphabetic indexing rules. Now that you have had some practice with the ten alphabetic indexing rules in this textbook, it's time to introduce how the computer stores, sorts, and retrieves filing segments. While the rules are the same for manual and computer indexing, there are a number of special features about the computer that need to be discussed.

OVERVIEW OF COMPUTER ALPHABETIC INDEXING

Why use a computer for any office operations? The computer can classify, sort, and repeat processes tirelessly and accurately for long periods of time. The computer is faster for sorting operations and can store more in less space. It gives great attention to detail and can "remember" faster and better than humans—*if* the input is accurate.

Computer Processing

In Figure 4-1 there are two lists. The one labelled "As Written" shows a computer printout of example names from Rules 1-10. The names were entered into the computer as they were written. The

Computer Sort, AS-WRITTEN Order			
AS WRITTEN	**KEY UNIT**	**UNIT 2**	**UNIT 3**
# Away Center	POUNDS	AWAY	CENTER
$ Saver Motel	DOLLAR	SAVER	MOTEL
7 Day Market	007	DAY	MARKET
21st Century Styles	021	CENTURY	STYLES
707 Garage Service	707	GARAGE	SERVICE
"A-OK" Pilot Shop	AOK	PILOT	SHOP
E'Lan Medical Equipment	ELAN	MEDICAL	EQUIPMENT
El Amigo Restaurant	ELAMIGO	RESTAURANT	

Computer Sort, KEY UNIT Order			
AS WRITTEN	**KEY UNIT**	**UNIT 2**	**UNIT 3**
7 Day Market	007	DAY	MARKET
21st Century Styles	021	CENTURY	STYLES
707 Garage Service	707	GARAGE	SERVICE
"A-OK" Pilot Shop	AOK	PILOT	SHOP
$ Saver Motel	DOLLAR	SAVER	MOTEL
El Amigo Restaurant	ELAMIGO	RESTAURANT	
E'lan Medical Equipment	ELAN	MEDICAL	EQUIPMENT
# Away Center	POUNDS	AWAY	CENTER

Figure 4-1 ■ Comparison of As-Written and Key Unit Computer Sorts

printout labelled "Key Unit" shows the same list of names entered into the computer as Key Unit, Unit 2, and Unit 3.   Notice the difference in the alphabetic order.   What causes the difference? In order to understand the difference, you need some background on how the computer records and stores information.

The computer sorts differently from humans.

The computer is an electronic device that translates all programs and data into electrical impulses.   When you touch a key on the keyboard, you are sending an electrical impulse to the computer. We can say that the presence of an electrical impulse represents a completed circuit; the absence of an electrical impulse represents an incomplete circuit.   From the time computers were invented, the complete and incomplete electrical circuits have been represented to humans as ones (1) and zeros (0). We cannot interpret an electrical impulse; and the computer doesn't understand a "1" without electricity.

Because there are only two possible choices, this representation of 1s and 0s is a binary (two-part) number system.   Each number in a binary number system is referred to as a binary digit. A **binary digit** (or **bit**) is the coding used to record information in the computer. Using a binary number system, the four mathematical functions of add, subtract, multiply, and divide can be performed. This is important because the computer carries out its tasks by performing numerous mathematical operations.

A byte is eight bits and represents a symbol, letter, or number.

The smallest addressable unit of information a computer can process is called a **byte** which represents eight binary digits.   Only seven digits are shown in Figure 4-2 (on the next page) because the eighth bit is a "test" bit. This test bit is called a **parity bit**. A parity bit is a binary digit used to check the accuracy of the completed electrical circuits. To show how a byte would look to humans, seven bits (ones and zeros) are encoded. For example, an "A" is 1000001.

In order for the computer to perform its operations, each byte or unit of information must be unique.   In other words, the computer must have a different bit pattern for an uppercase "A" than for a lowercase "a".

ASCII Code. Let's take a closer look at the need to have different bit patterns. The computer needs 8 bits to make a byte, which is the same as a letter, number, or symbol. In other words, there must be eight different circuits for one letter.

Decimal Number	ASCII Character	ASCII Bit Pattern	Decimal Number	ASCII Character	ASCII Bit Pattern
32	Space	0100000	80	P	1010000
33	!	0100001	81	Q	1010001
34	"	0100010	82	R	1010010
35	#	0100011	83	S	1010011
36	$	0100100	84	T	1010100
37	%	0100101	85	U	1010101
38	&	0100110	86	V	1010110
39	'	0100111	87	W	1010111
40	(	0101000	88	X	1011000
41	)	0101001	89	Y	1011001
42	*	0101010	90	Z	1011010
43	+	0101011	91	[	1011011
44	,	0101100	92	\	1011100
45	-	0101101	93	]	1011101
46	.	0101110	94	^	1011110
47	/	0101111	95	_	1011111
48	0	0110000	96	'	1100000
49	1	0110001	97	a	1100001
50	2	0110010	98	b	1100010
51	3	0110011	99	c	1100011
52	4	0110100	100	d	1100100
53	5	0110101	101	e	1100101
54	6	0110110	102	f	1100110
55	7	0110111	103	g	1100111
56	8	0111000	104	h	1101000
57	9	0111001	105	i	1101001
58	:	0111010	106	j	1101010
59	;	0111011	107	k	1101011
60	<	0111100	108	l	1101100
61	=	0111101	109	m	1101101
62	>	0111110	110	n	1101110
63	?	0111111	111	o	1101111
64	@	1000000	112	p	1110000
65	A	1000001	113	q	1110001
66	B	1000010	114	r	1110010
67	C	1000011	115	s	1110011
68	D	1000100	116	t	1110100
69	E	1000101	117	u	1110101
70	F	1000110	118	v	1110110
71	G	1000111	119	w	1110111
72	H	1001000	120	x	1111000
73	I	1001001	121	y	1111001
74	J	1001010	122	z	1111010
75	K	1001011	123	{	1111011
76	L	1001100	124	|	1111100
77	M	1001101	125	}	1111101
78	N	1001110	126	~	1111110
79	O	1001111	127	Del	1111111

The first 31 numbers are reserved for non-printing characters, sometimes known as control characters.

Figure 4-2 ■ ASCII Values Chart

In order to standardize which circuits and patterns are which to a computer processor, the American Standard Code for Information Interchange (ASCII, pronounced Ask E) was developed. **ASCII** assigns specific numeric values (or "decimal numbers") to the first 128 characters of the 256 possible byte combinations. Each symbol, space, number, uppercase, and lowercase letter must have a unique bit pattern. The ASCII chart shown in Figure 4-2 identifies the decimal number, the character, and the bit-pattern for symbols, numbers, uppercase and lowercase letters.

Number Processing. What do the ASCII values have to do with alphabetic indexing rules? For one thing, remember that a computer only uses mathematical operations to process information. When you sort a list of names, you look at the letters to determine the order. A computer reads *each* character by its bit pattern. The bit pattern is a number to the computer, shown in the ASCII value chart as a decimal number. *Because these values are numbers, the computer places the lowest value first.* The bytes are read as numbers, then the numbers are sorted from lowest to highest. Consequently, symbols, such as $, % and /, are sorted before numbers. Capital letters have a lower value or number than lowercase letters, and thus, would come first in an alphabetic sort.

ASCII values were developed to provide consistency in computer processing.

In other words, a filing segment beginning with a space would be sorted before any filing segment that begins with a symbol, a number, an uppercase letter, or a lowercase letter. If two filing segments were the same, but one was in uppercase letters and the other was in lowercase letters, the uppercase letters would be sorted and listed before the lowercase letters. By understanding how a computer reads the ASCII values, you can make your computer input more accurate and more predictable.

Indexing and Coding Filing Segments

Whether you are indexing and coding filing segments for a manual storage system or for computerized storage, the choice of the filing segment is vitally important. Careful attention to detail, consistent application of the alphabetic indexing rules, and knowledge of how a computer processes words are important points to remember.

The alphabetic indexing rules presented in this textbook are meant to be used in either manual or computerized systems. In a later section of this chapter, some specific considerations for computerized systems are discussed. Before that topic is discussed, though, you need to become aware of computer records storage.

COMPUTER DATABASES

A computer **database** is a collection of facts or information organized especially for rapid search and retrieval. Large mainframe computers have been using databases for years. A variety of database programs are available for personal computers. The information stored in a database can fulfill numerous purposes for a business. The next section describes some databases for records management.

> A database is a collection of facts or information.

Records Management and Databases

When office records are computerized, a database program is used. Depending on the size of the company and the records it generates, a company will use the database on personal computers or on a large mainframe computer. In either case, the database has been designed to handle file management, information management, and/or records management.

File Management. A **file management database** is used to keep track of one or two relevant facts, such as names and addresses in a customer mailing list.

Information Management. An **information management database** is more complex than a file management database and deals with keeping track of the data in correspondence documents. This type of database enables the user to extract specific pieces of information. Often, the decision maker uses the information gained to effect changes in the business. This type of database is sometimes administered by the records management department.

Records Management. A true **records management database** is an index of stored records. A typical index would contain such information as where the records are stored, how long the records must be kept, how the records will be destroyed, when the records should be moved from active to inactive storage, and some of the keywords used in the record. A **keyword** is a word or phrase that identifies a specified topic for the business. You will learn more about indexes, records retention, and transfer in Chapters 6 and 7.

In each of the three types of databases, whether a mainframe or personal computer is used, there are common terms and processes, which will be discussed next. Then, some overall rules required by the computer's operating system will be discussed.

Designing a Database

The process of designing a database takes time and effort to ensure that all of the needed pieces of information are included. This requires an in-depth analysis of the business for its current information needs as well as its possible future needs. The identification of the pieces of information that will make up the database to ensure rapid search and retrieval is a critical task. A good database design is crucial to its usefulness and success within the business.

The database structure is what makes the database work.

The databases you will work with have probably been designed and in use before you start with the company. However, the designer of the database had to break down the facts and pieces of information about the company to fit the database structure. The **database structure** defines the categories of information that make up the database. These categories are field, record, and file.

A **field** is a combination of characters to form words, numbers, or a meaningful code. Your first name, middle name, and last name would each be a field. Your date of birth, social security number, telephone number, the day you started school, and the month and year you finished high school are all examples of fields.

Each database software program follows general rules and each has its own specific rules. The general rules for creating fields are:

1. *The field must have a name.* Usually the name of the field cannot be longer than 8 to 11 characters.
2. *The field must have a specific character length.* The length of the field must accommodate the longest average entry. For last names, a common field length is 20 characters.
3. *The type of field must be identified.* Usually the type of information determines the type of field, such as:

   Character field—the most common type of field; combines alphabetic, numeric, and/or symbol characters to form words.
   Numeric field—used to perform mathematical operations.
   Date field—used for measuring length of time.

Logical field—used for answering yes or no and true or false questions.

Text field—used for recording sentences and/or paragraphs.

By identifying the type of field, further categorizing of information is possible. See Figure 4-3 below for an example of a database structure and a sample record.

Structure for database: A:\MAIL_LST.DBF
Number of data records: 155
Date of last update: 05/29/92

Field	Field Name	Type	Width	Dec	Index
1	Key_Unit	Character	20		Y
2	Unit_2	Character	15		N
3	Unit_3	Character	10		N
4	Unit_4	Character	10		N
5	Unit_5	Character	10		N
6	Address	Character	25		N
7	City	Character	20		N
8	State	Character	2		N
9	ZIP	Character	9		N
10	Phone	Character	8		N
11	Order_Dt	Date	8		N
12	Amt_Due	Number	8	2	N

Customer Name:	ABC COMPANY INC
Address:	1224 SW MERIDIAN
	CONCORD MA 01742
Phone Number:	555-2906
Date Ordered:	01/15/90
Amount Due:	$1,024.50

Figure 4-3 ■ Example of Database Structure and a Sample Record

When all the fields have been determined, the finished product is called a computer record. A **computer record** is the total collection of fields or specific pieces of information about one person or item.

When all the facts about one person are put together in a computer, a record has been created. For instance, all the specific facts about you listed in one place is a database record.

When all the records of similar items, like the students in a class or the customers of a business, are joined together, a file has been created. Because the **file** is a collection of related records, it can also be called a database. See Figure 4-4 below for an example of the relationships among fields, records, and files.

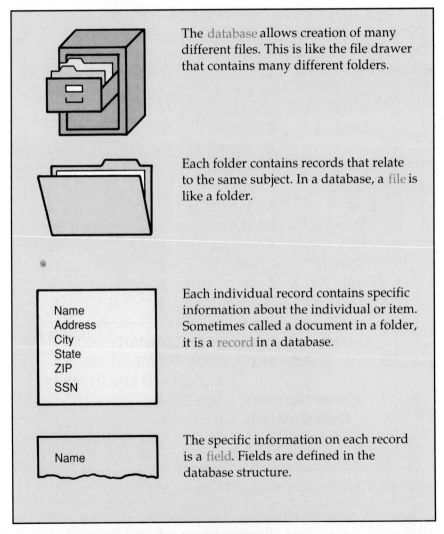

The database allows creation of many different files. This is like the file drawer that contains many different folders.

Each folder contains records that relate to the same subject. In a database, a file is like a folder.

Name
Address
City
State
ZIP
SSN

Each individual record contains specific information about the individual or item. Sometimes called a document in a folder, it is a record in a database.

Name

The specific information on each record is a field. Fields are defined in the database structure.

Figure 4-4 ■ Relationships of Database Parts

Example of a Computer Database

Let's plan a simple file management database to keep track of subscriptions for *Records Management Times*, a fictitious monthly magazine. We'll start by listing the facts or pieces of information required to keep track of the yearly subscriptions. Your job is to add new subscribers' names and change addresses and names as needed. You have determined that the best way to keep track of subscribers' names is to alphabetize the list of subscribers. With your knowledge of the alphabetic indexing rules, you know that for each subscriber, there will be a key unit, and at least a second unit, if not a third and fourth unit. Another factor here, though, is the need to mail subscribers their renewal notices. If the input to the database is by indexing units only, the mail labels will not be printed properly. Therefore, an additional field is needed for personal names. That field can simply be "Name." When the time comes to sort alphabetically, you tell the computer to use the indexing unit fields. When it is time to print mailing labels, you tell the computer to use the "Name" field.

> The database accepts input, then sorts and reports.

The next step is to create the computer database. The fields must be defined by name, type, and length. What type of information does the field contain? As mentioned earlier, the common types of fields are character, numeric, date, logical, and text. Each field type allows further categorization of the information in the field.

The Date of Renewal and Expiration Date fields are date fields. The Subscription Fee field is numeric. The rest are character fields.

Next, the longest average length of the field must be determined. For personal names, remember that the key unit is the surname. The key unit is usually the longest, and 20 characters is adequate. The second unit is usually 15 characters, and each succeeding unit is usually 10 characters.

The street address is usually 25 to 30 characters; city fields are usually 20; states are 2; and ZIP Codes are 9 digits, plus one space for the hyphen. Date fields are 8 characters (MM/DD/YY). The length of the Subscription fee field must include the decimal and two places after the decimal, so 6 characters is adequate.

Finally, the name of the field is determined. The field name has a limit of 8 to 11 characters; and no spaces are allowed. By using an underline instead of a space, the field names are a little easier to read and the database program accepts the entry.

On the next page is a list of the fields for our subscriber database file that includes the name, type, and length of the fields.

Field	Field Name	Type	Length
Subscriber's Key Unit	KEY_UNIT	Character	20
Second Unit of Subscriber's Name	UNIT_2	Character	15
Third Unit of Subscriber's Name	UNIT_3	Character	10
Fourth Unit of Subscriber's Name	UNIT_4	Character	10
Name	NAME	Character	40
Subscriber's Street Address	ST_ADDRESS	Character	25
Subscriber's City	CITY	Character	15
State	ST	Character	2
ZIP Code	ZIP	Character	10
Date of Renewal	RENEWAL	Date	8
Expiration Date	EXP_DATE	Date	8
Subscription Fee	SUB_FEE	Number	6

Working with a Database

There are three major categories of work that can be accomplished with a database — input, changing (editing), and reporting.

Input. After the database structure is defined and entered into the database program, the next step is to input or actually enter the information into the fields of the database. This is what the Subscriber Database looks like after the records have been entered.

KEY_ UNIT	UNIT_2	UNIT_3	ST_ADDRESS	CITY	ST	ZIP	RENEWAL	EXP_ DATE	SUB_ FEE
NEWMAN	NINA		301 E LANSDOWN RD	ARCOLA	MO	65603-1348	06/30/90	03/31/90	21.50
REMACK	THOMAS		117 CIRCLE DRIVE	CLINTON	PA	15026-7835	06/30/92	08/31/92	21.50
OWCYARK	LARRY		676 BLACKFORD CT	SAN JOSE	CA	95117-1134	06/30/92	08/31/92	21.50
BERRY	STEPHEN	S	4416 BRUNSWICK ST	CRYSTAL	MN	55422-2138	07/31/92	09/30/92	21.50
REISS	MICHAEL	R	2533 ELM STREET	ANCHORAGE	AK	99504-4238	07/31/92	09/30/92	21.50
SCHMIDT	LOUIS	B	3222 PAWNEE PLACE	ENID	OK	73702-4238	07/30/92	09/30/92	22.50
NUNAN	NATHAN	M	1652 CEDAR DRIVE	LONGMONT	CO	80501-3456	07/31/92	09/30/92	22.50
OWENBY	LAURA	J	1023 WALNUT LANE	AMARILLO	TX	79107-1204	07/31/92	09/30/92	22.50
LOWE	MARY	ANN	4914 ASHTON PKWY	CHICAGO	IL	60652-3456	07/31/92	09/30/92	21.50
REISS	MARK		21100 NW 29 AVE	OCALA	FL	32670-3647	07/31/92	09/30/92	21.50

Changing. The second category of work in a computer database involves *editing* or changing the data by inserting, deleting, or otherwise changing. The ability to use this database function makes the database dynamic and more useful to the business. This is what the Subscriber Database looks like after corrections have been made and the database has been sorted alphabetically by the KEY_UNIT field.

KEY_ UNIT	UNIT_2	UNIT_3	ST_ADDRESS	CITY	ST	ZIP	RENEWAL	EXP_ DATE	SUB_ FEE
BERRY	STEPHEN	S	4416 BRUNSWICK ST	CRYSTAL	MN	55422-2138	07/31/92	09/30/92	21.50
LOWE	MARY	ANNE	4914 ASHTON PKWY	CHICAGO	IL	60652-3456	07/31/92	09/30/92	21.50
NEWMAN	NINA		301 ELANSDOWN RD	ARCOLA	MO	65603-1348	06/30/90	03/31/90	21.50
NUNAN	NATHAN	M	1652 CEDAR DRIVE	LONGMONT	CO	80501-3456	07/31/92	09/30/92	21.50
OWCYARK	LARRY		676 BLACKFORD CT	SAN JOSE	CA	95117-1134	06/30/92	08/31/92	21.50
OWENBY	LAURA	J	1023 WALNUT LANE	AMARILLO	TX	79107-1204	07/31/92	09/30/92	21.50
REISS	MARK		21100 NW 29 AVE	OCALA	FL	32670-3647	07/31/92	09/30/92	21.50
REISS	MICHAEL	R	2533 ELM STREET	ANCHORAGE	AK	99504-4238	07/31/92	09/30/92	21.50
REMACK	THOMAS		117 CIRCLE DRIVE	CLINTON	PA	15026-7835	06/30/92	08/31/92	21.50
SCHMIDT	LOUIS	B	3222 PAWNEE PLACE	ENID	OK	73702-4238	07/31/92	09/30/92	21.50

Reporting. The last category of work for the database to perform is reporting. Database reports are printouts that give the user a summary of the information included in the database. Here is a report of the renewal dates in our sample subscriber list:

RENEWAL	KEY UNIT	UNIT 2	UNIT 3
06/30/90	NEWMAN	NINA	
06/30/92	OWCYARK	LARRY	
06/30/92	REMACK	THOMAS	
07/31/92	BERRY	STEPHEN	S
07/31/92	LOWE	MARY	ANNE
07/31/92	NUNAN	NATHAN	M
07/31/92	OWENBY	LAURA	J
07/31/92	REISS	MARK	
07/31/92	REISS	MICHAEL	R
07/31/92	SCHMIDT	LOUIS	B

Here is an example of what mailing labels would look like for the Subscriber Database:

STEPHEN S BERRY   MARY ANNE LOWE
4416 BRUNSWICK ST   4914 ASHTON PKWY
CRYSTAL MN 55422-2138   CHICAGO IL 60652-3456

The renewal date report and the sample mailing labels appear in different forms; yet, both reports were generated from the same database.

Working within the Computer's Operating System

Whether the database program is run from a mainframe, mini-computer, or microcomputer, it performs according to the operating system of the computer. An **operating system** is the link between the computer hardware, the user, and the application software. The most common operating system for IBM and IBM-compatible microcomputers built from 1981 through 1992 is called DOS, an acronym for **D**isk **O**perating **S**ystem. There are other operating systems specific to the type of computer and microprocessor. For instance, the Macintosh operating system is called *the System*. The IBM PS/2 operating system is called *OS/2*.

When you actually begin working with a database program, each database you create must have a filename. A **filename** is a unique name given to a file stored for computer use; the filename must follow the computer's operating system rules. Current DOS versions limit the filename to eight characters. These characters can include all of the letters of the alphabet, A through Z; digits, 0 through 9; and these special characters: ! @ # $ % ^ & ( ) _ { } ~ '. In the filename, you may not use mathematic and common punctuation symbols, such as: * + = : ; " , . ? / and space, or tab.

In some applications, a three-letter extension can be used. In most database programs, however, the extension is assigned by the database program and cannot be changed. For example, the file that contains the database records will often have an extension of DBF or DTA; a report may have an extension of RPT or REP; and mailing labels might have an extension of LBL.

Take a look at the following list of filenames and extensions:

SUBSCRIB.DTA is the file that contains all of the records about the subscribers to *Records Management Times*.

SUBSCRIB.REP is a report file for the subscriber database.

SUBSCRIB.NDX is an index file for the subscriber database.

SUBSCRIB.LBL is a label file for the subscriber database.

ALPHABETIC INDEXING RULES FOR COMPUTER DATABASES

The alphabetic indexing rules in this textbook work well for both manual and computer systems. This last section of the chapter deals with the input of filing segments to the computer database.

Some overall assumptions about computer database input are:

1. Each indexing unit is entered into a separate field.
2. All uppercase letters are used with no punctuation marks, like the examples in Chapters 2 and 3.

In the following discussion, specific assumptions about the rule will be listed first. Then, if the computer input needs special care, a comparison list will be shown to highlight the differences for each rule.

Rule 1: Indexing Order of Units

Names are entered in indexing order according to Rules 1A and 1B, Chapter 2. There are no changes in the order of examples.

Consistent input is vital!

Rule 2: Minor Words and Symbols in Business Names

Symbols and minor words are spelled out. Thus, sorting by ASCII values is similar to manual sorting where you use letters. Remember that in computer sorting symbols have the lowest value. Compare the similar names in the computer sort shown below:

Computer Sort, Rule 2

EX	KEY_UNIT	UNIT_2	UNIT_3	UNIT_4	UNIT_5
1A	#	AWAY	DIET	CENTER	
2A	$	SAVER	MOTEL		
3A	BARB	&	SAM	MINIATURE	GOLF
3B	BARB	AND	SAM	MINIATURE	GOLF
4A	BILTMORE	HOTEL	THE		
2B	DOLLAR	SAVER	MOTEL		
1B	POUNDS	AWAY	DIET	CENTER	
4B	THE	BILTMORE	HOTEL		

Notice the difference in examples 1A and 1B. The symbol "#" is spelled out in 1B and becomes the next to the last name in the list. Notice also how the indexing units must be in the correct field. In example 4A and 4B "THE" is indexed differently. This makes a critical difference in the alphabetic placement of the filing segments. The difference between entering a symbol or spelling the word is shown in examples 2A and 2B and 3A and 3B.

Spell out symbols.

Rule 3: Punctuation and Possessives

No punctuation is used.

Punctuation marks are not entered; when they are used, punctuation marks have a lower ASCII value and are sorted before letters of the alphabet. Take a look at examples 1A and 1B, 2A and 2B, 3A and 3B, and 4A and 4B shown below. In each case, the punctuation is sorted before an alphabetic letter.

Computer Sort, Rule 3

EX	KEY_UNIT	UNIT_2	UNIT_3	UNIT_4
3A	ALICE'S	CUSTOM	DESIGNS	
3B	ALICES	CUSTOM	DESIGNS	
2A	ALL-IN-ONE	STORE		
1A	ALLEN-MILLER	LAW	FIRM	
1B	ALLENMILLER	LAW	FIRM	
2B	ALLINONE	STORE		
4A	ON/OFF	FREEWAY	HOTEL	THE
4B	ONOFF	FREEWAY	HOTEL	THE

Rule 4: Single Letters and Abbreviations

Single letters are entered as written. Consistent input is critical. If a business name with spaces between initials has been coded as one unit one time and as several units the next time, the sort order would be completely different. In all three of the examples below, the units have not been entered in the same manner. This makes a big difference in the alphabetic order of the items.

Computer Sort, Rule 4

EX	KEY_UNIT	UNIT_2	UNIT_3	UNIT_4	UNIT_5
3A	I	B	M	CORP	
1A	I	C	I	REALTY	INC
3B	IBM	CORP			
2B	ICI	REALTY	INC		
2A	K	NINE	KLIPS		
2B	KNINE	KLIPS			

Rule 5: Titles and Suffixes

Names with titles and suffixes are indexed according to Rule 5, Chapter 2. If the units are correctly coded, the only problem to develop will be if the seniority title is in Roman numerals.   Fortunately, "I" has a lower ASCII value than "J" in Junior or "S" in Senior. If the Roman numeral was higher or more than "V," (VI, VII, VIII, IX, X), "J" in Junior or "S" in Senior would be listed before the Roman numeral. The computer reads Roman numerals as letters. To sort Roman numerals correctly, they must be entered as Arabic numerals. In that case, input the Roman numerals as Arabic numerals (1, 2, 3, 4, 5, 6, etc.).

Rule 6: Prefixes—Articles and Particles

Articles and particles are entered as a part of surnames, according to Rule 6, Chapter 3. Consistency of input is the key factor again. The rule states that the surname should be indexed as a single unit. Careful attention to detail makes this rule no different in either manual or computer systems. In each example below, the articles and particles have been treated differently. Consistency in the application of the rule is very important here.

Computer Sort, Rule 6

EX	KEY_UNIT	UNIT_2	UNIT_3	UNIT_4
2A	LA	BELLE	BEAUTY	SALON
1A	LA	BELLE	BOB	
2B	LABELLE	BEAUTY	SALON	
1B	LABELLE	BOB		
3A	VAN	DER	HOUT	WILLIAM
3B	VANDER	HOUT	WILLIAM	
3C	VANDERHOUT	WILLIAM		

Rule 7: Numbers in Business Names

Numbers are entered in such a way that all numbers have an equal number of digits and are aligned on the right. A zero, known as a **leading zero**, is added to the front of the number in order to sort in numeric order. As you and I know, 2 comes before 10. To the computer, though, 1 is first, then 10 through 19, then 2, followed by 20 through 29, continuing to 100. By adding a leading zero before a one-digit number, however, you are forcing the computer to read the number as a two-digit number for correct numeric sorting.

Notice the difference in examples 1A and 1B in Computer Sort, Rule 7. In 1A, a leading zero has been added and the filing segment is in the correct order. In examples 2A and 2B, the difference is adding

Numbers must have leading zeros.

letters to the number. The second unit in 5A has a leading zero and is in the correct order. The especially troublesome examples are 4A and 4B. Remember, Rule 5 states that Roman numerals come after Arabic numerals but before alphabetic characters. Roman numerals are shown in parentheses.

Computer Sort, Rule 7

EX	KEY_UNIT	UNIT_2	UNIT_3	UNIT_4
1A	07	DAY	FOOD	MARKET
2A	21	CENTURY	GRAPHICS	INC
4A	21(XXI)	CLUB		
2B	21ST	CENTURY	GRAPHICS	
1B	7	DAY	FOOD	MARKET
5A	HIGHWAY	026	CAFE	
6A	HIGHWAY	210	MALL	
5B	HIGHWAY	26	CAFE	
4B	XXI	CLUB		

Rule 8: Organizations and Institutions

Names of organizations and institutions are coded as written. There should be no difference between the filing order in manual systems and in computer systems.

Rule 9: Identical Names

Identical names are indexed according to Rule 9, Chapter 3. Rule 9 could become interesting with the computer. So much would depend on the field structure of the database and the sort order. The correct field structure to match Rule 9 requires separate City, State, and Street fields. The sort should be in the following order: Key Unit, Succeeding Units, City, State, and Street. Take a look at Computer Sort, Rule 9, Part A:

Computer Sort, Rule 9, Part A

EX	KEY_UNIT	UNIT_2	UNIT_3	CITY	ST	STREET
2A	FAST	EDDIES	DINER	LUBBOCK	TX	12 STREET
2B	FAST	EDDIES	DINER	LUBBOCK	TX	12500 GRANT
2C	FAST	EDDIES	DINER	LUBBOCK	TX	17000 GRANT
2D	FAST	EDDIES	DINER	LUBBOCK	TX	18650 GRANT
2E	FAST	EDDIES	DINER	LUBBOCK	TX	36 STREET
3A	FIRST	CHRIST	CHURCH	DALLAS	OR	150 SE CONCORD

3B	FIRST	CHRIST	CHURCH	DALLAS	TX	725 N 48 STREET
4A	NELSON	JULIANA		DAYTON	OH	4550 ELM STREET
4B	NELSON	JULIANA		DAYTON	OH	975 CEDAR STREET
5A	SANDPIPER	MOTEL	THE	GLADSTONE	MI	
5B	SANDPIPER	MOTEL	THE	GLADSTONE	NJ	

In example 2 shown above, the sort order is correct. However, the building number interferes with the sorting of the street name. Notice how 12 and 36 Streets are separated by 12500 Grant, 17000 Grant, and 18650 Grant. To overcome this problem, the numbers should have leading zeros. Next, the street names and building numbers should be in separate fields. This would solve the problem of examples 3 and 4. Study Computer Sort, Rule 9, Part B for the difference in input with the street names and building numbers indexed as separate fields.

Computer Sort, Rule 9, Part B

EX	KEY_UNIT	UNIT_2	UNIT_3	CITY	ST	STREET	BLDG_NO
2A	FAST	EDDIES	DINER	LUBBOCK	TX	12 STREET	04350
2D	FAST	EDDIES	DINER	LUBBOCK	TX	36 STREET	00350
2B	FAST	EDDIES	DINER	LUBBOCK	TX	GRANT STREET	12500
2C	FAST	EDDIES	DINER	LUBBOCK	TX	GRANT STREET	17000
2E	FAST	EDDIES	DINER	LUBBOCK	TX	GRANT STREET	18650
3A	FIRST	CHRIST	CHURCH	DALLAS	OR	SE CONCORD	00150
3B	FIRST	CHRIST	CHURCH	DALLAS	TX	N 48 STREET	00725
4B	NELSON	JULIANA		DAYTON	OH	CEDAR STREET	00975
4A	NELSON	JULIANA		DAYTON	OH	ELM STREET	04550
5A	SANDPIPER	MOTEL	THE	GLADSTONE	MI		
5B	SANDPIPER	MOTEL	THE	GLADSTONE	NJ		

Rule 10: Government Names

Government names are indexed in computers the same as in manual systems.

This chapter has presented an overview of how the computer processes information in computerized databases. By applying the ASCII values when inputting information to a computer database, you should achieve the same alphabetic order whether in a computer or manual system.

IMPORTANT TERMS

ASCII	byte
binary digit (bit)	computer record

database	information management database
database structure	keyword
field	leading zero
file	operating system
file management database	parity bit
filename	records management database

REVIEW AND DISCUSSION

1.   What is a bit and a byte? (Goal 1)
2.   What is a field, record, and file? (Goal 1)
3.   What does an ASCII value represent? (Goal 1)
4.   Place the following items in ASCII value order. Use Figure 4-2. (Goal 2)
     a.   # One Storage
     b. $ Rite Store
     c.   AT A GLANCE HAIR SALON
     d.   @ Once
     e.   ADAMS GROCERY
     f.   adams grocery
5.   List three important points to remember whether you are indexing and coding filing segments for manual or computer storage. (Goal 3)
6.   Identify and briefly describe three types of records management computer databases. (Goal 4)
7.   Describe the process you would use to set up a name and address computer database for a club membership. (Goal 5)
8.   How are fields, records, and files related in database terminology? (Goal 6)
9.   List and briefly describe the types of operations that are performed on a computer database. (Goal 7)
10. Code the indexing units in each of the following names. Then, describe how you would input each of the following items into a computer database. (Goal 8)
     a.   7 Gnomes Mining Company
     b.   21st and Main Cafe
     c.   11 Main Place Gallery
     d. $ Days Again!
     e.   KOST Radio Station

11. Which, if any, of the following filing segments might need to be adjusted for input into a computer database? (Goal 8)
    a. U & I Antiques, Inc.
    b. Andrea Hastings, CPA
    c. St. Andrew's Catholic Church
    d. 235 North Plains Mall
    e. #1 Storage Company
    f. George Peterson III
    g. Betty Jones, 123 First Street, Gordon, Alaska
    h. Betty Jones, 123 First Street, Gordon, West Virginia

APPLICATIONS (APP)

APP 4-1. Video Connection Database

You have just been hired to work at Video Connection, a video rental store. Video rentals are handled through a computer database. The database is set up to print a list of customers in alphabetized card form. The first thing you notice is that the list is not in true alphabetic order. You then discover that there is a difference in how the names have been input. Some of the names are in all capital letters; some are mixed. Some of the names have punctuation included in the name; some do not. What reasons can you give for how and why the list would not be in order? What steps can you take to make the customer listing more consistent? (Goals 2, 3, 6, and 8)

APP 4-2. Business Club Database

You are the newly elected secretary of your business club. The officers have decided that it's time for the 150-member club to use a computer database. The purpose of the database is to keep track of members' names and addresses and yearly dues. The officers have also determined that the membership list should be in alphabetic order, and member mailing labels should be generated by the computer. (Goals 5, 7, and 8)
    a. Describe how you will design and set up the database.
    b. Describe in detail how you will input the members' names and addresses.

APPLYING THE RULES

Job 3, Card Filing Review.

5 CORRESPONDENCE RECORDS STORAGE

GOALS

After completing this chapter, you will be able to:

1. Explain terms used in correspondence records storage systems.
2. Identify the basic types of correspondence records storage equipment.
3. Identify the different types of storage supplies used in correspondence records storage and explain their use.
4. Describe the criteria for selecting storage equipment and supplies.
5. List the advantages and disadvantages of the alphabetic method of records storage.
6. Explain the necessity for careful selection and design of an alphabetic records storage system.
7. Explain how color can be used in correspondence records storage.
8. Describe the six steps that must be followed in order to store a record properly according to the alphabetic method.
9. Explain the purpose of a tickler file and how it is arranged.
10. Explain the process you would use to find misfiled or lost records.

So far in your study of *Records Management*, Fifth Edition, you have worked with cards. Manual card records provide an excellent place to learn how to index, code, and cross-reference filing segments. In Chapter 4, you were introduced to records in computer databases. However, most business records are in the form of letters or memos. Beginning with this chapter, you will start to work with correspondence — the type of records that are found in all kinds of businesses. You will continue to index, code, and cross-reference according to the ten alphabetic indexing rules in Chapters 2 and 3. In this chapter, you will study the three remaining steps in alphabetic storage procedures: inspecting, sorting, and storing.

In Chapter 1 you learned how the information explosion has increased the number of business records. One of the major goals of records management is to get the right record to the right person at the right time at the lowest possible cost. You have discovered that a set of written rules for alphabetic indexing gives consistency for storing and retrieving records. Consistent application of the alphabetic indexing rules is one part of an efficient records management program. Using effective, appropriate equipment and supplies is another part of the records management program. This chapter introduces various records storage equipment and supplies available and describes criteria for their selection.

OVERVIEW AND TERMINOLOGY OF CORRESPONDENCE RECORDS STORAGE

You have identified filing segments for card and database records in Chapters 2, 3, and 4. You have indexed, coded, and cross-referenced a variety of personal and business names. It's time to add correspondence records. Business letters, reports, and memorandums are all part of the daily correspondence that business transacts. The process of determining how correspondence will be stored is a bit more complex than for cards. The same rules apply, though. Your task is still the same: index, code, and cross-reference the filing segment. What is different is the addition of the inspecting, sorting, and storing steps and the equipment and supplies required for correspondence records.

> Correspondence includes business letters, memos, and reports.

You are familiar with some of the specific terms and meanings regarding storage procedures in records management. Part of your study of Chapter 5 includes understanding the following definitions:

1. **System. System** as used in records storage means any storage plan devised by a storage equipment manufacturer. System has a broader meaning in management, however (See Figure 10-1, page 231).
2. **Storage. Storage** is the actual placement of materials into a folder, on a section of a magnetic disk, or on a shelf, according to a plan. The term *filing* may be used to mean storage, but filing is usually associated with paper records only.
3. **Storage (Filing) Method.** A **storage (filing) method** is a systematic way of storing records according to one of the following ar-

rangements: alphabetic, subject, numeric, geographic, or chronologic. This chapter's focus is the alphabetic storage method.

4. **Storage Procedures. Storage procedures** are a series of steps for the orderly arrangement of records as required by a specific storage method.

The storage method discussed here and in previous chapters has been alphabetic. Records management professionals do not agree on the number of methods of records storage. Some say there are just two: alphabetic and numeric. Others add a third: alphanumeric. Still others add a fourth: chronologic. To make storage systems easy for you to understand, this text will consider four storage methods: alphabetic, subject, numeric, and geographic. With the exception of chronologic storage, each storage method uses alphabetic concepts in its operation. The other storage methods are described in detail in Chapters 7, 8, and 9.

ARMA offers guidelines to ensure that records storage procedures are followed consistently.

The professional organization for records management, ARMA, has developed many helpful publications designed to simplify records management procedures. In this chapter, you will note reference to ARMA's *Filing Procedures Guidelines*. These guidelines are developed by ARMA committee members who bring the best and most efficient storage procedures to this publication. As with the ARMA *Alphabetic Filing Rules*, the *Filing Procedures Guidelines* offers records managers methods to gain the consistency so important to records storage and retrieval efficiency.

BASIC STORAGE EQUIPMENT AND SUPPLIES

We've all heard the adage, "A place for everything, and everything in its place." The records manager or person in charge of purchasing the equipment and supplies for the records center must certainly heed this advice! The filing systems industry has wholesale sales in excess of $8 million annually. Filing cabinet sales are increasing by 18 percent per year as 95 percent of all information is still stored on paper[1]. At this point let's consider these questions: What type of equipment and supplies are used most often in the office? What is the specific vocabulary for records management equipment and supplies?

---

[1]*ISDA Office Systems Management Quarterly*, Rod Exelbert Associates, Fort Lauderdale, FL, Fall, 1989, p. 20.

Storage Equipment

Types of storage equipment most commonly used for paper records are (1) vertical file cabinets, (2) lateral file cabinets, (3) shelf files, and (4) mobile shelving. Other types of storage equipment and their special uses will be discussed in later chapters.

Vertical File Cabinets. A **vertical file cabinet** is the conventional storage cabinet in one- to five-drawer sizes. The popular four-drawer vertical file cabinet is shown in Figure 5-1A. The type and volume of records to be stored will determine the width, depth, number, and size of drawers. The most common sizes of vertical file cabinet drawers are for cards, letters, and legal records. You will note that in order to place or remove items in a vertical file cabinet, a lifting up-and-down (vertical) motion is required.

Lateral File Cabinets. A **lateral file cabinet** has drawers that open from the long side and looks like a chest of drawers or bookcase with doors. Figure 5-1B shows a lateral file cabinet with roll-back drawer fronts.

Figure 5-1B ■ Lateral File Cabinet
TAB Products Co.

Figure 5-1A ■ Vertical File Cabinet

Because the long (narrow) side opens, lateral file cabinets are particularly well suited to narrow spaces. They are available in a variety of shapes and sizes, depending on the number and depth of the drawers. To place and remove items in a lateral file cabinet, a sliding (horizontal) motion is required.

Shelf Files. **Shelf files** are simply shelves arranged horizontally and used for storing records. Shelf files may be the open style or have roll-back or roll-down fronts. Shelves may be arranged in rotary form (see Figure 5-1C), as a stationary book-shelf (see Figure 5-1D), or may be mobile with shelves that move as needed for storage and retrieval (see Figure 5-2).

Figure 5-1C ■ Rotary Shelf Files
RICHARDS-WILCOX OFFICE SYSTEMS GROUP

Figure 5-1D ■ Open-Shelf Files
TAB Products Co.

Mobile Shelving. In **mobile shelving**, record containers (folders and boxes, as a rule) are stored on shelves that move on tracks attached to the floor. In some cases, these shelving units are not motorized and thus must be physically moved by the operator. More often, the units are electrically powered, which saves time and energy for the operator. One type of mobile shelving is the **mobile aisle system** (see Figure 5-2A) which is electrically powered so that shelves can be moved to create an aisle between any two shelf units.

In some movable shelving equipment, the shelves slide from side to side as shown in Figure 5-2B. The records on shelves behind the moved shelves are then exposed for use.

Figure 5-2A ■ Mobile Aisle System (Tab-Trac)
TAB Products Co.

Figure 5-2B ■ Side-to-Side Mobile Shelving (Tab Spacefinder)
TAB Products Co.

Motorized rotary storage revolves horizontally around a central hub much like the movement of seats on a Ferris wheel. Shelves that house documents in folders, cards, or microforms are available in sideways positions found in lateral files or more commonly in the regular forward position.

To retrieve records from motorized rotary storage, as shown with the Lektriever by Kardex in Figure 5-3, the operator consults a register

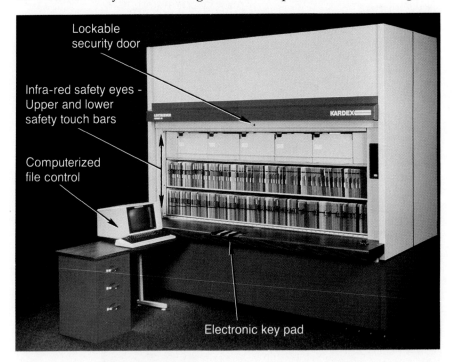

Figure 5-3A ■ Lektriever Motorized Rotary Storage Equipment
Kardex Systems, Inc.

Figure 5-3B ■ Electronic Key Pad (close-up)
Kardex Systems, Inc.

for the number of the shelf holding the requested record. (This register is maintained and kept up-to-date by the files operator.) Next, the operator presses a button on the keypad of the storage unit for the number of the shelf to be retrieved. The desired shelf then rotates to a position directly in front of the operator. This unit has a computerized file control option. The Lektriever also has several safety features such as a combination lock, lockable security door and lower access panel, infra-red safety eyes, and safety touch bars.

When choosing storage containers, a comparison of space used and file capacity is useful for determining cost effectiveness. Figure 5-4 compares the number of filing inches to the amount of floor space used by each of the storage containers shown.

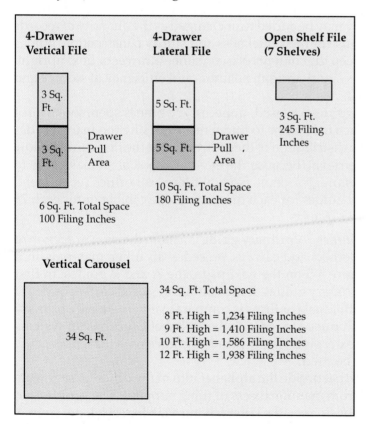

Figure 5-4 ■ Floor Space Consumption vs. Filing Capacity
(*All figures are approximate as manufacturers change.*)
Adapted from a drawing by Nick Hanson, Filing Systems Specialists, Portland, Oregon.

Storage Supplies

Efficient storage and retrieval requires the use of not only the right equipment but also the right supplies. The principal supplies used in manual storage of paper records are discussed briefly below.

Guides make storage and retrieval faster.

Guides. A **guide** is a rigid divider that, as the name implies, guides the eye or points the way to the location of the folder being sought. Guides are made of heavy material such as pressboard, plastic, or lightweight metal. Some guides have reinforced tabs of metal or acetate to give added strength for longer wear.

The proper placement of guides eliminates the need to spend time searching through similar names to find the part of the alphabet needed. The same set of guides may be used year after year with no change, or they may be added to or changed as the quantity of records expands. Because of their thickness and sturdy construction, guides serve also to keep the contents of a container (drawer or box) upright. When contents stand upright, neatness and efficiency of storage and retrieval result.

If too few guides are used, unnecessary time is spent looking for the correct place to store or to find a record. Using too many guides and an uneven distribution of them throughout the files can also slow storage and retrieval, because the eye must look at so many tabs to find the right storage section. Several filing authorities recommend using about 20 guides for each drawer in a file cabinet or for each 28 inches of stored records.

Primary Guides. A **primary guide** is a main division or section of the storage method and always precedes all other materials in a section. In Figure 5-5 on the next page, the A and B guides, in first position, are primary guides. If the volume of stored correspondence with many individuals or firms is comparatively small, only primary guides need to be used to indicate the alphabetic sections. In systems that use color extensively, only primary guides with the letters of the alphabet may be used.

Guide sets that divide the alphabet into many different segments are available from manufacturers of filing supplies. The simplest set is a 23- or 25-division set, the latter having a tab for each letter from A to W, a tab labeled Mc, and a last tab with the combination XYZ. A more complex set of guides, with the alphabet subdivided into 40, 80, 120, and 160 sections may be necessary if the volume of stored records

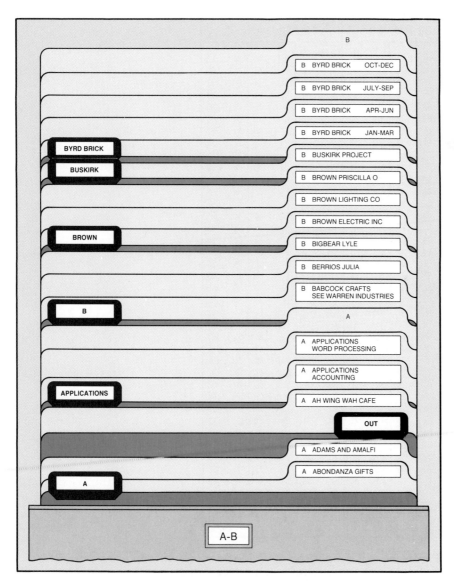

Figure 5-5 ■ One Section of an Alphabetic Arrangement

is great. Suppose, for example, you have hundreds of folders for names beginning with A. Instead of just one A guide, you might need a sequence of guides that would have tabs reading Aa, Ah, Am, An, Ar, and At. An 80-division and a 120-division breakdown of guides printed by manufacturers is shown in Figure 5-6 on the next page. Up to 10,000 alphabetic divisions are available for A to Z.

80 Div. A to Z				120 Div. A to Z					
A	1	L	41	A	1	Gr	41	Pe	81
An	2	Le	42	Al	2	H	42	Pi	82
B	3	Li	43	An	3	Han	43	Pl	83
Be	4	Lo	44	As	4	Has	44	Pr	84
Bi	5	M	45	B	5	He	45	Pu	85
Bo	6	Map	46	Bar	6	Hen	46	Q	86
Br	7	McA	47	Bas	7	Hi	47	R	87
Bro	8	McH	48	Be	8	Ho	48	Re	88
Bu	9	McN	49	Ber	9	Hon	49	Ri	89
C	10	Me	50	Bl	10	Hu	50	Ro	90
Ce	11	Mi	51	Bo	11	I	51	Rog	91
Co	12	Mo	52	Br	12	J	52	Ru	92
Coo	13	N	53	Bre	13	Jo	53	S	93
Cr	14	O	54	Bro	14	K	54	Sch	94
D	15	P	55	Bu	15	Ke	55	Scho	95
De	16	Pl	56	C	16	Ki	56	Se	96
Do	17	Q	57	Car	17	Kl	57	Sh	97
Dr	18	R	58	Ce	18	Kr	58	Shi	98
E	19	Re	59	Ci	19	L	59	Si	99
En	20	Ro	60	Co	20	Lar	60	Sm	100
F	21	S	61	Com	21	Le	61	Sn	101
Fi	22	Sch	62	Cop	22	Len	62	Sp	102
Fo	23	Se	63	Cr	23	Li	63	St	103
G	24	Sh	64	Cu	24	Lo	64	Sti	104
Ge	25	Si	65	D	25	M	65	Su	105
Gi	26	Sm	66	De	26	Map	66	T	106
Gr	27	St	67	Di	27	McA	67	Th	107
H	28	Sti	68	Do	28	McD	68	Tr	108
Har	29	Su	69	Du	29	McH	69	U	109
Has	30	T	70	E	30	McN	70	V	110
He	31	To	71	El	31	Me	71	W	111
Her	32	U	72	Er	32	Mi	72	Wam	112
Hi	33	V	73	F	33	Mo	73	We	113
Ho	34	W	74	Fi	34	Mu	74	Wh	114
Hu	35	We	75	Fo	35	N	75	Wi	115
I	36	Wh	76	Fr	36	Ne	76	Wil	116
J	37	Wi	77	G	37	No	77	Wim	117
K	38	Wo	78	Ge	38	O	78	Wo	118
Ki	39	X-Y	79	Gi	39	On	79	X-Y	119
Kr	40	Z	80	Go	40	P	80	Z	120

Figure 5-6 ■ Comparison of Guide Sets for A to Z Indexes
Esselte Pendaflex Corporation

As you study the columns in Figure 5-6, you will note that some parts of the alphabet have more subdivisions than do others; notably, B, C, H, M, S, and W. Subdivisions within those letters are necessary because there are more names that begin with those letters than with other letters in the alphabet. Similarly, names beginning with I, O, Q, U, V, X, Y, and Z occur far less frequently and, therefore, no subdivisions of those letters are usually needed.

The number of guides furnished by different manufacturers may vary even though each one may divide the alphabet into 40 subdivisions. Manufacturers may elect to omit Mc, subdivide letters differently, or combine different letters. Before a set of guides is purchased, the records manager needs to get a list of the subdivisions of the alphabet from the manufacturer to see if they fit specific office requirements.

Some guides may be purchased with preprinted tabs. Others have tabs with slotted holders into which can be inserted labels showing whatever sections of the alphabet are needed. (The guides in Figure 5-5 are of this kind.)

Special Guides. To lead the eye more quickly to a specific place in the file, a **special** or **auxiliary guide** may be used. This guide may:

1. Indicate the location of the folder of an individual or a company with which there is a large amount of correspondence. In Figure 5-5, the guides labeled BROWN, BUSKIRK, and BYRD BRICK are special (auxiliary) name guides.
2. Introduce a special section of subjects, such as one pertaining to Applications, Bids, Conferences, Exhibits, Projects, or Speeches, that may be found in an alphabetic name arrangement. Figure 5-5 shows a special subject guide, APPLICATIONS, placed in alphabetic order in the A section. All correspondence concerning applications for positions in accounting and word processing is stored behind APPLICATIONS, in properly labeled folders.
3. Introduce a section reserved for names that have the same first indexing unit. In Figure 5-5, the BROWN auxiliary guide leads the eye to the section with numerous folders labeled with Brown as the first indexing unit.

Guides for open-shelf equipment are similar to the guides used for drawer filing except that their tabs are at the side (see Figure 5-7 on the next page). Because materials stored in open-shelf equipment are visible at one edge instead of across the top (as is true in drawer files), the alphabetic or other divisions must extend from the side of the guide so that they can be seen easily. The printing on these side-guide tabs may be read from either side.

Folders. A **folder** is a container used to hold stored records in an orderly manner and is usually made of heavy material, such as manila, Kraft, plastic, or pressboard. Folders are creased approximately in half; the back is higher than the front. A folder may be

Folders hold the stored records.

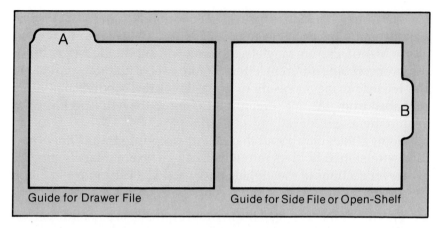

Figure 5-7 ■ Guides Used in Drawer Cabinets and Open-Shelf Files

reinforced across the top of the back edge because that is the place receiving the greatest wear, as it is usually grasped by that edge.

Folders are available with a straight edge or with tabs in various positions. A **tab** is a portion of a folder or guide that extends above the regular height or beyond the regular width of the folder that is immediately visible to the filer. If the folder or guide has a tab extending across its complete width, it is said to be *straight cut* (see Figure 5-8). One-third cut tabs extend only one third the width of a folder and may be in any of three positions (see Figure 5-8).

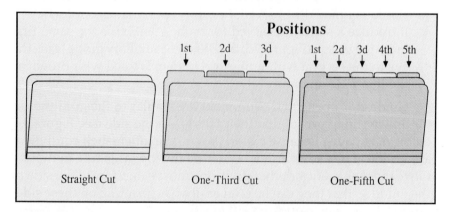

Figure 5-8 ■ Commonly Used Folder Cuts and Positions

Position refers to the location of the tab at the edge of the folder or guide as seen from left to right. First position means the tab is at the left; second position means the tab is second from the left; and so on.

Folders may have all tabs in one position, known as *straight-line position*. If the tabs on the folders are in a series of several different positions from left to right according to a set pattern (as are the one-fifth cut folders pictured in Figure 5-8), this is known as *staggered position*. Straight-line position is increasing in usage because of ease in reading; the eye travels faster in a straight line than it does when it jumps back and forth from left to right. The most efficient position for folders is third, with third-cut tabs; and the most efficient position for guides is either first or third with fifth-cut tabs.

Folders for open-shelf equipment have their tabs on the side edge (see Figure 5-9) in various positions according to the manufacturer's system or the customer's preference.

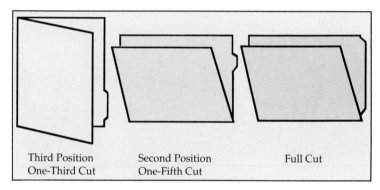

| Third Position | Second Position | Full Cut |
| One-Third Cut | One-Fifth Cut | |

Figure 5-9 ■ Open-Shelf File Folders

Behind every guide are folders that are used to keep like records together. The three main types of folders used in alphabetic storage are general folders, individual folders, and special folders.

General Folders. Every primary guide has a correspondingly labeled general folder bearing the same caption as that on the guide. A **general folder** contains records to and from correspondents with a small volume so that an individual folder is not necessary. In Figure 5-5, the A folder is a general folder and is the last folder in that section.

Within the general folder, records are arranged first alphabetically by the correspondents' names. Then, within each correspondent's records, the arrangement is by date with the most recent date on top (see Figure 5-10 on the next page).

Individual Folders. An individual folder is used to store the records of an individual correspondent. Within an individual folder,

What is the difference between a general folder, an individual folder, and a special folder?

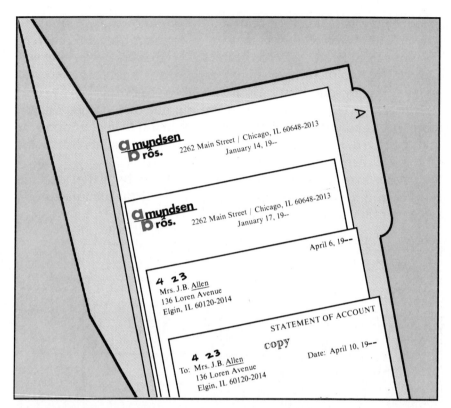

Figure 5-10 ■ Paper Arrangement in a General Folder

records are arranged chronologically, with the most recently dated record on top. In Figure 5-5 (page 95), all individual folders are third cut, third position.

When records pertaining to one correspondent accumulate to a pre-determined number in the general folder, they are removed and placed in an individual folder. Individual folders are usually placed in alphabetic order between the primary guide and its general folder.

Special Folders. A **special folder** follows an auxiliary or special guide in an alphabetic arrangement. In Figure 5-5, three special folders are shown: two behind APPLICATIONS and one behind BUSKIRK. Within the APPLICATIONS ACCOUNTING folder, all records pertaining to accounting positions are arranged first by the names of the correspondents who applied. If a correspondent has more than one record in the folder, those records are arranged by date with the most recent date on top. Within the BUSKIRK PROJECT folder, records are arranged by date, the most recent one on top.

Care of Folders. Proper care of folders is necessary so that records that have been stored will be readily accessible. When records start to "ride up" in any folder, it is overloaded — there are too many papers. The number of records that will fit into one folder obviously depends on the thickness of the papers. Records should never protrude from the folder edges and should always be inserted with their tops to the left. The most useful and most often recommended folders have *score marks* (indented or raised lines or series of marks) along the bottom edge to allow for expansion of the folder. As it becomes filled, the folder is refolded along a score mark and expanded to give it a flat base on which to rest. Most folders can be expanded from 3/4 to 1 inch. If folders are refolded at the score marks (see Figure 5-11), the danger of folders bending and sliding under others is reduced, papers do not curl readily, and a neater looking file results.

> Refolding a folder on the score marks will create a neater looking file drawer.

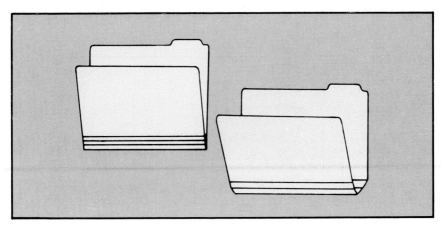

Figure 5-11 ■ Flat Folder and Expanded Folder

A folder lasts longer and is easier to use if it is not stuffed beyond its capacity. If too many papers are contained in an individual folder, it is time to make a second folder for that correspondent. The folders may then be labeled to show that the records are arranged chronologically in them (see the four BYRD BRICK folders in Figure 5-5). Sometimes the papers are redistributed in folders by subjects instead of by dates, as is the case with APPLICATIONS in Figure 5-5.

New folders may be needed because:

1. A new group of names is to be added to the file.
2. Older folders have become full and additional ones must be added to take care of the overload.

> When are new folders needed?

3. Enough records have accumulated for certain correspondents so that their records can be removed from the general folders and put into individual folders.
4. Folders have worn out from heavy use and must be replaced.
5. The regular time of the year has arrived for replacing folders and transferring infrequently used folders to semiactive or inactive storage. Further explanation of records transfer is contained in Chapter 6.

Other types of folders often used in offices include (1) the **suspension or hanging folder** with built-in hooks that hang from the parallel bars on the sides of the storage equipment (Figure 5-12, left); (2) the **bellows (expansion) folder**, which is made with creases along its bottom and sides so that it can expand like an accordion, used when the volume of stored records is small (Figure 5-12, middle); and (3) the **pocket folder**, a folder with a great deal more expansion at the bottom than that of the ordinary folder (Figure 5-12, right).

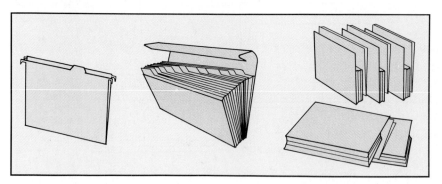

Figure 5-12 ■ Special Folders Used to Store Paper Records

Follower Blocks or Compressors. Failing to use proper means to hold drawer contents upright causes folders to bend and slide under one another. Folders are kept upright by using the proper number of guides and by the correct use of a follower block behind the guides and folders. A **follower block** (or **compressor**) is a device placed at the back of a file drawer that may be moved to allow for contraction or expansion of the drawer contents (see Figure 5-13). A follower block that is too loose will allow the drawer contents to sag; one that is too tight will make it very difficult to get a folder in or out of the drawer. In an over-compressed drawer, as in an overcrowded drawer, locating and removing a single sheet of paper is almost impossible.

Adjusting the follower block in a file drawer will compress or expand the space available for folders.

Instead of follower blocks, some file drawers have slim steel upright dividers placed permanently throughout the file drawer to keep the contents vertical.

Figure 5-13 ■ Follower Block (Compressor)

OUT Indicators. OUT indicators are control devices that show the location of records at all times. When a borrowed record is returned to storage, the OUT indicator is removed, to be reused, thrown away, or saved and later used to check the activity at the files or to determine which records are active or inactive. The more commonly used indicators are OUT guides, OUT folders, and OUT sheets; examples are shown in Figure 5-14.

Figure 5-14A ■ OUT Guide
TAB Products Co.

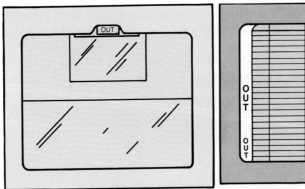 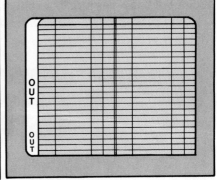

Figure 5-14B ■ OUT Folder   **Figure 5-14C** ■ OUT Sheet

OUT Guide. An **OUT guide** is a special guide used to replace any record that has been removed from storage. When the borrowed record is returned, the filer can quickly find the exact place from which the record was taken. An OUT guide is made of the same sturdy material as other guides with the word OUT printed on its tab in a large size and in a distinctive color. In Figure 5-5 an OUT guide is located between the ADAMS AND AMALFI and the AH WING WAH CAFE individual folders. Instead of an OUT guide, however, one of the two indicators explained next may be used.

OUT Folder. An **OUT folder** is a special folder used to replace a complete folder that has been removed from storage. The OUT folder remains in the file as a temporary storage place for records that will be transferred to the permanent folder when it is returned to storage.

OUT Sheet. An **OUT sheet** is a form that is inserted in place of a record or records removed from a folder. An OUT sheet is often the same size and color as an OUT guide, but its thickness is that of a sheet of paper. An OUT sheet, too, remains in the file until the borrowed material is returned to storage.

OUT indicators let the filer know that a record or folder has been removed from storage.

OUT guides and sheets have spaces on them for writing the name of the person borrowing the record, the date it was borrowed, a brief statement of the contents of the record, and the date it should be returned to storage. An OUT folder has a pocket or slot into which a card is placed bearing the same information concerning who took the folder, the date it was taken, its contents, and the date the folder should be returned to storage.

Labels. The containers, guides, and folders will help you store records efficiently. However, each of these items must be labeled to quickly guide the eye to the appropriate storage location. A **label** is a device by which the contents of a drawer, shelf, folder, or a section of records is identified. A **caption** is the content identifying information on a label. Label captions may be typewriter or computer printed with briefly worded, inclusive, and clear descriptions of the contents of the container, guide, or folder.

Container Labels. The labels on drawers, shelf files, or other storage containers should be as briefly worded, inclusive, and as clear as possible. The containers usually have holders on the outside where card stock labels can be inserted. Various colors are available on perforated card stock sheets. The ARMA *Filing Procedures Guidelines* recommend centering the information for the container in all caps with no punctuation. The caption on the drawer illustrated in Figure 5-5 reads A-B, indicating that the records of the correspondents whose names are within the A and B sections of the alphabet are stored in that drawer.

Guide Labels. Labels on guides consist of words, letters, or numbers (or some combination of these items). In Figure 5-5, the guides shown have window tabs into which typed information has been inserted (A, APPLICATIONS, B, BROWN, BUSKIRK, BYRD BRICK). Some guides come with preprinted information. The ARMA *Filing Procedures Guidelines* recommend keying the information for blank guides two spaces from the top edge and two spaces from the left edge in all capital letters with no punctuation.

Folder Labels. Rolls of labels in boxes, continuous folded strips, separate strips, or pressure-sensitive adhesive labels are only four of the various ways in which labels are packaged. The use of pastel-colored labels is preferable to deeper colored ones because the typing on the pastel labels can be read easily. Sometimes a colored stripe across the top is used on a white or buff-colored label, for the same reason.

The ARMA *Filing Procedures Guidelines* recommend keying folder labels two spaces from the left edge and as near the top of the label or the bottom of the color bar as possible. Wrap-around side-tab labels for lateral file cabinets are keyed both above and below the color bar separator so that the information is readable from both sides. The letter of the alphabet is keyed first, followed by five spaces, then the

Labels are printed in all caps with no punctuation.

actual filing segment is keyed. In all cases, the label is keyed in capital letters with no punctuation as shown in Figure 5-15 below. Figure 5-15 shows commercially prepared folder labels (upper left), lateral folder labels (upper right), and vertical folder labels.

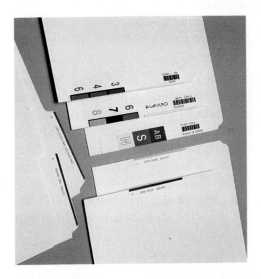

Figure 5-15 ■ Folder Labels
Commercially prepared labels supplied by Engineered Data Products, Inc.

When new folders are prepared, care should be taken to make sure the placement of the labels and the typing format are the same as those on other folders. One way to achieve uniform placement of labels is as follows: When a new box of folders is opened, remove all the folders, keep them tightly together, and stand them upright on a flat surface. Place a ruler or stiff card over the tab edges at the spot where all the labels are to be affixed. Make a pencil mark across the top edge of all the tabs. A very small pencil mark will show on each of the tabs at the same place and will serve as a guide for attaching all the labels.

Sorters. A **sorter** is a device used to hold records temporarily and serves to separate the records into alphabetic or numeric categories to be stored later. The records are organized in a roughly alphabetic order so that they may be stored quickly when time is available for the storage function. The type of sorter to be used in any office depends on the volume of records to be stored.

One sorter that will accommodate records with one dimension as large as ten inches (such as checks, sales slips, time cards, correspondence, and ledger sheets) is shown in Figure 5-16.

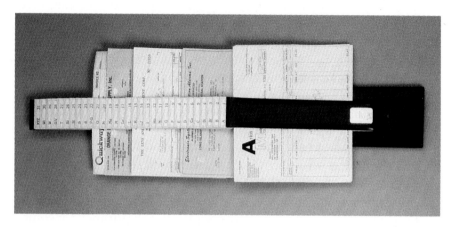

Figure 5-16 ■ General Purpose Sorter
Reprinted with permission of Esselte Pendaflex Corporation, Garden City, NJ, 11365 © 1990

Other specialized supplies will be discussed in later chapters of the text, as their use becomes necessary. The supplies just explained and illustrated are basic ones and are applicable to all storage methods.

Selection of Storage Equipment and Supplies

Efficiency, increased productivity, and overall savings result when the right type, size, number, and quality of storage equipment and supplies are used. Records managers should keep themselves up-to-date on new and improved products by reading business periodicals, trade magazines, and manufacturer's catalogs and brochures; by attending business shows; and by participating in professional records management association meetings.

Appropriate storage equipment and supplies increase efficiency and productivity.

The selection of storage equipment and supplies requires that each of the following interrelated factors be taken into consideration:

1. *Type and volume of records to be stored and retrieved.* An inventory of what is to be stored may reveal papers, cards, books, disks, microrecords, architectural drawings, computer printouts, etc. Such an inventory will also show the current volume of records

already stored. Future volume must be forecast as well as any anticipated changes in method of storage, such as the possibility of microfilming records.

2. *Degree of required protection of records.* Confidential or classified records may require equipment with locks; and irreplaceable records will need fireproof or fire-resistant storage equipment.

3. *Efficiency and ease of use of equipment and systems.* The ease with which records can be found is another consideration. The simpler the system is to understand, the easier it is to use. Also, less training of new employees is needed when the system is a simple one. Time saved by personnel who store and retrieve records means dollars saved. The ease of expansion or modification of a system or the addition to it of compatible equipment will be important in meeting the changing needs of an organization.

4. *Space Considerations.* Floor-weight restrictions, usage of space to the ceiling or the advisability of counter-type equipment or something in between, and the possibility of transferring part of the records to off-site storage facilities—all of these affect space which, in an office, is costly. The effect of new equipment on present layout and work flow should also be considered.

5. *Cost.* After all other criteria have been examined, cost and the company budget may be the final determinants as to which equipment and supplies may be acquired. The astute records manager realizes that the least expensive equipment and supplies may not provide the most economical records storage. Quality in construction and in materials is important; inferior materials or lightweight stock may need frequent and costly replacement. In determining costs, keep in mind the following points:

    a. Cost of the personnel needed to work with the records.
    b. Compatibility of supplies and equipment.
    c. Advisability of using local vendors rather than purchasing from out-of-town vendors.
    d. Possibility of discounts for quantity purchases.
    e. Feasibility of choosing used rather than new equipment.
    f. Volume of records that can be stored within the equipment. Lateral, shelf, or rotary equipment can house more square feet of records than can conventional drawer file cabinets in the same square footage of floor space.

What factors need to be considered when choosing a storage system?

Other factors may need to be added to your list of considerations because of the special needs of your organization. Also, it will be helpful to consult with users of the same equipment that you are now considering acquiring.

CORRESPONDENCE STORAGE PROCEDURES

This last section of the chapter examines the advantages and disadvantages of alphabetic records storage; some criteria for selecting an alphabetic storage system; and finally, procedures for storing correspondence alphabetically.

Advantages and Disadvantages of Alphabetic Records Storage

The advantages of alphabetic records storage are as follows:

1. You can refer directly to an alphabetic arrangement to find a name. This is called **direct access** — you look directly for a specific name in the file without referencing an index.
2. The dictionary (A to Z) order of arrangement is simple to understand.
3. Storage is easy if standard procedures are followed.
4. Misfiles are easily checked by examining alphabetic sequence.
5. Costs of operation may be lower than for other methods because of the direct access feature.
6. Only one sorting is required—by alphabet.

The disadvantages of alphabetic records storage are:

1. Misfiling is prevalent when there are no established rules for alphabetic storage and filers follow their own preferences.
2. Similar names may cause confusion, especially when spellings are not precise.
3. Transposition of some letters of the alphabet is easy, causing filing sequence to be out of order.
4. Selecting the wrong name for storage can result in lost records.
5. Names on folders are instantly seen by anyone who happens to glance at an open storage container. Consequently, confidential or classified records are not secure.

Selection and Design of Alphabetic Records Storage Systems

At the time a new office is opened, a decision must be made on the kind of storage system to be selected or designed. For already established offices, the system in use may prove to be ineffective because it no longer serves the needs of those who request records. If the records are to be requested by names of individuals, businesses, and organizations with few subjects, then an alphabetic system is best for that office.

When the alphabetic method of storage is selected, utmost care should be exercised in its selection or design because, once installed, it is likely to be used for a long time. In order to select an alphabetic system, or to redesign one, the records manager should know:

1. The total volume of records to be stored.
2. The number of records in each alphabetic section and which letters of the alphabet contain a large number of records.
3. The expected activity in the files—an estimate of how many times records may be requested.
4. The length of time records are to be kept.
5. The efficiency of the filing personnel.
6. The training time available for personnel.

In some cases, the person in charge of the records may seek the help of a records management consultant or a representative of a filing system manufacturer. These people study the needs of the office, consult with the person in charge of the records, and make recommendations.

It is important that the person in charge of the records keep the needs of the office in mind rather than being swayed by the beauty of a system, the expert sales techniques of a representative, or the apparent low cost of one system as compared to another. The ultimate test of any successful storage system (alphabetic or any other) is whether or not records that have been stored within the system can be quickly found when needed.

Examples of Alphabetic Records Storage Systems

Many manufacturers have produced trade-named alphabetic systems with special characteristics intended to speed records storage and retrieval and to provide a double check against misfiling. These systems use color extensively, as you will see in the illustrations. Other trade-named alphabetic systems are available; the ones shown here are representative of the systems available.

The use of color has two meanings: (1) **color coding**, where different colors are used to divide the alphabetic sections in the storage system; and (2) **color accenting**, where different colors are used for the different supplies in the storage system—one color for guides, various colors for folders, one color for OUT indicators, and specific colors of labels or stripes on labels. Both color coding and color accenting are found in the systems illustrated here.

How is color used in storage systems?

To gain a maximum understanding of each system, study the text material carefully and refer to the illustrations frequently. Give special attention to the sequence of items in the illustrations.

TAB Products Co. TAB Products Co., 1400 Page Mill Road, Palo Alto, CA 94303, uses color in simple to complex filing systems. TAB's AlphaCode is shown in Figure 5-17. The color bars correspond to the first letters of the file's name. TAB claims 40 percent faster retrieval because the use of color eliminates the need to stop and read letters. Notice the blocks of color. For instance, the B guide shows the same first color; the BE guide shows a different second color on the label. Misfiles would stand out because the color pattern would be broken.

Figure 5-17A ■ TAB Alphacode Filing System
TAB Products Co.

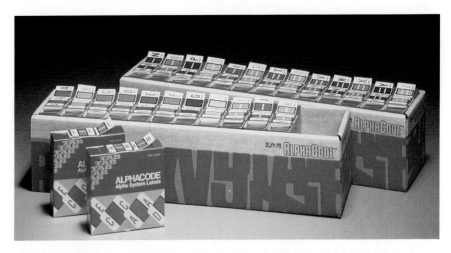

Figure 5-17B ■ Labels of the TAB Alphacode Filing System
TAB Products Co.

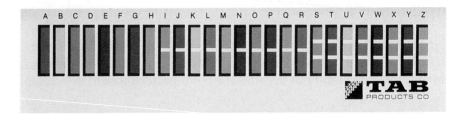

Figure 5-17C ■ Colors of the TAB Alphacode Filing System
TAB Products Co.

TAB's AlphaCode assigns a letter and color for the key unit of the filing segment and then a second color for the second letter of the key unit. Supplies for the AlphaCode come in handy rolls of self-sticking labels. The folders are ordinary manila colored. A records manager can also choose to have TAB generate computer AlphaCode folders from a list of folder names or a tape or disk containing the names.

Other TAB systems assign a letter and color for the key unit of the filing segment, a second color for the second letter of the key unit, and a third color for the first letter of the second unit.

Kardex Systems, Inc. Kardex Systems, Inc., Marietta, OH 45750, also uses color for a variety of filing systems. The LetterScan system is shown in Figure 5-18. The first letter of the key unit indicates the main alphabetic division (A, B, C, etc.); the first letter of the second unit indicates the color of the folder. The color wheel shown is for the folder colors. For example, the file for Jim Lewis would appear behind the alphabetic guide L in a white folder. Likewise, the file for Kardex Systems would appear behind the alphabetic guide K in a violet folder. According to Kardex, the use of bright colored folders speeds filing and retrieval and reduces misfiles by up to 90 percent.

Figure 5-18A ■ Kardex LetterScan System
Kardex Systems, Inc.

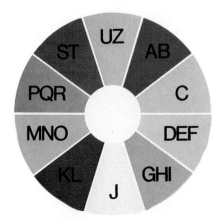

Figure 5-18B ■ Kardex LetterScan Code
Kardex Systems, Inc.

The Kardex ColorScan System is shown in Figure 5-19. The difference between this system and LetterScan is the use of preprinted alphabetic folder tabs by ColorScan. The first letter of the key unit still indicates the alphabetic division, and the first letter of the second unit indicates the color of the folder. Kardex states that ColorScan filing is 50 percent faster and retrieval is 30 percent faster than the LetterScan

Figure 5-19A ▪ Kardex ColorScan System
Kardex Systems, Inc.

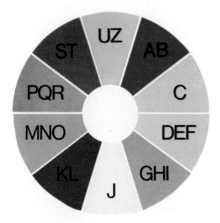

Figure 5-19B ▪ Kardex ColorScan Code
Kardex Systems, Inc.

system. In the ColorScan system, a black tab is placed over the correct alphabetic letter. When the folders are filed in the alphabetic divisions, the black tabs form a solid line that helps you detect misfiles.

Procedures for Storing Correspondence Records

The actual storing operation is an exacting responsibility. It must be done with concentration and the knowledge that a mistake may be costly. No matter whether records storage is centralized, decentralized, or centrally controlled, the filing procedures remain the same: Records must be (1) inspected, (2) indexed, (3) coded, (4) cross-referenced if necessary, (5) sorted, and (6) stored (see Figure 5-20 on the next page). Therefore, the filer must enjoy detailed work, be dexterous, have a good memory, be willing to follow set procedures, be interested in developing new and better procedures, and realize the importance of correctly storing all records so that they may be found immediately when needed. Each of the procedures will be discussed, in turn.

Inspecting. Checking a record for its readiness to be filed is known as **inspecting**. A business record must not be stored until its contents have been noted by someone with authority. And storing must not take place before whatever needs to be done with the record has been done. Anyone who stores records should be absolutely certain that the actions required by the contents of the records have been taken or noted on a reminder calendar so that the records will be brought to the attention of the proper person at a future date. Storing records before their contents have been noted and before appropriate action has been taken can sometimes cause embarrassment to a business and might even result in financial loss or loss of goodwill.

> A record is inspected for its readiness to be stored.

It may be assumed that the copy of an outgoing letter or other communication is ready to be stored when it is received by the filer for storage. But in most offices every original (or incoming) record to be stored must bear a **release mark** showing that the record is ready for storage (See "RK" on Figure 5-21). This release mark, usually put on the record by the person who has typed the reply or otherwise handled the matter, may be in the form of initials, a code or check mark, a punched symbol, a stamped notation, a lightly drawn pencil line through the contents, or some other agreed-upon mark. A missing mark is a signal to the filer to inquire why the release mark

	**Inspecting**	Look for release mark!
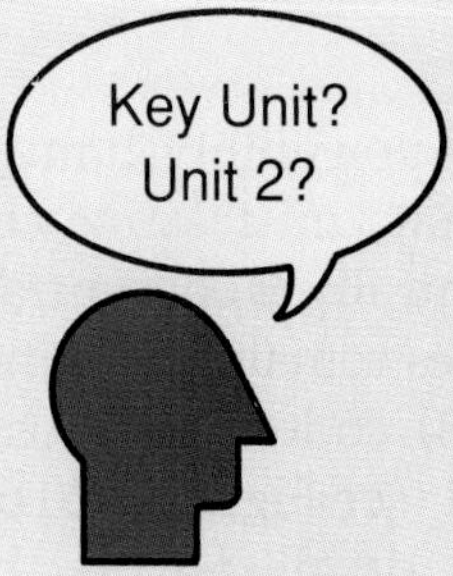 Key Unit? Unit 2?	**Indexing**	Most important step!
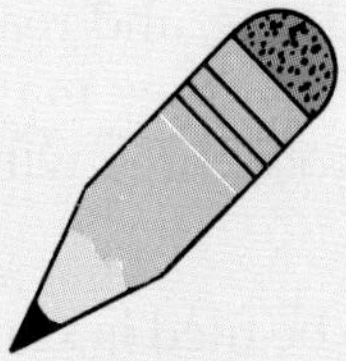	**Coding**	Mark the filing segment.
	**Cross-Referencing**	Think! Use the rules.
	**Sorting**	Rough sort. Then, fine sort. Coordinate these steps to handle the record just once.
	**Storing**	Prepare record for storage. Check again to match filing segments. Most recent date on top.

Figure 5-20 ■ Storage Procedures for Correspondence

is missing. A time stamp (See JUN 22, 19— 2:30 PM in Figure 5-21 on the next page) is not a release mark. The person who opens mail often stamps the correspondence with a time stamp showing the date and time received, for reference purposes only. A cardinal rule that all filers must observe, therefore, is: **Be sure that the record to be stored has been released for storage.**

Indexing. You have indexed filing segments on cards. On correspondence, however, the name may appear in various places on the page. As you know, the selection of the right name by which to store the record means that the record will be found quickly when it is needed. If the wrong name is selected, much time will be wasted trying to locate the record when it is eventually requested. Here are some rules to keep in mind when indexing correspondence — incoming and outgoing:

Incoming Correspondence

1. On incoming correspondence, the most likely name for storage purposes is usually in the letterhead.
2. If a letterhead has no relationship with the contents of the letter, the location of the writer, or the business connection of the writer, the letterhead name is disregarded for filing purposes. An example is a letter written on hotel stationery by a person who is out of town on a business trip.
3. Incoming correspondence on plain paper (paper without a letterhead — usually personal) is most likely to be called for by the name in the signature line, which will then be the one used for storage.
4. When both the company name and the name of the writer seem to be of equal importance, the company name is used.

Outgoing Correspondence

1. On the file copy of an outgoing letter, the most important name is usually the one contained in the inside address.
2. When both the company name and the name of an individual are contained in the inside address of the file copy of an outgoing letter, the company name is used for filing unless the letter is personal or unless a name in the body is the correct name to index.
3. On the copy of a personal letter, the name of the writer may be the most important and should be used for storage.

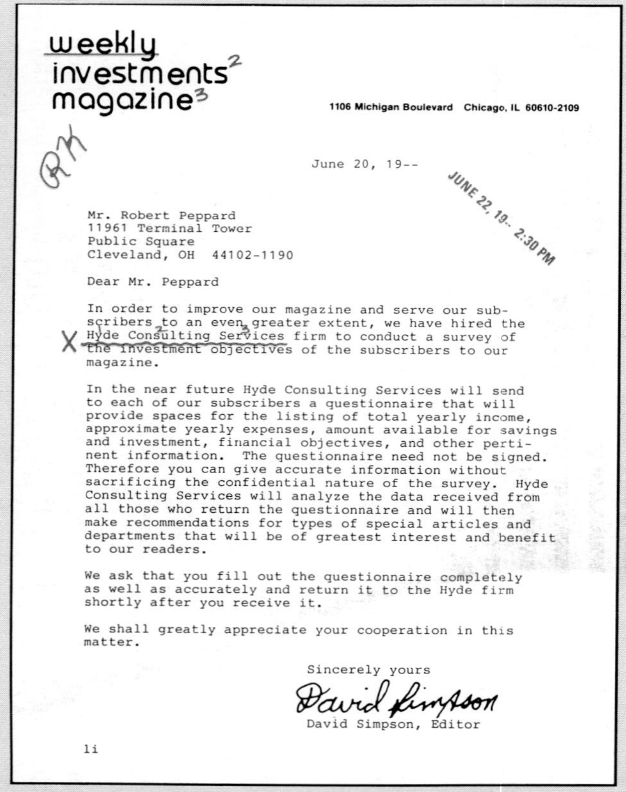

weekly investments[2] magazine[3]

1106 Michigan Boulevard Chicago, IL 60610-2109

RP

June 20, 19--

JUNE 22, 19-- 2:30 PM

Mr. Robert Peppard
11961 Terminal Tower
Public Square
Cleveland, OH 44102-1190

Dear Mr. Peppard

In order to improve our magazine and serve our subscribers to an even greater extent, we have hired the X Hyde Consulting[2] Services[3] firm to conduct a survey of the investment objectives of the subscribers to our magazine.

In the near future Hyde Consulting Services will send to each of our subscribers a questionnaire that will provide spaces for the listing of total yearly income, approximate yearly expenses, amount available for savings and investment, financial objectives, and other pertinent information. The questionnaire need not be signed. Therefore you can give accurate information without sacrificing the confidential nature of the survey. Hyde Consulting Services will analyze the data received from all those who return the questionnaire and will then make recommendations for types of special articles and departments that will be of greatest interest and benefit to our readers.

We ask that you fill out the questionnaire completely as well as accurately and return it to the Hyde firm shortly after you receive it.

We shall greatly appreciate your cooperation in this matter.

Sincerely yours

David Simpson

David Simpson, Editor

li

Figure 5-21 ■ Letter Properly Released and Coded

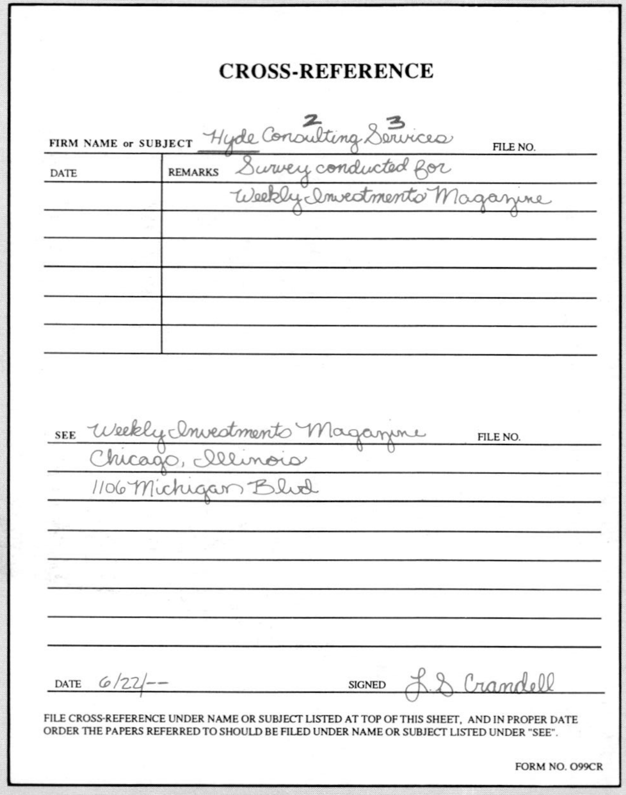

CROSS-REFERENCE

FIRM NAME or SUBJECT Hyde Consulting[2] Services[3] FILE NO.

DATE REMARKS Survey conducted for Weekly Investments Magazine

SEE Weekly Investments Magazine FILE NO.
Chicago, Illinois
1106 Michigan Blvd

DATE 6/22/-- SIGNED L. S. Crandell

FILE CROSS-REFERENCE UNDER NAME OR SUBJECT LISTED AT TOP OF THIS SHEET, AND IN PROPER DATE ORDER THE PAPERS REFERRED TO SHOULD BE FILED UNDER NAME OR SUBJECT LISTED UNDER "SEE".

FORM NO. O99CR

Figure 5-22 ■ Cross-Reference for Letter Shown in Figure 5-21

If a special subject is used in an alphabetic arrangement (such as Applications), the subject is given precedence over both company and individual names appearing in the correspondence. Often, the subject name is written on the correspondence at the top right.

Sometimes two names seem equally important. One name is selected as the name by which the record is to be stored and the other name is cross-referenced according to the rules learned in Chapters 2 and 3. In case of real doubt as to the most important name, clarification should be requested from the supervisor or the department from which the record came. If a records manual is in use in the office, it should be consulted.

Coding. Often the filer is responsible for coding the record. In coding, the filing segment may be marked in any one of several ways. Figure 5-21 shows a straight underline and numbering method of coding. In some offices a colored pencil is used for coding to make the code stand out; in other offices, coding is done with a regular lead pencil, to keep distracting marks at a minimum.

Coding saves time when refiling is necessary. If an uncoded record is removed from storage and returned at a later date to be refiled, it must be re-indexed and re-coded. Coding that is done too quickly may result in choosing the wrong name or incorrectly coding the right one, resulting in storing the record in the wrong place.

Cross-Referencing. The same cross-reference rules learned in Chapters 2 and 3 apply for storing correspondence. Here's an example: Assume that the letter shown in Figure 5-21 comes to the filer for storage. The record is indexed and coded for Weekly Investments Magazine by underlining the key unit and numbering the other units. The letter is then coded for cross-referencing since it may be called for by Hyde Consulting Services. A wavy line is drawn under Hyde Consulting Services; an X is written in the margin; and the units are numbered for the cross-referenced name. The cross-reference coding marks are different from those used for the regular coding of a record. Figure 5-22 shows the cross-reference made for the letter shown in Figure 5-21.

A separate cross-reference sheet, as shown in Figure 5-22, may be prepared for the alternative name, or an extra copy of the original record may be coded for cross-reference purposes. The cross-reference sheet shown in Figure 5-22 is a type that may be purchased in quantity and filled in with the required information as needed. Note that the name at the top of the cross-reference sheet is coded for storage in exactly the same way as is any record—the key unit is underlined with a straight line and the succeeding units are numbered.

At times a **permanent cross-reference** takes the place of an individual folder. The permanent cross-reference is a guide with a tab in the same position as the tabs on the individual folders. The caption on the tab of the permanent cross-reference consists of the name by which the cross-reference is actually filed, the word "SEE," and the name by which the correspondence may be found. In Figure 5-5, a permanent cross-reference guide for BABCOCK CRAFTS SEE WARREN INDUSTRIES appears in proper alphabetic sequence in the file drawer.

A permanent cross-reference may be used, for instance, when a company changes its name. The company's folder is removed from the file, the name is changed on the folder, and the folder is refiled under the new name. A permanent cross-reference guide is prepared under the original name and is placed in the position of the original folder in the file. For example, assume that MAYNARD AND PHELPS changes its name to BAYSHORE PRODUCTS, INC. The MAYNARD AND PHELPS folder is removed from the file, the name on the folder is changed to BAYSHORE PRODUCTS INC and the folder is filed under the new name. A permanent cross-reference guide is made and filed in the M section of the file:

MAYNARD AND PHELPS
SEE BAYSHORE PRODUCTS INC

Sorting. **Sorting** is the act of arranging records in a predetermined sequence according to the storage method used as an aid to final filing. In most instances, a sorting step precedes the actual storing. It is very important that sorting be done as soon as possible after coding and cross-referencing, especially if storage must be delayed. Sometimes coding and **rough sorting** are done in sequence. After each record has been coded, it is rough sorted into a pile of like pieces — all of the As, Bs, and Cs are together, all of the Ds, Es, and Fs are together, and so on. Coordination of inspection, indexing, coding, and sorting means handling each record only once. Records can be found with less delay if they have been roughly sorted instead of being put in a stack on a desk or in a "to-be-filed" basket.

The efficient filer will handle a record once during inspecting, indexing, coding, cross-referencing, and sorting.

A delay in sorting until all records have been coded means handling each record twice, consumes more time and energy, and results in greater record-handling costs. If sorting is delayed until all coding is finished, the records may then be grouped into another rough-sort arrangement: all the As together in no special order; all the Bs together at random; all the Cs together in mixed order; and so forth. This sorting may be done on top of the desk, with the records placed in separate piles. Use of a desktop sorter that has holders or pockets for various sections of the alphabet will make such sorting easier.

After the records have been roughly sorted according to the alphabetic sections, they are removed section by section, alphabetized properly within each section, and replaced in order in the sorter for temporary storage. This step is often called **fine sorting** or arranging the records in the exact sequence prior to storing. The records in all sections have thus been alphabetized and are now ready to be stored. The records are removed in sequence from all divisions of the sorter and taken to the storage containers.

Using these rough and fine sorting procedures saves time. Wasted motion will be minimized because all records are in strict alphabetic order. The greater the number of records to be stored, the more precise or fine the sorting should be so as to make the work easier, quicker, and less tiring.

Storing. **Storing** is the actual placement of records in containers, a physical task of great importance in an office. A misfiled record is often a lost record; and a lost record means loss of time, money, and peace of mind while searching for the record.

The time that records are actually put into the storage containers depends on the work load during the day. In some offices, storing is the job performed first in the morning; in others, all storing is done in the early afternoon; in others, storing is the last task performed each day. In still other offices, storing is done whenever records are ready and when there is a lull in other work. In a centralized filing department, there is no lull; storage takes place all day every day — storing, retrieving, and restoring.

Prior to the actual storage of records, the filer must remember to:

1. Remove paper clips and pins from records to be stored.
2. Staple records together (if they belong together) in the upper right corner so that other records kept in the folder will not be inserted between them by mistake.

What preparation is needed before a record is stored?

3. Mend torn records.
4. Unfold folded records to conserve storage space unless the folded records fit the container better than when unfolded.

Then, when at the storage equipment, the filer should:

1. Glance quickly at the label on the container to locate the place to begin storage.
2. After locating the place, scan the guides until the proper alphabetic section is reached.
3. Pull the guides forward with one hand, while the other hand searches quickly for the correct folder.
4. Check to see if an individual or a special folder for the filing segment has been prepared. If there is none, locate the general folder.
5. Slightly raise the folder into which the record is to be placed. Avoid pulling the folder up by its tab, however, as continual pulling will separate the tab from its folder. If the folder is raised, the record will be inserted into the folder and not in front of or behind it.
6. Glance quickly at the label and the top record in the folder to verify further the fact that the piece to be stored is correctly placed, since all records will bear the same coded name.
7. Place each record in the folder with its top to the left (see Figure 5-23). When the folder is removed from storage and placed on a desk

Figure 5-23 ■ Proper Insertion of Papers into a File Folder

to be used, the folder is opened like a book with the tab edge to the right; all the records in it are then in proper reading position.

8. Jog the folder to straighten the records if they are uneven.

9. Never open more than one drawer in a cabinet at the same time; a cabinet can fall forward when it becomes overbalanced because two or three loaded drawers are open.

Special points to be remembered include:

1. The most recently dated record in an individual folder is always placed at the front and therefore is on top when the folder is opened. The record bearing the oldest date is the one at the back of the folder.

2. Records that are removed from a folder and later refiled must be placed in their correct chronologic sequence, not on top of the contents of the folder.

3. Records within a general folder are arranged first alphabetically by correspondents' names and then by date within each correspondent's records. The most recently dated record is therefore on top of each group.

Tickler File Usage

A **tickler file** is a chronologic arrangement of information that "tickles" the memory by serving as a reminder that specific action must be taken on a specific date. Other names sometimes used to describe such a file are **bring-up file, suspense file,** and **pending file.** The basic arrangement of a tickler file is always the same: chronologic. A manual arrangement usually takes the form of a series of 12 guides with the names of the months of the year printed on their tabs. One set of guides or folders with tabs printed with 1 through 31 for the days of the month are also used. A computer tickler file is usually in the form of some type of calendar or schedule program.

Many office workers use a tickler system to remind them of events that happen yearly, such as birthdays and anniversaries; membership expiration dates and dues payments; insurance premium payments; weekly, monthly, or annual meetings; subscription expiration dates; and the dates on which certificates of deposit or bonds are due. In records management, tickler files can be used to keep track of records that are borrowed or to keep track of records that do not have a release mark.

On the last day of each month, the person in charge of the tickler file checks through the date folders to be certain that nothing has been inadvertently overlooked during the month. Then that person removes all the papers from behind the next month's guide and redistributes them behind daily guides (numbered 1 through 31). At the end of March, for instance, the spaces behind all the daily guides would be checked, the March guide would be moved to the back of the file, and the April guide would be put in the front. All reminders that were filed behind April would then be redistributed behind the daily guides according to the dates on the reminders.

The tickler file must be the first item checked each day by the person in charge of it. Information on the notes found in the tickler file serves as a reminder to act or follow through on specific instructions.

Misfiled and Lost Records

Even with care, some records are misfiled and become lost. If storage is done haphazardly or with no concern for the importance of following consistent procedures, lost records are even more numerous. Lack of attention to spelling, careless insertion of records into the storage equipment, and distractions often cause records to be misfiled and, therefore, lost.

Experienced filers use the following techniques in trying to find missing records:

What techniques are used to locate lost or misfiled records?

1. Look in the folders immediately in front of and behind the correct folder.
2. Look between the folders.
3. Look under all the folders, where the record may have slipped to the bottom of the drawer of shelf.
4. Look completely through the correct folder because alphabetic or other order of sequence may have been neglected due to carelessness or haste.
5. Look in the general folder in addition to searching in the individual folder.
6. Check the transposition of names (HAYES BENJAMIN instead of BENJAMIN HAYES).
7. Look for the second, third, or succeeding units of a filing segment rather than for the key unit.
8. Check for misfiling because of misreading of letters — e for i, n for m, t for l, k for h, C for G, etc.

9. Check for alternate spellings (JON, JAHN).
10. Look under other vowels (for a name beginning with Ha, look also under He, Hi, Ho, and Hu).
11. Look for a double letter instead of a single one (or the reverse).
12. Look for anglicized forms of a name (Miller, Moller, or Muller for Mueller).
13. Check for transposition of numbers (35 instead of 53).
14. Look in the year preceding or following the one in question.
15. Look in a related subject if the subject method is used.
16. Be aware that the records may be en route to storage.
17. Look in the sorter.
18. Ask the person in whose desk or briefcase the record may be to search for it.

If every search fails to produce the missing record, some records managers try to reconstruct the record from memory, typing as much as is known. This information is placed in a folder labeled "LOST," in addition to the name of the original folder. This new folder is stored in its correct place as a constant reminder to the filer to be on the alert for the missing record.

Efficient correspondence records storage is the result of:

1. Good planning to choose the right equipment, supplies, and system.
2. Proper training of personnel who recognize the value of the release mark, know and consistently apply the rules for alphabetic indexing, code papers carefully, prepare cross-references skillfully, invariably sort papers before storing, and carefully store records in their proper containers.
3. Constant concerned supervision by records managers or others responsible for the storage and retrieval functions.

IMPORTANT TERMS

bellows (expansion) folder
caption
color accenting
color coding
direct access
fine sorting
folder
follower block or compressor

general folder
guide
individual folder
inspecting
label
lateral file cabinet
mobile aisle system
mobile shelving

motorized rotary storage
OUT folder
OUT guide
OUT sheet
permanent cross-reference
pocket folder
position
primary guide
release mark
rough sorting
shelf files
sorter

sorting
special folder
special (auxiliary) guide
storage
storage (filing) method
storage procedures
storing
suspension (hanging) folder
system
tab
tickler file
vertical file cabinet

REVIEW AND DISCUSSION

1. Compare and contrast the terms *storage system* and *storage method*. (Goal 1)
2. List and briefly describe four kinds of commonly used storage equipment for correspondence records. (Goal 2)
3. List and briefly describe four important supplies used in records storage. (Goal 2)
4. Why is the straight-line arrangement of tabs on folders and guides easier to use than the staggered arrangement? (Goal 3)
5. Why are OUT indicators important? How are they used? (Goal 3)
6. Of what value would a set of guide and folder tabs preprinted by a manufacturer be? When would blank ones be of greater use? (Goal 3)
7. What five criteria should be considered when choosing storage equipment and supplies? (Goal 4)
8. What are the advantages and disadvantages of the alphabetic storage method? (Goal 5)
9. Why is it important to inspect and study an alphabetic records storage system carefully before purchasing? (Goal 6)
10. Explain how color can be used in correspondence records storage. (Goal 7)
11. List and briefly describe (in order) the six steps to properly store a record properly. (Goal 8)
12. What are the kinds of release marks you might find on records that are ready to be stored? (Goal 8)

13. What is a tickler file and how is one arranged? (Goal 9)
14. A record was requested and you were unable to find it in the proper folder. Describe at least five techniques you would use to try to find the lost record. (Goal 10)

APPLICATIONS (APP)

APP 5-1. Changing Storage Equipment

Assume that you work in an office where correspondence is stored alphabetically in traditional four-drawer vertical file cabinets. Everyone in the office has access to the file cabinets. You usually must retrieve 10 to 20 stored records daily, one paper at a time. You believe open-shelf files would be better. Why do you think so? What factors would contribute to your decision? Whom would you consult to help you assemble the facts needed to approach your supervisor with a suggestion for change? List the facts you believe would help you to present your suggestion for change. (Goals 2, 3, and 4)

APP 5-2. Coding Correspondence

On the copy of an outgoing letter, both the company name and the name of the individual receiving the letter appear in the inside address:

Dr. Jayne DeSales Bertram, President
Microform Equipment Sales & Services, Inc.
Conway Towers #47
Dallas, TX 75202-1847

Which name is coded for storage? Why? (Goal 7)

APPLYING THE RULES

Job 4, Correspondence Filing—Person's Names; Job 5, Correspondence Filing—Business, Organization, and Government Names; and Computer Applications 4 and 5 (optional).

GOALS

After completing this chapter, you will be able to:

1. Define and explain requisition, retrieval, charge-out, and follow-up procedures.
2. Define and explain the use of a retention schedule.
3. Define and explain the three classifications of records, two transfer methods, and transfer procedures.

As you will recall from previous chapters, two stages (or phases) in the records life cycle are *retrieval* and *transfer* of stored records. These two steps, as they relate to the retrieval of records or to the information retrieved from them, are discussed in this chapter along with *retention* of records.

In the records cycle, *retrieval* refers to the process of comparing requested information with stored information. **Records transfer** refers to the physical movement of active records from the office to inactive or archive storage areas. The basis for making the decision to transfer records is the frequency of use of the record. **Retention** refers to policies and procedures of *what* documents to keep, *where* the documents are kept, and *how long* these documents are to be kept. Both the transfer records policy and the retention schedule policy is usually written in your company procedures manual.

Remember that all retrieval consists of comparing requested information with stored information.

All retrieval consists of comparing requested information with stored information. Whether the retrieval is done manually, mechanically, or electronically, the process of comparison takes place. When the information being searched for matches the information found, retrieval is accomplished. Figure 6-1, on the next page, shows that retrieval occurred when "Velders F" (the only match possible in the file) was keyed in the computer database.

SCREEN 1

Key *Ve*.

SCREEN 2

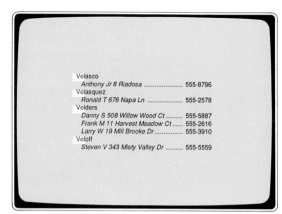

Key next letter *l*.

SCREEN 3

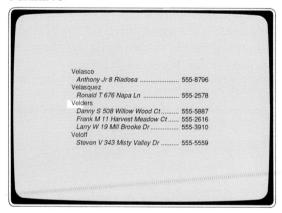

Key next letter *d*.

SCREEN 4

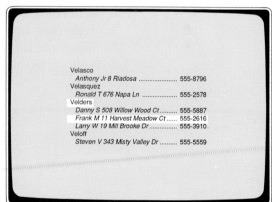

Key *ers* **F**.

Figure 6-1 ■ Steps in Retrieving Information on Frank M. Velders From a Computer Database

RECORDS RETRIEVAL

With the development of more refined records systems, records terminology takes on even more important meanings. Initially, to "retrieve" information meant only to find it. Now, however, **retrieval** is the process of searching for and finding records and/or information. For example, a common storage and retrieval activity is that of finding a name and telephone number in a telephone directory. The storage method is an alphabetic listing of names on the pages of a book; the system is a table search (scanning of tabulated telephone lists) according to name. Similarly, nonfiction library books are stored on shelves in numbered sequence; the shelves are searched by reference number to retrieve a desired book.

Retrieval of a record or of information from it can be done in three ways:

Ways to retrieve:
1. Manually
2. Mechanically
3. Electronically

1. *manually*—A person goes to the storage container and takes by hand the record wanted or makes a note of the information requested from it.
2. *mechanically*—A person uses some mechanical means to locate a record, such as pressing the correct buttons to make movable shelves rotate to the correct location of the document.
3. *electronically*—A person uses some means such as a computer to locate a record. The physical record may not need to be removed from storage; but the requester is informed as to where it can be found, or the information requested is shown to the requester in some way, perhaps on a screen (see Figure 6-2).

SCREEN 1—Author Search

SCREEN 2—Title Search

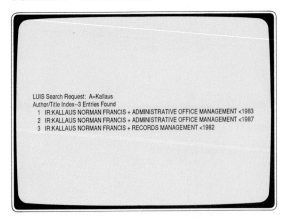
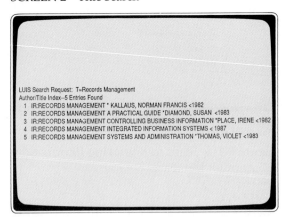

LUIS Search Request: A=Kallaus
Author/Title Index--3 Entries Found
1 IR:KALLAUS NORMAN FRANCIS + ADMINISTRATIVE OFFICE MANAGEMENT <1983
2 IR:KALLAUS NORMAN FRANCIS + ADMINISTRATIVE OFFICE MANAGEMENT <1987
3 IR:KALLAUS NORMAN FRANCIS + RECORDS MANAGEMENT <1982

LUIS Search Request: T=Records Management
Author/Title Index--5 Entries Found
1 IR:RECORDS MANAGEMENT * KALLAUS, NORMAN FRANCIS <1982
2 IR:RECORDS MANAGEMENT A PRACTICAL GUIDE *DIAMOND, SUSAN <1983
3 IR:RECORDS MANAGEMENT CONTROLLING BUSINESS INFORMATION *PLACE, IRENE <1982
4 IR:RECORDS MANAGEMENT INTEGRATED INFORMATION SYSTEMS < 1987
5 IR:RECORDS MANAGEMENT SYSTEMS AND ADMINISTRATION *THOMAS, VIOLET <1983

Figure 6-2 ■ Computer Search of Author/Title Index for this Textbook

Requests may be oral or written.

Requests for stored records may come in many ways: either orally (from the next desk, over the telephone or intercom, or by messenger) or in writing (by memo, by letter, or on a special form). The request may be delivered in person or sent by some mechanical means such as a conveyor system. A typical request, for example, might be, "Please get me the most recent letter from Ralston Purina that has the prediction of how much bird food will be produced for next quarter." Or, "Let me have the tape that has Jane's annual report to the stockholders." Or, perhaps, "Get me the microfilm of the current price list for patio enclosures." All of these records have previously been stored manually according to some agreed-upon method of storage. The letter, tape, or film must be found quickly in storage and given to the requester. Every minute of delay in finding the record is costly — in user or requester waiting time and in filer searching time — to say nothing of possible loss of business as an ultimate result.

If filer and requester use the same filing segments for storing and for requesting a record, the system works well. If, for instance, records relating to a company named Huffman Refrigerator were stored under Huffman but requested under Refrigeration Company, retrieval would be extremely difficult because the searcher would look in the R section of the storage instead of the H section.

Retrieval and Restorage Cycle

The same set of basic steps to retrieve are used for handling manual records (see Figure 6-3 below). Only the specific operating

> The basic steps in retrieval are used for manual records.

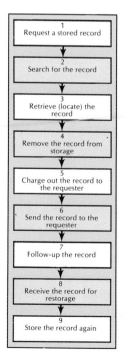

Figure 6-3 ■ Steps in Manual Retrieval and Restorage

procedures will differ. The crucial step, the point at which a problem is most likely to arise, is in Step 1 with the words used to request a record. Ideally, the person who stores the record should be the one who searches for and removes it from storage when it is requested. Realistically, however, the record may be stored by one person and retrieved by someone else when that record or information is requested.

Effective records control enables the records manager or searcher to retrieve requested records on the first try and to answer correctly these following five questions:

1. *Who* took the records?
2. *What* records are out of storage?
3. *When* were the records taken?
4. *Where* will the records be refiled when they are brought back to storage?
5. *How long* will the records be out of storage?

Control is achieved and the questions can be answered if standard procedures have been established and are followed. Each of these procedures will be discussed.

Requisition, Charge-Out, and Follow-Up Procedures

Effective records control includes following a standard procedure for requesting records, charging them out, and seeing that they are returned. In records management terminology, *requisition, charge-out,* and *follow-up* is the procedure that includes following a standard system for requesting records, charging them out, and seeing that they are returned.

Requisition Procedures. Preparation of a requisition is the first step in the retrieval sequence. A **requisition** is a written request for a record or information from a record. Even if the borrower orally requests the information or record, that request is put in writing and referred to as a requisition. The form may be (1) prepared by the requester or (2) made out by the filer from information given orally or in writing by the requester. Two of these forms are described below.

Requisition Form. One of the most frequently used requisition forms is a 5 x 3- or 6 x 4-inch card or slip of paper printed with blanks to be filled in. Figure 6-4 shows an example of such a requisition.

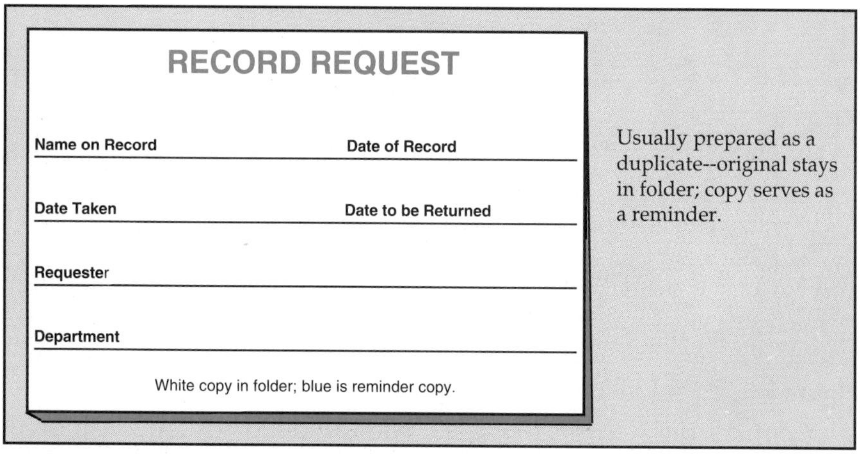

RECORD REQUEST

Name on Record	Date of Record

Date Taken   Date to be Returned

Requester

Department

White copy in folder; blue is reminder copy.

Usually prepared as a duplicate--original stays in folder; copy serves as a reminder.

Figure 6-4 ■ Requisition Form

By studying Figure 6-4, you see that this form answers the five questions (Who? What? When? Where? How Long?) discussed above. This form may be prepared in duplicate: the original stays in the folder from which the document was retrieved to serve as an OUT indicator (this will be discussed shortly); the copy (usually placed in a tickler file as discussed in Chapter 5) reminds you to be sure that the record is returned on time.

On-Call (Wanted) Form. Occasionally, a record that has already been borrowed will be requested. When you go to your files to retrieve the record, there in its place is the requisition form. When this occurs, you should notify the requester that the record is out and when it should be returned. If the request is urgent, you notify the original borrower that someone else wants the record and ask that it be returned to storage. The notification may be made orally and/or in writing on an on-call form or a wanted form. An **on-call form** (or **wanted form**) is a written request for a record that is *out* of the file. (See Figure 6-5 on the next page). This form is similar to an OUT form.

Two copies of an on-call form are made—one copy goes to the borrower; the other is attached to the original OUT indicator in storage. As soon as the borrowed record is returned to storage, it is charged out to the second borrower by the standard method of charge-out or by noting on the on-call form the date on which the record was delivered to the second borrower. (Note the "Delivered" column at the right of the card in Figure 6-5.)

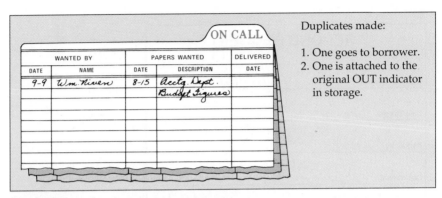

Figure 6-5 ■ On-Call or Wanted Form

Confidential Records Requests. All stored records are considered valuable or they would not be stored. Some are so valuable that they are marked *Confidential, Classified, Secret, Vital,* or *Personal.* You must be sure not to release these types of records from storage without proper authorization — following the standard office procedure. In some offices, a written request bearing the signature of a designated officer of the company is required for the release of such records.

> Be sure to follow company procedures for handling confidential records.

Some records may be so valuable or confidential that they are not to be removed from the storage under any circumstances. They must be inspected at the storage container. This inspection is not accompanied by any requisition form other than the required signature of someone in authority before the inspection is allowed.

Charge-Out Procedures.   **Charge out** is a procedure used to account for records that are removed from storage. A record is charged-out to the borrower who is held responsible for returning it to storage by an agreed-upon date. A standard procedure for charging out and following up records should be observed in every instance, regardless of who removes material from storage. Less than one minute is needed to note the name of a person who borrows a record, while hours can be spent searching for a lost or misplaced record. Borrowers seem to be more conscientious about returning records to storage when they know that records have been charged out in their name. Typically, the supplies needed to charge-out records consist of:

> Remember that it only takes a minute to record who took what file on what date.

1. OUT indicators to show that records have been removed from storage.
2. carrier folders to transport borrowed records while the original folder remains in the file.
3. a charge-out log.

OUT Indicators. When requested records are found, they are removed from storage and an OUT form is inserted in place of the record just removed. The location of these forms show where to refile the record when it is returned. The four types of OUT indicators in general use were explained in Chapter 5—OUT guides, folders, cards, and sheets.

Disposing of OUT Indicators. When borrowed records are returned to storage, all OUT forms inserted while the records were gone must be immediately removed. If the charge-out information has been written on the OUT form itself, this information is crossed out and the form is stored for reuse. In some offices, OUT forms are kept for tallying purposes, to see how many records are being requested, to determine the work load of employees, and to see which records are being used frequently and which are not. Totals may be kept daily, weekly, monthly, or yearly as determined by the standard office procedure in effect. Requisition forms that are removed from files may be destroyed. Any duplicates of OUT forms should be located and immediately destroyed.

Follow-Up Procedures. Whoever is responsible for retrieving records from storage and charging them out is also responsible for checking on their return within a reasonable length of time. The procedure is known as follow-up. **Follow-up** is checking on the return of borrowed records within a reasonable (or specified) time. The length of time records may be borrowed from storage depends on (1) the type of business, (2) the number of requests that come in for the records, (3) the use of a copying machine, and (4) the value of the records. Experience shows that the longer records remain out of the files, the more difficult their return becomes. Many businesses stipulate a week to ten days, with two weeks being the absolute maximum time records may be borrowed. Other businesses allow less time because records can be so easily and quickly copied that the original may be returned to storage within a few hours. Doing a follow-up may mean calling a borrower as a reminder that records must be returned to storage or sending a written request that borrowed records be returned.

Following Up Confidential Records. The rule concerning confidential records is generally that the records (if they may be borrowed at all) must be returned to storage each night. You should use a special memory device as a reminder to see that these records are returned.

Follow the same charge-out procedures used for other records; however, an *additional* reminder must be made to make sure that you will not forget to obtain the record before you leave for the day. This reminder may be a note prominently displayed on your desk or a special flag or signal on your desk to serve as a memory jogger. The memory jogger used should be something unusual because it must never fail to remind you that some confidential records are out of storage and must be recovered.

Charge-Out Log. Usually a company will have a charge-out log for you to complete for all records leaving storage. A **charge-out log** is a form used for recording the following information:

1. WHAT record was taken
2. WHEN it was taken
3. WHO took the record(s)
4. DATE BORROWED
5. DUE DATE
6. DATE RETURNED
7. DATE OVERDUE NOTICE WAS SENT

The log is always kept current and used in the follow-up procedure. Refer to Figure 6-6 for an example of a portion of a charge-out log that may be used.

Name on Borrowed Record	Date of Record	Name of Person or Department Borrowing Record	Date Borrowed	Date Due	Date Returned	Date Overdue Notice Sent	Extended Date
Desoto Auto Repair	3-1	Bill Hartman	3-6	3-11	3-11		
Applications Word Processing Lute, Renee	2-24	Michelle Nienkemper	3-7	3-12	3-8		
Mom's Restaurant	1-4	E. Kinworthy	3-8			3-14	3-16
St. Charles' Graphics	2-20	James Daniel	3-10	3-15			

Figure 6-6 ■ Charge-Out and Follow-Up Log

RECORDS RETENTION

Once a record is stored, it does not stay there forever. Just think of the thousands of storage containers, shelves, and so forth that would be required in offices if that were the case!

With the value of each record determined, the records manager must then determine how long records are to be kept (retained). A **records retention schedule** is a listing of an organization's records along with the stated length of time the records must be kept.

For making retention decisions, one useful classification system divides records into four categories: (1) *records that are not worth keeping*, such as bulk mail announcements, simple acknowledgments, bulletin board announcements, and the like; (2) *records for short-term storage* of up to three years, used mainly for active files of business letters and interoffice memorandums, business reports, and bank statements; (3) *records for long-term storage* of, say, seven to ten years for retaining more important financial and sales data, credit histories, and statistical records; and (4) *records for permanent storage*, such as student transcripts, customer profile records, and business owner-ship records, which have lasting value.

Information needed to create and keep a records retention sched-ule up-to-date can be obtained at little or no cost from various sources. The U.S. Government annually publishes the *Guide to Records Reten-tion Requirements*, which is available from the Superintendent of Documents, U.S. Government Printing Office. Each of the 50 states has developed statues of limitations that specify the time after which legal rights cannot be enforced by civil action in the courts. Once a record reaches an age beyond which the statute of limitations applies, the record has no value as evidence in a court of law. Chapter 12 discusses records retention scheduling in detail.

RECORDS TRANSFER

In the record cycle, **records transfer** is the physical movement of active records to inactive storage areas. The basis for making the decision to transfer records is the activity (frequency of use) of the record.

Records analysts define three degrees of records activity:

Active records: Records that are used three or more times a month. They are stored in very accessible equipment in the active storage file.

Inactive records: Records that are referred to less than 15 times a year. They are stored in a less expensive storage area.

Archive records: Records that have historical value to the organization and are preserved permanently. Archives can have many uses: maintain public relations; prepare commemorative histories; preserve corporate history; provide financial, legal, personnel, product, or research information; provide policy direction.

Careful management of stored records requires that agreed-upon procedures be followed. Procedures to handle all situations should be listed on the retention schedule your organization has developed. In most cases, the current year's records plus those of the past year are all that are needed in the active files. However, several other factors must be considered when making the transfer decisions.

First of all, transfer helps to reduce equipment costs, because inactive records may be stored in cardboard containers that are less expensive than the steel cabinets used for storage of active materials. Second, the cabinets or shelves formerly used by the transferred files provide additional space for the active files. Finally, efficiency of storage and retrieval is improved because crowding of files has been eliminated; and, as a result, the work space in drawers, cabinets, or shelves has been increased.

Records are either:
1. Destroyed
2. Kept permanently
3. Transferred from active to inactive storage.

At some point in the life of a record, it is usually moved. You either decide to (1) destroy the record, (2) retain the record permanently, or (3) transfer the record to inactive storage. This movement is made according to a retention schedule that has been set up by one with special knowledge of records management. If the records are transferred, the main basis for making that decision is often how active or inactive the use of the record is. The following reasons also have a great influence on when and why transfer takes place.

1. No more records storage space is available.
2. Costs of more storage equipment and extra office space are rising and less costly areas of nearby storage or off-site storage become attractive alternatives.

3. Stored records are no longer being requested and, therefore, are ready for transfer.
4. Workloads have lightened and there is time for records transfer activity.
5. Case or project records have reached a closing or ending time (the contract has expired, the legal case is settled or closed).
6. Established company policy requires every department to transfer records at a stated time.

Once transfer is decided upon, the records manager must find answers to four important questions:

1. WHAT records are to be moved?
2. HOW are the records to be prepared for transfer?
3. WHEN are the records to be transferred?
4. WHERE are the records to go?

The answers to the first three questions will depend on the transfer method selected and the company's records retention schedule. The answer to WHERE will depend on the method selected *and* on the availability of in-house or off-site records storage areas. After answering those questions, the records manager then follows perpetual or periodic transfer procedures discussed below to move the selected records.

Transfer Methods

Two of the most common methods of transferring records are the perpetual transfer method and the periodic transfer method. Each will be discussed along with the procedure to ensure efficient transfer.

Perpetual Transfer Method. Under the **perpetual transfer method**, records are continuously transferred from active storage to inactive storage areas whenever the records are no longer needed for reference. Examples of records that can be transferred by the perpetual method include legal cases that are settled; research projects when results are finalized; medical records of cases no longer needing attention; prison and law-enforcement case records; and construction or architectural jobs that are finished.

The perpetual transfer method is not recommended for business correspondence or records that are often referred to and that must be quickly available.

Periodic Transfer Method. The **periodic transfer method** is a method of transferring active records at the end of a stated period of time, usually one year, to inactive storage. New folders are made for records that are then allowed to accumulate in active storage until the next transfer period. A method of transferring records at the end of one period of time, usually once or twice a year, is called the **one-period transfer method.** At the end of *one period of time*, records are transferred. The main advantage of this method is its ease of operation. The main disadvantage is that some frequently requested records will be in inactive storage, and time will be lost in making frequent trips to the inactive storage area. At times, records of some correspondents will need to be retrieved from both active and inactive storage if the requested records cover several time periods.

Transfer Procedures

Once the transfer method has been determined, transfer procedures are communicated to every department. The records manager must see that adequate storage equipment is available and at the correct place to receive transferred records before the actual transfer begins.

Transfer from Active to Inactive Storage. Preparing records for transfer involves completing the necessary forms (see Figure 6-7) and

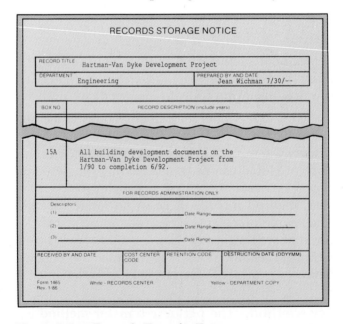

Figure 6-7 ■ Records Transfer Form

boxing the records for inactive storage. The forms used will vary; Figure 6-7 shows a records transfer form used by a large pharmaceutical company. Note that the form should be typed or clearly written because it will be attached to the outside of the storage box and used to locate inactive records that may be requested at a later date. Also note that on the form is information about its contents, such as a description, the time span the records cover, the department name, and retention data.

At the time records are transferred, the transferring department completes a multi-copy set of the records transfer form. One copy is retained by the transferring department when the box is in transit to storage. The original and two copies accompany the box to inactive storage where the box is logged in and its location on the storage shelves is noted on all copies. One copy of the form is returned to the sending department and retained there for reference when a record from that box is required. The copy that was first retained in the department is now destroyed.

Information for the records transfer form is either keyed into or read into automatic equipment (discussed further in Chapter 10). When records are borrowed from inactive storage, the same controls are needed as used in active storage — requisition, charge-out, and follow-up.

If the records center does not provide boxes of uniform size in which to store records to be transferred, the records manager must see that all departments use the same size box, to facilitate stacking and to use space most economically. Transfer cases are made of heavy fiberboard with sliding drawers. Transfer boxes, also of heavy fiberboard, have lift-up or lift-off tops or lift-out sides and are more difficult to retrieve records from than are transfer cases. Refer to Figure 6-8 on the next page for an illustration of boxes stored in an inactive records storage center.

Transfer from Inactive to Archive Storage.   Preparing records for transfer from inactive to archive storage (permanent storage) involves completing the necessary forms, labels, and possibly boxing the records for archive records storage. Depending on the size of the company, there may be a special storage area especially designed for archive records to be displayed or reviewed. While archive records may be on display, others may be boxed, labeled, and stored.

Figure 6-8 ■ Inactive Records Storage Center

At the time that records are transferred to the archives, careful notes must be kept on what is being archived and where. This information may either be keyed in or read into automated equipment (discussed further in Chapter 10). When records are borrowed from the archive storage and removed, the same controls are needed as used in active storage—requisition, charge-out, and follow-up.

IMPORTANT TERMS

active record
archive record
charge out
charge-out log
follow-up
inactive record
on-call (wanted) form

one-period transfer method
periodic transfer method
perpetual transfer method
records retention schedule
records transfer
requisition
retrieval

REVIEW AND DISCUSSION

1. How has the meaning of the phrase "to retrieve records from storage" changed over the years? (Goal 1)
2. Name at least three ways that requests for stored records are made. (Goal 1)

3. Explain storage and retrieval. (Goal 1)
4. What procedure should the records manager establish to maintain control over stored records? (Goal 1)
5. Three dates are usually written on a requisition form. What are they? Why are all three necessary? (Goal 1)
6. Explain why an on-call or wanted form is used. (Goal 1)
7. How are OUT indicators used in the charge-out procedure? How are they disposed of? (Goal 1)
8. What is the reason for the follow-up procedure? (Goal 1)
9. Explain what a retention schedule is and why it is important. (Goal 2)
10. Why is it necessary to transfer records? (Goal 3)
11. What are four important questions to be answered before records transfer takes place? (Goal 3)
12. Explain the two most common methods of records transfer. (Goal 3)
13. How is a records transfer form used? (Goal 3)

APPLICATIONS (APP)

APP 6-1. Solving Retrieval Problems

You are one of two administrative assistants in the office of a small certified public accounting firm where there are two CPAs, one junior accountant, and two administrative assistants — you and Bob. Because you do not have a records manager, you and Bob are responsible for keeping the records stored so that they can be found quickly. All of the five people in the office have access to the files — removing and refiling records as needed. You and Bob do the refiling about 50 percent of the time.

Because the office is small, no controls are presently being used; there is no way to tell who has a client's records except to ask. Misfiling occurs frequently because someone is in a hurry when records are refiled, and you and Bob spend unproductive time searching for records you *know* should be in storage but that are not there.

What kind of records control procedures would you recommend? Do you believe additional supplies or equipment are needed to provide adequate control of records? If not, explain why. If so, what would you recommend? Be specific in your answers. (Goals 1, 2, 3)

APP 6-2. Recommending Records Transfer Methods

What method of records transfer would you recommend for each of the following records situations? Explain your decision. (Goal 3)

1. Medical clinic office: Medical cases of deceased patients.
2. Law office: Client folders with 10 years' accumulation in the folders.
3. Department store: Correspondence and billing records of customers, kept for five years in active storage.
4. Shopping center developer: All folders related to a shopping center that has just been completed, all space rented, and the Grand Opening held last Saturday. Folder are those of contractors, lessees, insurance carriers, and governmental agencies containing permits.

APPLYING THE RULES

Job 6, Correspondence Storage—Other Names and Tickler File Usage; Job 7, Requisition and Charge-Out Procedures; Job 8, Transfer Procedures; and Computer Application 6 (optional).

3

Subject, Numeric, and Geographic Storage and Retrieval

Part 3 represents an extension of the alphabetic method because subject, numeric, and geographic storage and retrieval are based on the alphabetic method. The procedures and equipment used with these three methods of records storage are discussed, and the advantages and disadvantages of each method are presented.

7 SUBJECT RECORDS STORAGE

GOALS

After completing this chapter, you will be able to:

1. State the differences and similarities found in the alphabetic and subject records storage methods as well as advantages and disadvantages of the subject method of records storage.
2. Explain the straight dictionary and the encyclopedic arrangements of subjects.
3. List the supplies used with the subject records storage method.
4. Describe a master index and a relative index used with the subject method and tell how they differ.
5. Store and retrieve records by the subject method.

In Part 1 of this textbook you studied, in considerable depth, the alphabetic method of records storage. You will recall that within the alphabetic records storage method, several subjects might be found, such as applications, projects, branch office memos, etc. Storing records solely by subject matter or by topic instead of by the name of an individual, business, or organization is known as the **subject records storage method**.

As you study this chapter, you will see the similarities between the subject and alphabetic methods. You will also see the necessity to use the rules for alphabetic indexing presented in Chapters 2 and 3, as you store records according to subjects. The ARMA International Guideline, *Subject Filing*, contains an in-depth discussion of subject records storage.

Subject filing should be used when other systems will not be effective or when documents cannot be filed by any other single filing characteristic. Some indications that a subject filing system may be needed are:

1. When time is wasted in filing and retrieving information by other storage methods.
2. When there is an extreme number of misfiles (records are not filed where they should be filed).
3. When office workers request documents from a file by numerous key units instead of by a common key unit.
4. When the volume of records exceeds two file drawers/shelves or when a series of documents cannot be filed by any other single filing feature or document characteristic.

The subject storage method is used somewhere in almost every office. Subject filing is suitable for filing correspondence, reports, catalogs, clippings, research data, excessively long inventory lists, or product development plans, just to name a few examples. Some of the types of organizations and their uses of this method are:

> Subject filing is used in almost every office.

1. Department stores that keep all records together relating to such subjects as advertising, appliances, customers, home furnishings, housewares, men's wear, special promotions, store maintenance, and window displays.
2. School offices where records are stored according to such subjects as accidents, accreditation, athletics, budget, cafeteria, curriculum, graduation, library, personnel certification, and student records.
3. Airplane manufacturers where records may be stored according to the types of planes being manufactured.
4. Construction companies whose records are stored by such types of construction as apartment houses, bridges, condominiums, individual homes, multifamily homes, office buildings, and roads.
5. Purchasing agents who keep records according to the names of the items being bought or being considered for purchase, rather than according to the names of the vendors: dryers, freezers, microwave ovens, refrigerators, and washers.

THE NATURE AND PURPOSE OF THE SUBJECT STORAGE METHOD

In an alphabetic system, the filing segment that is selected is a name, and the name Smith is not confused with the name Jones. With the subject method, however, two persons can easily think of one topic by similar or synonymous terms, such as Supermarket for Grocery Store; Rugs for Carpets; and Seafood for Shrimp. Because of the similarity of terms and because some records refer to more than one subject, much cross-referencing is necessary, as will be explained later in this chapter.

The selection of a word or phrase to be used as a subject (the filing segment) is of prime importance. The persons responsible for choosing subjects must be thoroughly familiar with the material to be stored, which implies a considerable knowledge of every phase of the operations and activities of their business. The subject must be short and clearly descriptive of the material it represents. Once a subject has been chosen, it must be used by everyone in the organization; and all future subjects should be chosen so that they will not duplicate or overlap any subject previously assigned.

If filers use headings or subjects assigned at random by members of different departments, soon the same type of material may be stored under two or more synonymous terms. Such storage of related records at two or more places will not only separate records that should be stored together but will also make retrieval of all related records very difficult. Good subject selection means (1) *agreement* by file users on the subjects to be used, (2) *flexibility* to allow for growth within the subjects chosen and for expansion to include new material, and (3) *simplicity* so that the users of the records can understand the system.

With the rapid acceptance and use of word processing and the storage of information in computers and on magnetic media, the importance of proper selection of subjects is further increased. To find information that has been stored on any medium, searchers must know what subject or filing segment has been used to store that information. Then they can key into the equipment the words needed to retrieve the information quickly. Further discussion of automated storage and retrieval is found in Chapter 10.

Advantages of the Subject Storage Method

Subject storage saves time because all written records on a specific topic, a specific product, a project, or a problem requiring a managerial decision are grouped rather than being separated into folders by the names of the correspondents.

Margin notes:

Every record must be read thoroughly to determine its contents.

Good subject selection means: Agreement, Flexibility, and Simplicity.

Subject storage saves time.

Subject lists can be expanded easily by adding subdivisions to main subjects. For example, if Transportation were a main heading and Airplanes, Automobiles, Buses, and Trains were subheadings, Space Shuttles could easily be added.

All related material in a subject system is brought together at a common point of reference; consequently, statistical relationships stand out and statistical data become available.

When you have finished studying Chapter 8, Numeric Records Storage, you will find additional advantages that result when numbers and subjects are combined. All the advantages found in numeric storage are also found in the combination of numbers and subjects.

Disadvantages of the Subject Storage Method

The disadvantages of the subject method are many. Unless extreme caution is taken, subject lists and subdivisions grow until there are too many overlapping subjects chosen. The selection of subject classifications is difficult in that subject titles must be concise, clearly defined, and uniformly stated. The development and installation of subject storage usually requires the assistance of experienced records analysts.

Many disadvantages of the subject storage method are found.

Unless the chosen subjects are used consistently, new personnel will find retrieval extremely difficult because the original filer deviated from the subject list. An inadequate subject index often prevents or seriously delays records retrieval. Furthermore, a subject classification is not effective when the titles used are not clear.

The subject method of storage is the most expensive method to maintain because it requires very experienced filers. Preparation of materials for subject storage always takes longer than for any other method of storage, because the content of every record must be thoroughly and carefully read; skimming will not suffice. When a subject folder contains records that are often called for by the name of the writer, and no cross-reference has been prepared, a delay in retrieval results. The use of folders for names of officers in a business firm leads to difficulty when the name of an officer is unknown or forgotten or when personnel changes have been made. Too often records are stored in folders made for the name of the officer (Ben Chu) who is in charge of the department, instead of for the name of the department (Accounting Department). Personnel may change in organizations, but the name of the department or position usually remains. If cards are not prepared for the alternate subjects by which records may be requested, retrieval is delayed. An up-to-date relative index (see page 158) is necessary as well as a master list of subjects.

Records that are stored by subject in order that statistical information may be easily compiled or that mailing lists can be quickly prepared require an extensive cross-referencing system that is impractical. It would be costly, for instance, to store customers' correspondence and orders under the headings of ACCOUNTS—OUT-OF-TOWN and ACCOUNTS—CITY just to find sales statistics for each sales representative's territory or for each state or city.

Most of the disadvantages mentioned here are based on inappropriate uses of the subject method. If reference to records is to be made by a person's name, by a firm name, or by location, subject storage is not the recommended method. However, after careful study of the needs of a company, a records manager may rightly decide that a subject arrangement is the best method by which to store a portion of the company's records.

Even the most thoughtful selection of subjects is worthless unless the subjects are arranged so that the storage of records can be done easily and their retrieval can be quick. Suggestions for the arrangement of records stored by subject follow.

ARRANGEMENT OF RECORDS STORED BY SUBJECTS

The standard arrangements for subject storage are (1) the straight dictionary arrangement and (2) the encyclopedic arrangement, both of which are explained in the following paragraphs. Other arrangements using numbers are explained in Chapter 8.

Straight Dictionary Arrangement

In the **straight dictionary arrangement**, the subject folders are arranged behind A-to-Z guides in their correct alphabetic order according to the subject title. The dictionary subject arrangement should be used when the volume of records is no greater than two file drawers. Subjects that are exceptionally active may be made conspicuous by the use of auxiliary guides (See OWNERS in Figure 7-1). Color coding is often used to distinguish one subject from another. The illustration in Figure 7-1 shows a drawer of file folders arranged in straight dictionary order, used by the secretary of a condominium

The dictionary subject arrangement should be used when records volume is no greater than two file drawers.

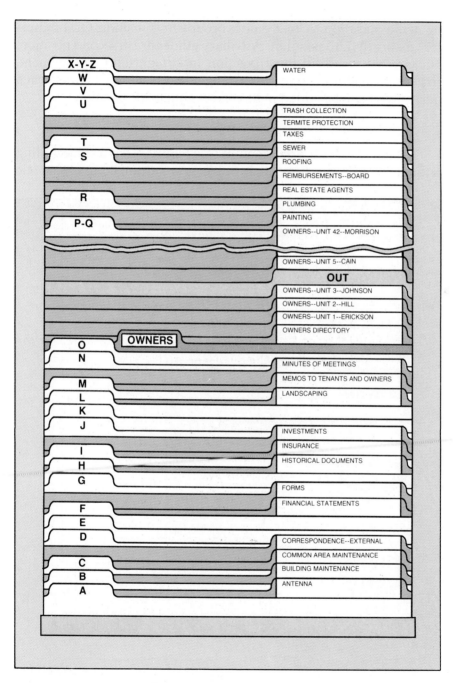

Figure 7-1 ■ Straight Dictionary Arrangement of Subjects

owners association. A-to-Z guides occupy first position. OUT indicator tabs are in third position. Auxiliary guides are in second position. Subject folders are in third position in straight-line arrangement. Expansion within this type of arrangement is simple because each new subject can be added in its correct alphabetic position.

Encyclopedic Arrangement

Subjects are subdivided in the encyclopedic arrangement.

The **encyclopedic arrangement** (see Figure 7-2) is a subject filing arrangement in which the main subjects are arranged in alphabetic

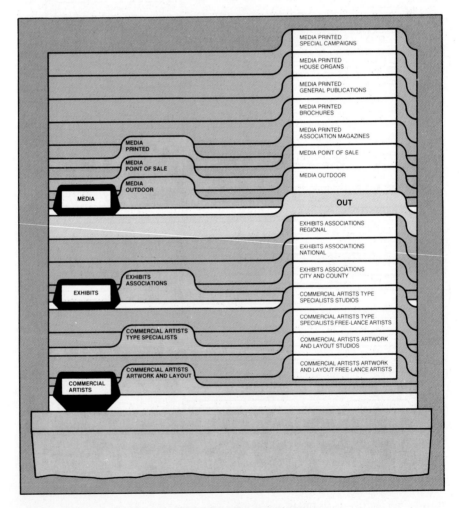

Figure 7-2 ■ Encyclopedic Arrangement of Subjects

order with their subdivisions also arranged alphabetically. The labels on these folders show them to be subdivisions of the main subject. Figure 7-2 shows part of an encyclopedic arrangement used by an advertising agency. The main subjects are arranged in alphabetic order in first position. Subject labels have been typed and inserted into the metal holders of the one-fifth cut first position guide tabs. The typed subdivision labels are affixed to guides in second position one-fifth cut and bear the main subject title and the subdivision subject. Individual folders have typed labels attached to one-third cut tabs in the third position. These tab captions include the main subject and the subdivision subject of the folders.

Refiling is easy when the main subject heading and its subdivision are typed on the folder labels: The storage section into which the folder should be returned is easily found because that subject is typed on the label. Very often, each subject will have a color band that is repeated on all guides and folders of that subject. Sometimes, all captions of one subject will be one color, the color changing when the subject title changes. A third possibility is that each subject will have guides and folders of one color only; another color will be used for guides and folders of the next subject.

Note that the OUT indicator has a third-cut, third-position tab in Figure 7-2. The OUT indicator could be a distinctive color and placed in the drawer to show the removal of a folder.

The equipment needed for the subject storage is the same as that used for alphabetic storage. There is one difference in supplies, as will be explained in the following section.

Refiling is easy when the main subject and its subdivision are on the folder labels.

SUPPLIES FOR SUBJECT RECORDS STORAGE

The supplies used for the subject arrangement are guides, folders, labels, and OUT indicators. All of these items have been explained briefly in Chapter 5.

Guides and Labels

The guides used in subject records storage are determined by the kind of subject arrangement used. If the subject headings are long, subject codes as explained on page 161 may be used to accommodate the words needed for the subjects chosen. Primary guides contain the main subject headings; secondary guides contain the main subject headings and their subdivisions. The guide labels should be prepared on the typewriter or on the computer. The label information is typed two spaces from the left edge and two spaces from the top of the label. The information is typed in capitals with no punctuation and corresponds with the coding system. Keep the label information as brief as possible (see Figure 7-3).

Guide label captions are typed in capitals with no punctuation.

Figure 7-3 ■ Primary and Special Guide Labels

Folders and Labels

The folders used in subject arrangement have captions that include the main subject and any subdivisions. Individual folders following each subject guide have one-third cut tabs. Labels for the folders should be typed on the typewriter or on the computer. The information begins two spaces from the left edge and as near the top of the label or the bottom of the color bar as possible. The information is typed in all capitals with no punctuation (see Figure 7-4).

Folder label captions are in capitals with no punctuation.

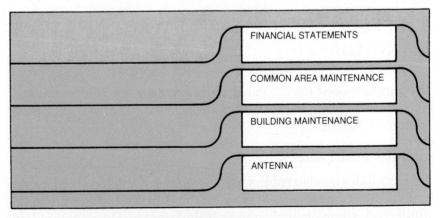

Figure 7-4 ■ Subject Folder Labels

The size of the label used is determined by the size of the tab to which it is to be affixed. If color is used, the typist must be careful to select the correct color for the subject title to be typed.

OUT Indicators

OUT indicators were discussed in Chapter 5. You may want to review briefly page 103 to refresh your memory on OUT indicators.

INDEXES FOR THE SUBJECT METHOD

After the coding system for the subject storage method is determined, some type of index is prepared. The subject storage method cannot function efficiently without indexes. The use of indexes in the subject storage method is the one difference between the supplies used for alphabetic storage and those used for subject storage.

Before discussing the various indexes, let's look at the index format. There are two common formats available. The first format is just a simple list of headings in alphabetic order (see Figure 7-5). Key words are inverted when necessary in order to have the key word first.

ADVERTISING—DIRECT MAIL
ADVERTISING—NEWSPAPER
ADVERTISING—OUTDOOR
ADVERTISING—RADIO
ADVERTISING—TELEVISION

Figure 7-5 ■ Subject Index (Format 1)

The second format is an alphabetic list with related terms indented under the key heading making more than one level of indention possible (see Figure 7-6 at the top of the next page).

Indexes can be printed lists. The printed lists may be manually typed on sheets of paper, cards, or some kind of visible file (described in Appendix B)—or it may be entered on the computer. A subject list on sheets of paper or on visible strips is easier to see at a glance than are subjects typed on individual cards. If a word processor or computer is available, adding and deleting subjects can be done

Indexes may be on printed lists, cards, visible files, or on a computer screen.

<u>Subject</u>		<u>Filed Under</u>
Expenses	SEE	ACCOUNTS—EXPENSE
Leave	SEE	ABSENCES
Maternity		ABSENCES—MATERNITY
Personal		ABSENCES—PERSONAL TIME
Professional		ABSENCES—PROFESSIONAL DEVELOPMENT
Sabbatical............		ABSENCES—SABBATICAL
Sick		ABSENCES—SICK
Personnel Records	SEE	DOCUMENTS
Administrators		DOCUMENTS—ADMINISTRATORS
Clerical		DOCUMENTS—CLERICAL STAFF
Faculty		DOCUMENTS—FACULTY
Student		DOCUMENTS—STUDENTS

Figure 7-6 ■ Subject Index (Format 2)

quickly and easily. See Figure 7-7 on the next page. Note that the top illustration shows a manually typed subject list on a sheet of paper. The lower illustration shows a subject list appearing on a computer screen. Subject information on visible strips is arranged alphabetically. As subjects change, the strips can be easily slipped in and out of the strip file. The important point is that the list must be kept up-to-date at all times.

If a card file is used, each card bears a subject name and the cards are filed alphabetically by subject. One advantage the use of cards has over the use of printed lists is that color can be used beneficially. Cards of one color might identify main subjects; another color might identify subdivisions. Another way to use color is similar to color coding on file folders: All cards pertaining to one subject (the main subject and its subdivisions) are of one color; when the subject changes, the card color changes. Usually, the sequence of color is kept the same throughout the file. For example—pink, buff, green, white, yellow, blue; and then the color sequence begins again with pink, buff, green, etc., through the entire range of subjects. The disadvantages are that the cards can take up excess space and the supplies can cost a considerable amount. With computers, corrections can be made and printed in just minutes, and all information is stored on one disk.

Three types of indexes are extremely valuable to the filer—the master index, the relative index, and the numeric index. In addition, a name index can be helpful.

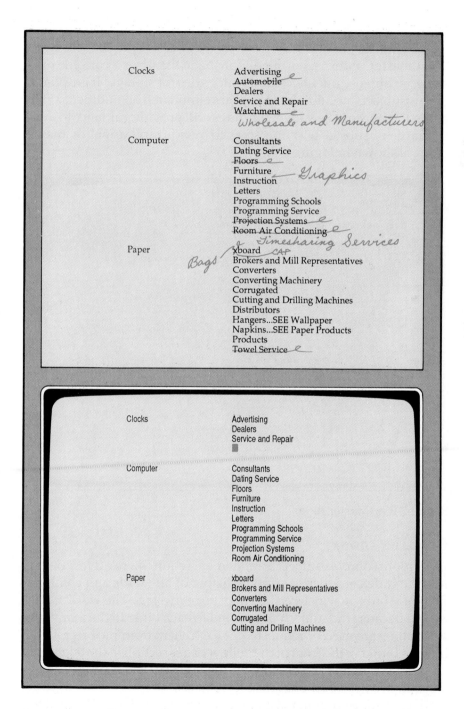

Figure 7-7 ■ Comparison of Manual and Computer Index Corrections

Master Index

A master index is necessary with subject storage.

A **master index** is a printed alphabetic listing or a card file of all subjects (filing segments) used as categories for storage. It is updated as new subjects are added and old ones eliminated or modified. When new subjects are to be added, the index will provide guidance to those in charge of subject selection so as to avoid duplication. A master index is shown in Figure 7-8.

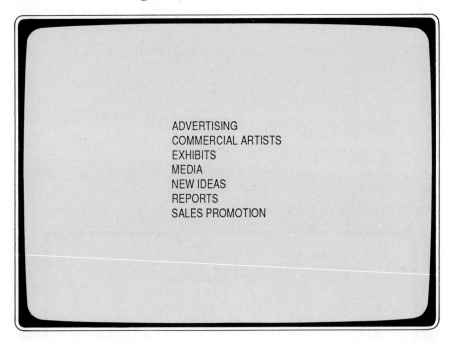

ADVERTISING
COMMERCIAL ARTISTS
EXHIBITS
MEDIA
NEW IDEAS
REPORTS
SALES PROMOTION

Figure 7-8 ■ Master Index

Relative Index

A more complex subject arrangement requires a relative index. A **relative index** is a dictionary-type listing of all words and combinations of words by which records may be requested. The word *relative* is used because the subjects are related to each other in the manner in which they are used or requested. An excellent example of a relative index is found in the front of the Yellow Pages section in the telephone directory. This index contains all the subjects listed in the Yellow Pages as well as additional related subjects.

The relative index may be a printed list or a card file. The card file previously was a preferred method because of the ease of adding subjects to the file. The computer is now the preferred and the fastest method. A relative index is a cross-reference device because it contains all the subjects by which a record might be requested. Whenever someone requests a record by a subject that is not the one selected for use, the filer checks the relative index to see if that requested subject has been included with the correct subject beside it. If not, the filer adds the requested subject to the index listing as soon as the requested record has been located. Figure 7-9 shows a section of a relative index.

A relative index is a large cross-reference file.

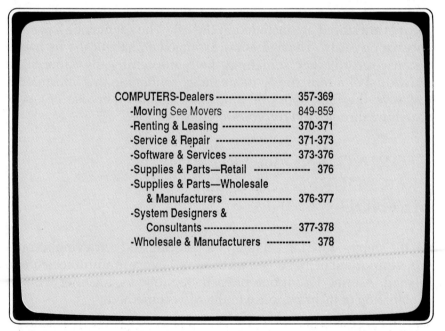

COMPUTERS-Dealers ----------------------- 357-369
        -Moving See Movers -------------------- 849-859
        -Renting & Leasing --------------------- 370-371
        -Service & Repair ---------------------- 371-373
        -Software & Services -------------------- 373-376
        -Supplies & Parts—Retail ----------------- 376
        -Supplies & Parts—Wholesale
                & Manufacturers -------------------- 376-377
        -System Designers &
                Consultants ---------------------------- 377-378
        -Wholesale & Manufacturers ------------- 378

Figure 7-9 ■ Relative Index

The relative index may contain SEE and SEE ALSO cross-references (see Figure 7-10). A SEE ALSO cross-reference is helpful in suggesting related materials and in explaining the nature of a subject.

AUTOMOBILES	CLAIMS	VELDERS CONSTRUCTION CO
SEE	SEE ALSO	SEE
BUSES PASSENGER CARS TRUCKS	ACCIDENTS INSURANCE	PLAZA SHOPPING CENTER

Figure 7-10 ■ Three Cross-References for a Relative Index

Numeric Index

A numeric index is a number list.

A **numeric index** is a current list of all files by the file number as opposed to an alphabetic list or subject list.

Name Index

A name index may be needed in some companies.

Customarily, an index used with a subject arrangement does not contain the names of individuals or companies. However, for many businesses, a **name index**—which is a special listing of correspondents' names used with subject filing—may be needed. The name and address of each correspondent and the subject under which the records are stored are included in the list. The list may be a printed sheet or on cards. The names are arranged alphabetically by name. Because records may sometimes be requested by the name of an individual or a company, a name index containing this information can save the filer hours of time that would otherwise be spent searching through the records stored by subject.

STORING AND RETRIEVING PROCEDURES FOR THE SUBJECT METHOD

All the steps studied in Chapter 5 for storing and retrieving records are as important in the subject method as they are in any other storage method. A brief description of each step follows, together with an explanation of its importance to the subject method.

Inspecting

In any storage system, the inspection of every record is necessary to see that it has been released for storage. No record should be stored until someone with authority has indicated that it is ready for storage.

Indexing

Indexing, or classifying, consumes more time with the subject method than with any other storage method. The filer must examine the contents of each record carefully in order to determine the filing segment under which it is to be stored. If the record relates to one subject only, indexing is comparatively simple; the correct subject is chosen from the subject list. If someone else has previously indicated the subject under which the record is to be stored, the filer must recheck the accuracy of the subject selection.

If the record contains information about more than one subject, indexing will consist of the determination of the most important subject by which the record is to be stored. An X is then placed beside the other subjects that must be cross-referenced.

Coding

Coding of the main subject heading and of any subdivisions consists of underlining or otherwise marking the selected words (filing segment) if they appear on the record. If the subject is not mentioned, it must be legibly written at the top of the record, sometimes with a colored pencil. Some filers prefer to write the filing segment on the material to be stored instead of underlining or circling the information. When more than one subject is indicated, only the most important one is coded; all other subjects are marked in some distinctive manner (with a wavy line, checked, X-ed, etc.) for cross-referencing.

The filer should not rely on memory to determine the subject under which a record should be stored. The subject list should always be consulted to make sure that the correct filing segment is selected and coded. Coding in an alphabetic subject filing system may include an entire subject heading such as PERSONNEL. To simplify a complex subject filing system, coding may include abbreviations. An abbreviation is created with the first alphabetic character of the heading followed by the next one or two consonants of the primary heading, such as PRS for PERSONNEL. The first character of each word in a multiple-word subject heading, such as RRS for RECORDS RETENTION SCHEDULE, may also be used. Consistency in developing a subject code system in which two-to-six-character abbreviations are used is essential. Everyone using the system must understand the codes and how to develop new ones when necessary. Subject letter codes are written on each record and used on individual folder labels.

Cross-Referencing

Many cross-references may be made for one record. If the record to be stored refers to several important subjects, sometimes copies (typed, photocopied, or otherwise reproduced) are made of the record, and those copies are stored under the different subject headings involved to eliminate the need for cross-references for that record.

In Figure 7-10, the illustration on the left shows a card of a distinctive color to show the filer the correct filing segments under which to look for information about automobiles. A cross-reference of this type is a SEE reference used for synonymous or similar terms. The SEE ALSO reference shown in Figure 7-10 is a reference to two places where helpful material connected with claims may be found.

The illustration on the right in Figure 7-10 shows a card made for a correspondent whose name is often used in calling for records. Because the records relate to the Plaza Shopping Center, they have been cross-referenced under that filing segment. This cross-reference card would be stored in the file containing correspondents' names (name index), not in the subject card file.

Instead of noting a cross-reference on a printed list or card, a permanent cross-reference guide may be placed in the regular storage container. No record would ever be stored under the permanent guide heading—this directs you to the correct place for storage.

Sorting

Subject records are sorted first by main subject.

The sorting of records to be stored alphabetically by subject is usually done in an A-to-Z sorter. Records are sorted by main subjects; any resorting by subdivisions is done at the time the records are inserted into the file folders. If the volume of records to be stored is great and many subdivisions are used, the sorter might be subdivided to save the filer's time.

Storing

Careful placement of records into folders is always important. A quick look at the folder tab to see that the subject on it agrees with the filing segment coded on the record will help to avoid misfiling. A slight raising of the folder by one hand before the record is inserted by the other hand will also avoid mistakes.

Records are stored by correspondent names in subject folders.

Records in a single subject folder are placed in alphabetic order according to the names of the correspondents. Each correspondent's records are then arranged by date with the most recent date in front.

Retrieving

Retrieval procedures for the subject storage method are the same as those used in any other method of storage. Knowing who has taken the records, the contents of those records, what date the records were borrowed, and when the records are supposed to be returned to storage is important in maintaining control over all records. Follow-up is necessary to ensure that the records are returned, to extend the charge-out time, or to call to the attention of someone any matters needing consideration in the future.

It must be reemphasized here that subjects are words and the words chosen to be used for retrieving *must* be the same as those used for filing/cross-referencing. For example, everyone must know to use *carpets* not *rugs*; *automobile* not *car*; *restaurant* not *fast foods*.

Subjects used for retrieving records must be the same as those used for storing.

IMPORTANT TERMS AND CONCEPTS

encyclopedic arrangement
master index
name index
numeric index

relative index
straight dictionary arrangement
subject records storage method

REVIEW AND DISCUSSION

1. What are the differences and similarities of the alphabetic and subject storage methods? (Goal 1)
2. Why is the subject storage method said to be more costly than the alphabetic storage method? (Goal 1)
3. List at least three advantages and at least three disadvantages of the subject storage method. (Goal 1)
4. What is the difference between the straight dictionary arrangement and the encyclopedic arrangement of subjects? (Goal 2)
5. What supplies are needed when using the subject storage method? (Goal 3)
6. What indexes are necessary for use with the subject storage method? Explain their use. (Goal 4)
7. What is the relationship between cross-referencing and the relative index? (Goal 4)
8. List the procedure followed in storing and retrieving records using the subject storage method. (Goal 5)

APPLICATIONS (APP)

APP 7-1. Selecting Subjects

Refer to Figure 7-1. You will recall that it shows a file drawer of subject folders used by the secretary of a condominium owners association. The secretary is contemplating the addition of folders to the drawer as labeled below. What do you think of the secretary's selection of new subjects? (Goals 4, 5)

1. CURRENT—folder in which matters needing attention at the next Board meeting will be placed.
2. BUDD PIPER ROOFING CO—folder in which all paid bills and correspondence related to building repairs for which this company is responsible will be placed. After each heavy rainstorm, the services of Budd Piper are necessary to caulk windows and fix leaky roofs of unit owners' condos.
3. APPLICATIONS—CONDO MANAGEMENT—folder in which correspondence to and from persons desiring to manage the condo complex will be placed.
4. H AND E DEVELOPMENT CO—folder in which memos and correspondence between the association and its developers, the H and E Development Co. will be placed.
5. DUES LEDGER SHEETS—folder in which all noncurrent ledger sheets for all owners will be placed. The sheets show the monthly record of payments made by the owners over the years.

APP 7-2. Storing Records by the Subject Method

You are in charge of storing all the records of three departments. You have set up a master index of subjects and a relative index of variations of the subjects. Records come to you:

1. with the filing segment coded that agrees with the subjects that are on your master index.
2. not coded at all.
3. coded with subjects that do not appear on your master or relative indexes. (Goals 4, 5)

What would be your procedure for storing each of the records in those three categories? For instance, in 1 you would read the records to see if the coded filing segment and the content of the records agree. If they agree, what would you do? If they do not agree, what would you do?

APPLYING THE RULES

Job 9, Correspondence Storage—Subject Method

8 NUMERIC RECORDS STORAGE

GOALS
After completing this chapter, you will be able to:

1. List and describe the basic features of the consecutive numbering method.
2. Describe in detail the procedure for storing records by the consecutive numbering method.
3. State the advantages and disadvantages of consecutive numeric records storage.
4. Explain the difference between consecutive and nonconsecutive numbering storage methods.
5. Explain the way in which records are stored by terminal-digit and middle-digit storage methods.
6. Describe block numeric storage.
7. Describe how records are stored chronologically.
8. Define mnemonic coding and give an example.
9. Explain duplex-numeric, decimal-numeric, and alphanumeric coding.

In previous chapters, alphabetic and subject methods of records storage were discussed. This chapter explains a third method by which records can be stored—**the numeric storage method**. As its name suggests, the numeric method of records storage is storage wherein records are assigned numbers and then stored in one of various numeric sequences. Two major reasons for using a numeric storage method are the infinite set of numbers available (relative to the limitation of 26 alphabetic characters) and the ease with which people recognize and use numbers. Machines, too, are capable of great speed in the use of numbers; and the increase in the use of machines is abundantly apparent in our lives.

OVERVIEW OF NUMERIC RECORDS FILING

Numbers as a means of classifying data are common in our everyday routines. For example, numbers identify our:

bank checks and accounts
social security records
driver's licenses
ZIP Codes
insurance policies
hospitalization/health plans
residential addresses
telephones
charge accounts
school courses
legal cases
permits of many kinds (boating, hunting, fishing)
post office boxes
safe-deposit boxes
student records

Products in grocery stores are coded with a Universal Product Code for use by computers. Mail-order houses sometimes store their merchandise in numbered areas, rows, and bins and retrieve the items by mechanical robots or arms called "pickers." As businesses become more reliant on computers, and as the number of personal computers in homes increases, the use of numbers to classify data further stresses the need for knowledge about the numeric method of storage.

The numeric method of records storage is particularly useful to:

1. Insurance companies that store records by policy and claim numbers.
2. Social welfare agencies that maintain records by case numbers.
3. Firms in the building trades that use contract or job numbers and stock or parts numbers.
4. Architects who assign contract numbers to their clients' projects to ensure clear-cut identification of all pieces of correspondence and other records pertaining to contracts and projects.
5. State automobile license departments and social security offices where records are arranged by number because of the offices' large-scale operations.

6. Physicians, dentists, and veterinarians who assign numbers to patient history records and to X-ray records.
7. Companies whose personnel records are stored by either employee number or social security number.
8. Savings and loan associations and banks whose mortgage and loan departments store records by the number assigned to the mortgage or loan.

This chapter contains a detailed description of the basic features of numeric arrangements and the procedures for storing records numerically.

CONSECUTIVE NUMBERING METHOD

The easiest-to-understand method of numeric storage uses numbers arranged in sequence. This method is called the consecutive numbering method, also sometimes referred to as serial or sequential numbering. The **consecutive numbering method** is numeric storage in which consecutively numbered records are arranged in ascending number order — from lowest to highest number. The numbers begin with 1 and progress upward; or they may begin with 100, 1000, or some other number and progress upward. For example, office forms such as invoices, sales tickets, and purchase orders are frequently numbered in consecutive order. Even though these forms may be filled in at various locations within a business, the forms are ultimately stored together in consecutive numeric sequence.

Correspondence may also be stored numerically by consecutive numbers. The supplies needed and procedures to be followed to store correspondence so that it may be found easily will be explained and illustrated. Storage and retrieval (access) for the numeric method is **indirect access**—an index must be referenced before a record can be stored/retrieved.

Indirect access requires more steps to retrieve records.

Basic Features of Consecutive Numbering

The consecutive numbering method requires the following supplies:

1. Numbered guides and folders
2. Alphabetic guides and folders
3. An alphabetic (card or computer) file
4. An accession log

Numbered Guides and Folders.   A straight-line arrangement of the contents of a consecutively numbered file drawer is shown in Figure 8-1. Primary guides, numbered 640 and 650, divide the drawer into easy-to-find numeric segments. The guides may be purchased with numbers printed on their tabs; numbered labels may be inserted into blank slots on the tabs; self-adhesive numbers may be attached to blank tabs; or numbers may be stamped on tabs with a numbering machine or typed on. Handwriting or printing should be avoided because of its lack of uniformity. Usually, one guide is provided for every ten folders.

In Figure 8-1 on the next page, consecutively numbered folders 640 through 650 are placed behind the guides that begin the correspondingly numbered sections. Folders at the right also show the names of the correspondents since secrecy is not a factor, and office policy requires names in addition to numbers. The names are stored in random order, not alphabetically, as names are assigned numbers; and the numbers are in consecutive order.

Alphabetic Guides and Folders.   An alphabetic general section found in many numeric arrangements holds records of correspondents whose volume of correspondence is very small. In most offices, an individually numbered folder is not used until at least five pieces of correspondence that relate to one correspondent have accumulated. Until those five pieces accumulate, correspondence is stored by customer or client name in the general section in the same manner as names are stored by the alphabetic method.

Because expansion occurs at the end of a consecutively numbered arrangement, placement of the general section at the beginning is recommended.

The general section contains a primary guide labeled GENERAL. This guide may be followed by other guides to indicate the alphabetic divisions. In Figure 8-1, the GENERAL guide is at the beginning of the drawer. Behind the GENERAL guide are the alphabetically captioned folders that hold records of correspondents who have not yet been assigned numbers.

Alphabetic File.   A numeric arrangement cannot function without an **alphabetic file** containing the names of the correspondents or any subjects used in a numeric file with the assigned numbers indicated. The file may be kept on cards (as has been the practice in the past) or on a computer disk (as is fast becoming the fashion). The cards or the

Alphabetic computer files are used often.

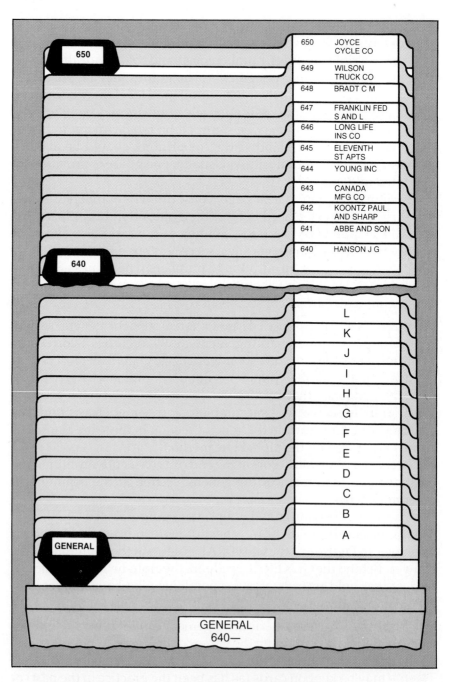

650	JOYCE CYCLE CO
649	WILSON TRUCK CO
648	BRADT C M
647	FRANKLIN FED S AND L
646	LONG LIFE INS CO
645	ELEVENTH ST APTS
644	YOUNG INC
643	CANADA MFG CO
642	KOONTZ PAUL AND SHARP
641	ABBE AND SON
640	HANSON J G

650

640

L
K
J
I
H
G
F
E
D
C
B
A

GENERAL

GENERAL
640—

Figure 8-1 ■ Consecutively Numbered Arrangement

computer list, arranged alphabetically, show the numbers that have been assigned to the filing segments. According to office policy, cards (or the computer list) may or may not be made for correspondents whose records are stored in the GENERAL section. If cards (or a computer list) are made for those correspondents, the cards (or computer list) bear the letter G to show that the correspondence with those individuals or companies is in the general section of storage. Figure 8-2 shows a portion of a card file with cards arranged alphabetically and a computer screen with the same list.

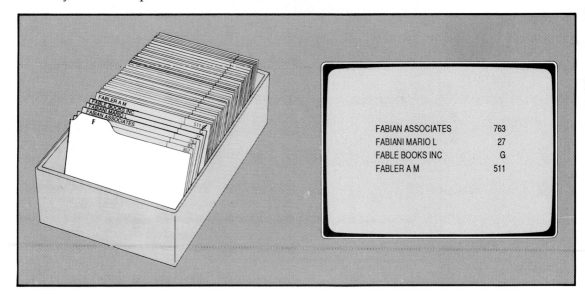

Figure 8-2 ■ Alphabetic Card and Computer Files for Consecutive Numbering Method

Because each correspondent is assigned a different number and thousands of correspondents' records may be in storage, remembering the numbers for all of those names is impossible. Therefore, the alphabetic card or computer file serves as the "memory," because each card or entry shows either the complete name and address of one correspondent and its assigned number or the name of one subject and its assigned number. Mistakes made in the card or computer file are very serious because the card or computer file is the first place to which the filer goes to locate any requested name or subject. Great care must be taken to keep the card or computer file up-to-date and accurate.

Accession Log. The **accession log** is sometimes called an accession book or a number list because it is a serial listing of numbers assigned in a numeric system. The log provides (1) those numbers already assigned to correspondents and subjects and (2) the next number available for assignment (see Figure 8-3). The proper use of an accession log prevents a filer from assigning the same number twice.

The accession log is crucial to numeric records storage.

```
759  NIENKEMPER MICHELLE E
760  HARTMANN JOSEPH
761  CHANCE CHARLOTTE M
762  WILSONHOLME RED
763  LUTE DANIEL MICHAEL
764  KINWORTHY EDNA A
765  VELDERS VELDERS AND VAN DYKE
766  SCHRADER KAREN M
767  HARTMAN BILL
768  LAVACK EDWARD L
769  BALTZ SYLVIA
770  MARTIN DORTHA
771  BISHOP TERI
772  HANCOCK DAVID
773  FULLER MARY B
774  . . .
775  . . .
776  . . .
```

Figure 8-3 ■ Printout of Computer File Accession Log

If a numbered folder is lost or misplaced, reference to the accession log would provide the name that had been assigned that number; and the full information can then be obtained from the alphabetic card or computer file to help in locating the folder. Only complete names, not addresses, need be in the accession log because the alphabetic card or computer file shows all the information about each correspondent. The accession log is never used to locate numbers previously assigned to correspondents because that information is instantly available in the alphabetic card or computer file.

Storage and Retrieval Procedures for Consecutive Numbering

The steps for storage (inspecting, indexing, coding, cross-referencing, sorting, and storing) and retrieval (requisitioning, charging out, and following up) are as important in the numeric method as they are in all other storage methods. The procedures to be followed in storing and retrieving records numerically are discussed below.

Inspecting and Indexing. Records are first inspected for release marks. Then records are mentally indexed to determine the name or subject by which each record is to be stored.

Coding. Coding for numeric storage requires two steps: (1) coding the name or subject (the filing segment) to which the record refers (as is done in all storage methods) and (2) assigning a number to the record.

If the alphabetic coding of the name or subject has been previously done, the filer checks the coding for accuracy. If the coding has not been done, the filer marks the record according to the practice of the office. If cross-references should be prepared, the coding should include a notation to that effect (usually an X written on the record).

When many records are to be stored, a rough preliminary alphabetic sorting at this time will speed the storing process later because reference to the alphabetic file is the next step. Consulting the alphabetic file will show whether or not a card or a computer entry has already been prepared for that correspondent or subject and, if so, whether a number or the letter G (indicating records in the general section of storage) has been assigned. In some offices, a number is automatically assigned to every correspondent when the first record arrives, or an officer of the company may indicate that a new correspondent is of such importance that a number is to be assigned immediately even though only one piece of correspondence has been received.

Correspondents or Subjects with Numbers Already Assigned. Because the alphabetic file will contain an entry for the correspondent, the record is coded with the number found in the upper right corner of the card (see Figure 8-2) or with the number found on the computer list. The number is written at the top right on the record to be stored, and the coded record is then placed in a numeric sorter for later storage in its properly numbered folder. The letter on the left in Figure 8-4 (on the following page) is coded by name for the alphabetic file and also coded "419" because the card or computer file showed that 419 had previously been assigned to the name of that organization.

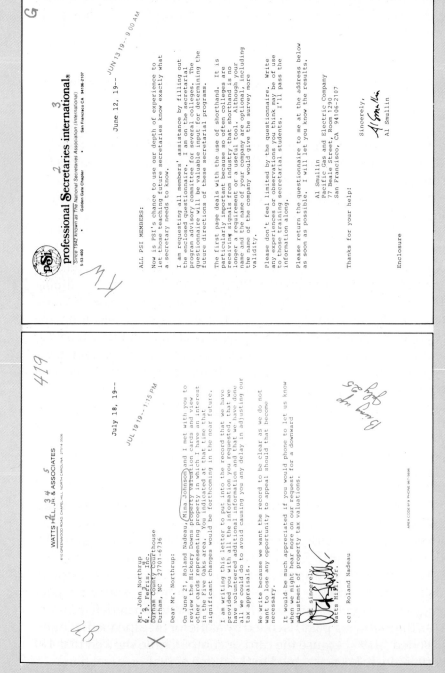

Figure 8-4 ■ Coding of Correspondence for Numeric Method

Correspondents or Subjects with the letter G Already Assigned. If the card or computer file shows a G, the previous correspondence for that person, organization, or subject has been stored in the general alphabetic section of numeric storage. The record now to be stored is therefore coded with G in the upper right corner. The record is then placed in an alphabetic sorter for later storage in the general section of numeric storage. The letter at the right in Figure 8-4 shows the G coding.

New Correspondents or Subjects to be Assigned Numbers. If a correspondent is to be immediately assigned a numbered folder, the filer should take the following steps:

1. Consult the accession log and on the first unused numbered line write the correspondent's name or the subject.
2. Write the assigned number on the record in the upper right corner.
3. Make a file entry for the correspondent or subject. For all correspondents, include complete information (see Figure 8-5 on page 176). For subjects, type the subject and the assigned number.

   Updating your alphabetic file is very important.

4. If any cross-referencing needs to be done, prepare a cross-reference entry to be placed in the alphabetic file.
5. Prepare a new folder, placing on its tab the assigned number (and, if the procedure in the office requires it, the correspondent's name or the subject).
6. Place the record with top to left in the folder.
7. Place the folder in the sorter to be stored later in numeric order. Or, the folder may be laid aside in a separate pile to be taken to storage at the time the storing of other records is done.

New Correspondents or Subjects to be Assigned the Letter G. If the filer does not find a card for the correspondent or subject in the card or computer file and the correspondent or subject does not warrant a numbered folder immediately, a card or computer entry is prepared for the name of that correspondent or the subject. G is typed in the upper right corner of the card. Any necessary cross-reference cards or computer entries are made also, and the letter G is placed on each of those cards. The card is marked G in the upper right corner and placed temporarily in the alphabetic sorter until it is stored. The newly typed cards are then inserted in their correct alphabetic sequence in the card file. Computer entries are inserted in their correct alphabetic sequence at the time the entries are keyed.

Cross-Referencing. Cross-referencing of names and subjects follows the same rules and procedures as were explained in Chapters 2 and 3. No cross-references are stored in numeric file folders—all cross-references are on cards placed in the alphabetic card file or entered in the computer file. In order to emphasize the fact that a card is a cross-reference, the filer should use a card of distinctive color. On the computer, you may want to use bold print or underline cross references. The cross-reference card should bear the number assigned to the original card, followed by an X to indicate clearly that the card serves as a cross-reference. Figure 8-5 shows an original card on the left with the number 690 assigned to the correspondent, Flavelle &

Cross-references appear in the alphabetic file *only*.

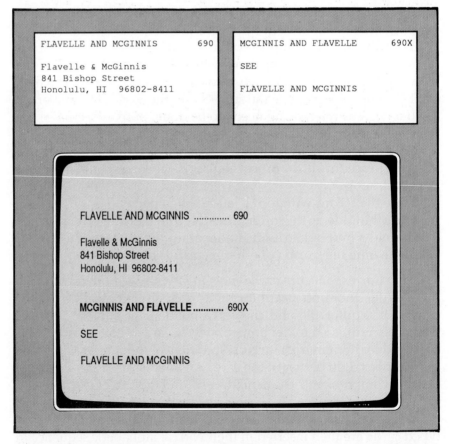

Figure 8-5 ■ Original and Cross-Reference Cards and Computer Screen for Alphabetic File

McGinnis. The accompanying card on the right in Figure 8-5 bears the number 69OX, showing that it is a cross-reference card. The typing format, capitalization, and punctuation should be consistent on all cards; the style shown here is an excellent one to use because it is simple and, therefore, can be typed rapidly. Note the computer entry uses bolding for cross referencing.

Sorting. If rough sorting has been done as the records were prepared for storage, the sorter and its contents may be moved to the storage area for ease of use. If sorting has not been done, a quick rough sorting before storage will save time. Stacking the records randomly in groups by hundreds is one helpful sorting method that eliminates moving back and forth from drawer to drawer or shelf to shelf. The filer would store all 100s, move to the 300s, and finally move to the 600s, eliminating much retracing of steps.

Storing. All records coded with numbers are stored in the correspondingly numbered folders, with the latest date on top. All records coded with G are stored in the general alphabetic folders, first alphabetically according to the units in the filing segments and then by date within each name group, with the most recent date on top.

Office policy governs the point at which accumulated records in the general folder require the assignment of a permanent number. When that accumulation has occurred, the filer should remove the records from the general folder and take the following steps:

1. Consult the accession log to ascertain the next number to be used and enter the name of the correspondent or the subject in the accession log beside that number.
2. Locate the alphabetic file entry that has already been prepared with the subject or the correspondent's name and address, showing the code letter G.
3. Change the G to the assigned number by crossing out the G and writing the assigned number above it or beside it on the card; on the computer, simply delete the old and insert the new number (see Figure 8-6 on the next page).
4. If cross-reference cards have been made, locate the cards, cross out the G on them and write the assigned number followed by an X in the upper right corner. On the computer, simply delete the G and insert the assigned number followed by an X; use bold or underlining for the entry to distinguish it as a cross-reference.

Figure 8-6 ■ Original Card and Computer Screen Records Showing Change from General to Assigned Numbers

5. Insert cards in their proper alphabetic sequence in the card file or insert the computer entry at the correct location.
6. Recode all records with the newly assigned number, crossing out G and writing the number beside it.
7. Prepare a new folder with the assigned number on its tab (and, possibly, the correspondent's name or the subject).
8. Place all records in the new folder, with the most recently dated record on top.
9. Place the numbered folder in its correct numeric sequence in storage.

Retrieving. Whenever records are removed from numeric storage, requisitions, charge-out cards or slips, and OUT indicators must be used in the same way as they are used for alphabetic or subject records storage. Many records are stored by number in computers and information is retrieved electronically from the computer file, either by being shown on a screen or by being printed on paper.

Follow-up procedures to locate borrowed records include the use of a tickler file or other reminder system. These procedures are identical to those used in the alphabetic method, as described in Chapter 6.

Conversion from Alphabetic Arrangement to Consecutively Numbered Arrangement

An organization may decide that a numeric arrangement would provide for quicker records storage and retrieval than would an existing alphabetic arrangement. Or, an organization may decide to change from alphabetic storage to consecutively numbered storage for security reasons. A number on a storage container or file folder does not convey information to inquisitive persons; a name on a folder is instantly recognizable to anyone who sees it. Whatever the reason for a conversion, the procedure is not difficult; it is only time consuming.

The conversion procedures are time-consuming.

In the conversion process, folders that are presently arranged alphabetically are relabeled with numbers assigned consecutively. As numbers are assigned, a card is prepared for each subject or for each correspondent's name (the filing segment) or the computer list is made on paper to be entered in the computer later. The alphabetic card file or computer entries and the sequence of numbered folders will parallel each other since folders are usually removed from their containers in A to Z order. As new folders are added to numeric storage, however, this parallel sequence will stop. The card or computer file will always be in alphabetic order, but new folders will be added at the end of the numbered sequence as they are assigned the next numbers in order.

Steps to be followed in converting from an alphabetic arrangement to a consecutively numbered arrangement are as follows:

1. Numbered guides are prepared for every 10 folders in storage according to the sequence of numbers decided upon, such as 1-10-20; 100-110-120; 1000-1010-1020; etc.
2. Each individual folder is removed from storage and is assigned a number from the accession log. Notation of the filing segment (the name of each correspondent or of any subject) is made in the accession log beside the assigned number.
3. A new label with only a number on it is made and affixed to the folder — or the newly assigned number is added to the old label. *Caution*: General folders must not be removed from alphabetic storage, as will be explained later.
4. An alphabetic file card is typed for each filing segment, or a computer entry is made, and all necessary cross-reference cards or computer entries are typed immediately. The assigned number is typed on each card or in each computer entry for reference purposes; the number and X are then typed on cross-reference cards or in the computer entry (bolding or underlining may also be used at this point).

5. Cross-reference sheets and SEE ALSO sheets are removed from the individual folders because the cross-reference cards or computer entries now take the place of those sheets.
6. If any permanent cross-reference guides are within the group of folders being converted to the numeric method, the guides are removed and cross-reference cards or computer entries are made bearing the same information as was on the guides.
7. All cards, including cross-reference cards, are placed in the card file alphabetically by name or subject or all computer entries are now entered alphabetically.
8. Each record in every folder is coded with its newly assigned number in the upper right corner of the record.
9. The numbered folders are returned to storage in their correct numeric sequence.
10. After all individual folders have been removed from alphabetic storage, converted to numbered folders, and refiled numerically, the folders remaining in alphabetic storage will be the general A to Z folders. These become the general section of the numeric storage arrangement. All records in each general folder are coded with the letter G.
11. A card or computer entry is typed for the name of each correspondent, or the subject, in every general folder. The cards are placed in the card file in alphabetic order or the computer entries are arranged alphabetically.

Advantages and Disadvantages of Consecutive Numbering

Every storage method has advantages and disadvantages. Consecutive numbering is no exception.

Advantages. The major advantage is speedy storage and retrieval because the majority of people know the sequence of numbers better than they know the sequence of the letters of the alphabet. Other advantages of the consecutive numbering method are:

1. Refiling of coded records is rapid because of the reason given above.
2. Expansion is easy and unlimited. New numbers may be assigned without disturbing the arrangement of the existing folders.
3. Transfer of inactive records is easy, especially in the offices where case numbers or contract numbers are used. The oldest cases or

contracts have the lowest numbers and are together in storage rather than being scattered throughout the storage equipment, as would be the situation if cases were stored by name. This transfer then provides space for active records, eliminating the need to buy more equipment.

4. All cross-references appear in the card or computer file and do not congest the file folders, drawers, or shelves.

5. A file drawer filled with guides and folders with tabs containing only numbers is secure from curious eyes or intentional seekers of information. This need for secrecy may be important for patents, research projects, formulas, or clients' names.

6. Orders, invoices, ledger accounts, and correspondence of one customer all bear the same number, keeping like records together. Fewer errors may occur in matching invoice and payment, for example.

7. A complete list of correspondents' names and addresses is instantly available from the alphabetic card or computer file.

8. Time and effort in labeling are saved because numbers can be affixed much more quickly than can correspondents' names or subjects. Folders may be numbered in advance of their use.

9. Misfiled folders may be easily detected because numbers out of place are usually easier to locate than are misfiled records arranged alphabetically.

Disadvantages. Disadvantages, too, are found in the consecutive numbering method. They are:

1. Transposition of numbers, inaccuracy in copying, and the omission of a digit are frequent errors that may not be easily detected. Carelessness results in misfiling—carelessness by the person who wrote the original number as well as carelessness by the filer who stored the record.

2. Numeric storage access is indirect. Reference to an alphabetic file is necessary to ascertain whether or not a number has been previously assigned to the case, contract, or correspondent whose records are being stored. Whenever more steps are required to store records, more mistakes can be made.

3. More guides are necessary for the numeric method than for other methods; the cost of numeric storage is therefore somewhat higher.

4. Because it is necessary to consult an alphabetic file in order to store records by the numeric method, congestion around the file can arise if there is frequent reference to its contents by more than one person. With the computer, depending on how many computers and/or updated copies of the computer list are available, this problem may or may not occur.
5. Two storage methods are involved—alphabetic and numeric. All of the disadvantages inherent in the alphabetic method are therefore found in the numeric method, in addition to the disadvantages of the numeric method.
6. Because it is necessary to check each record against an alphabetic file, sorting alphabetically must usually be done first. Then resorting is done numerically prior to storage. This double sorting requires extra time.
7. If the alphabetic file and the accession log are not very carefully kept, one correspondent's records might be assigned more than one number and be stored in more than one folder. Or a number could be assigned twice, resulting in a mixture of records within one folder.
8. If the alphabetic file is not checked, some of the records of one correspondent could be placed in a general folder, others in a numbered folder.
9. As the numbers used become larger, remembering them becomes harder and misfiling can easily result if memory fails.
10. In the consecutively numbered method, folders are added in consecutive order at the end of storage. Usually the folders with the highest numbers are the ones referred to most often, and reference to them by several people simultaneously is physically difficult because the filers get in each other's way.

The consecutively numbered method is used infrequently for ordinary correspondence storage because the alphabetic method is less costly to operate. However, in offices such as those mentioned at the beginning of this chapter, numeric storage can fill a definite need.

NONCONSECUTIVE NUMBERING METHODS AND CODING

Nonconsecutive numbering is a system of numbers that either has no logical sequence or that may have logical sequence but from which blocks of numbers have been omitted. Very useful storage methods and systems that use numbers in random order are the subject of this section. These methods include terminal- and middle-digit storage, and block numeric storage.

Terminal-Digit Storage

Terminal-digit storage was developed to avoid the disadvantage of working with large numbers. This method also overcomes the disadvantage of congestion at the storage area. The terminal-digit storage method is used most effectively with thousands of folders whose numbers have reached at least five digits (10,000 or more). The words *terminal digit* refer to the end digits of a number, and you will see how they are referred to first as you study this method.

Description. **Terminal-digit storage** is a numeric storage method in which groups of numbers are read from right to left. Numbers are assigned to records in the same manner as was explained previously under consecutive numbering, using an accession log and creating an alphabetic card or computer file. After the numbers are affixed to folders, they are sorted by being read in groups from right to left instead of from left to right. The digits in the number are usually separated into groups of twos or threes. For example, the number 22451 could be divided 022 451 or 02 24 51 (sometimes written with hyphens: 02-24-51). The numbers would be read as 51 24 02 (beginning with the terminal or end numbers). Because of this backward reading, the terminal-digit method seems difficult. Very careful study and some rereading of the explanation may be necessary before you understand it.

> In terminal-digit filing, read the number groups from right to left.

The groups of digits will be identified in this text as terminal, secondary, and tertiary numbers reading from right to left.

02   24   51

(tertiary) (secondary) (terminal)

The terminal digits usually indicate a drawer or shelf number. If the volume of records stored is great, more than one drawer or shelf may be needed to hold all records with numbers ending in the same terminal digits. (As you read this explanation, refer often to Figure 8-7 on the next page; the meaning of terminal digits will soon become clear.) Figure 8-7 shows the arrangement of folders or numbered cards in a portion of drawer 51. All records within that drawer bear numbers ending in 51.

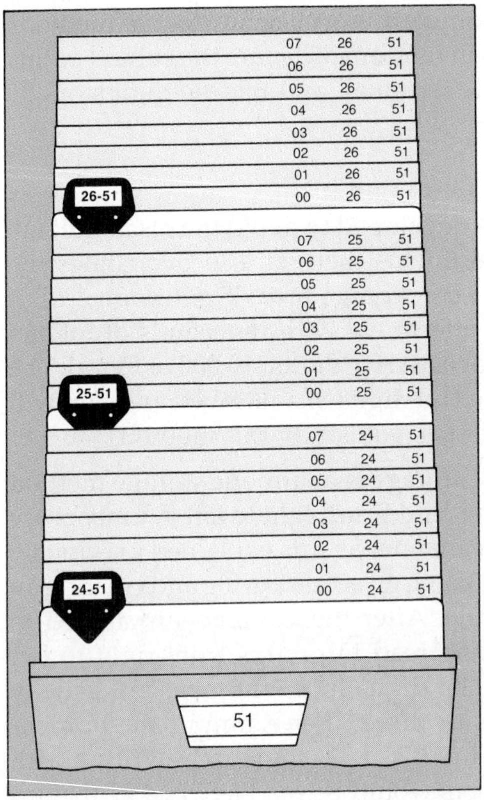

Figure 8-7 ■ Terminal-Digit Arrangement

The guide numbers in the drawer are determined by the numbers of the secondary digits, beginning with 00 and ending with 99 in each terminal-numbered section of storage. If space had permitted, the entire 51 section would show guide 00-51 at the beginning of the drawer and guide 99-51 at the end of the drawer, each followed by its numbered folders.

The order of arrangement behind a certain guide is determined by the tertiary digits. Remember, these are the digits at the extreme LEFT of the number.

As new folders are stored, it becomes necessary to add new guides to separate each group of 10 folders. In Figure 8-8 on the next page, the first section of the file shown in Figure 8-7 (the 24-51 section) has been expanded by the addition of folders bearing numbers 10-24-51 through 19-24-51. The terminal number is 51; the secondary number is 24; the tertiary numbers now have increased from the previous 00 through 07 to 00 through 19. Therefore, guides 00, 10, and 20 are necessary as dividers.

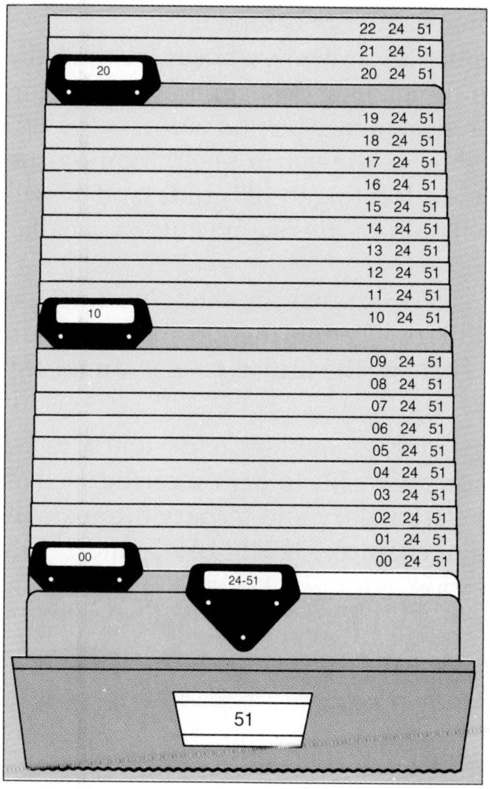

Figure 8-8 ■ Expansion of Terminal-Digit Arrangement

If the next folder added to storage were numbered 08-37-52, the folder would not be placed in this drawer but would be placed in the 52 drawer. Thus, as numbered folders are added to storage, the new folders will be distributed among different drawers according to the last two digits of the new numbers. (In a consecutively numbered drawer all new folders would go at the end, as numbers increase consecutively.)

Assume that folders having the following numbers are ready to be stored:

a. 67 38 24

b. 67 38 25

c. 00 52 93

d. 42 52 93

To store each of the folders correctly requires the following procedure:

a. Locating the terminal number 24 drawer or shelf; locating the secondary number 38-24 guide; locating the 60 guide and placing the 67 in its proper numbered sequence behind 66.

b. Locating the terminal number 25 drawer or shelf; locating the secondary number 38-25 guide; locating the 60 guide; and placing the 67 in its proper numbered sequence behind 66.

c. Locating the terminal number 93 drawer or shelf; locating the secondary number 52-93 guide; locating the 00 guide; and 00 will be the first folder behind that guide as there is no number smaller than 00!

d. Locating the terminal number 93 drawer or shelf; locating the secondary number 52-93 guide; locating the number 40 guide within the 52-93 section; and placing the 42 in its proper numbered sequence behind 41.

Although the terminal-digit storage method is designed to be used in a situation where there are many file folders, it can be used in smaller offices by arranging the secondary and tertiary numbers in combined numeric sequence. For example, 12345, 12445, and 12545 would all be stored in the 45 section, with 123, 124, and 125 stored in sequence.

Advantages and Disadvantages of Terminal-Digit Storage.
Because of the difference in the way numbers are read, some people are inclined to think that the terminal-digit method has few advantages. A thorough study of the method, however, will show the following advantages:

1. Fewer errors in number transposition are likely to occur with this method than with consecutive numbering because the numbers on the folders are divided into groups of two or three digits, and the filer is concerned with only two or three numbers at one time.

2. Misreading of numbers is less likely to occur with shorter groups of numbers than with one long number.

3. Several persons can be storing or retrieving consecutively numbered folders at the same time with no congestion or waiting for someone to move in the storage area because filers will be working at different places.

4. Folders are distributed throughout the drawers or shelves as new ones are added because the terminal numbers determine storage

placement. Additions to storage occur at various places in the storage area.

5. The use of color coding on folders reduces misfiling and in some systems eliminates the need for additional guides to separate every ten folders, as the change in color effectively separates every ten numbers. Eliminating guides cuts costs.

6. If a color system is used, the color association simplifies training of filers because they quickly learn the color associated with the secondary number.

7. Sorting by secondary number is eliminated when this sorting is accomplished on the basis of color.

8. In especially large storage installations, a filer is assigned to a specific section of the equipment and fixed responsibility for records storage and retrieval can be effectively placed.

Disadvantages of the terminal-digit storage method are:

1. People are fearful of the method because it appears complex.

2. Training of filers may take longer with this method than with any other method. Part of this difficulty is caused by the habit of reading numbers from left to right. It takes time to change to reading groups of numbers from right to left.

3. As is true with any filing method, inattention and carelessness will result in misfiled folders; a misfiled numbered folder (unless it is color coded in some way) is extremely hard to find because of number similarity.

4. When a large block of consecutively numbered folders is requested, the filer must go to each of many locations in storage to retrieve the folders. This retrieval takes much more time than would be required to retrieve a block of consecutively numbered folders from a consecutively numbered arrangement. Since such a request does not occur often, the disadvantage is not great.

Middle-Digit Storage

Middle-digit storage is another method of nonconsecutive numbering. Using this method can avoid working with large numbers and overcome the disadvantage of congestion at the storage area. The words *middle-digit* refer to the middle digits of a number, and you will see how they are referred to first as you study this method.

Description. **Middle-digit storage** is a numeric storage method in which the middle numbers are considered first. Numbers are usually

In middle-digit filing, read the middle, the left, and then the right number groups.

written with spaces or hyphens between the groups to aid the filer, with 053301 being written as 05 33 01. The number 33 (the middle group) is considered first; 05 is considered second, and 01 is the last number to be considered. In Figure 8-9 all records with the middle digits 33 are stored in one section. The sequence within the 33 drawer is determined first by the digits on the left and then by the digits on the right. Guide numbers are determined by the left digits.

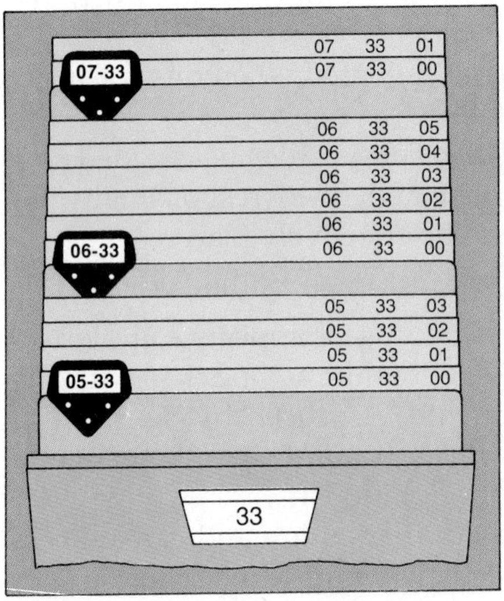

Figure 8-9 ■ Middle-Digit Arrangement

In the middle-digit method, a block of 100 (00 through 99) sequentially numbered records is kept together. Middle-digit arrangement is often used in large insurance companies where it is desirable to keep together blocks of policies issued by one agent. Each agent is assigned a number, which becomes the secondary number. In Figure 8-9 three agents' numbers are shown: 05, 06, and 07. Figure 8-9 shows that agent 05 has on file four policies (3300, 3301, 3302, and 3303) and that there is space in that section for storing 96 additional policies. The largest number that could be affixed to a folder for agent 05 would be 05 33 99, making 100 folders possible—00 to 99.

Reference again to Figure 8-9 shows that agent 06 has six policies on file (3300 through 3305). Agent 07 has two policies on file.

The middle-digit method is most effective with numbers not exceeding six digits. If more than six digits are used, the numbers are separated so that the left grouping has three digits instead of two: 246 81 39.

Advantages and Disadvantages of Middle-Digit Storage. Two advantages are claimed for middle-digit storage, and one major disadvantage is evident. The advantages are:

1. Conversion is easier from a consecutively numbered filing arrangement to a middle-digit filing arrangement than it is from a consecutively numbered arrangement to a terminal-digit arrangement. This is true because blocks of 100 consecutively numbered folders can be moved at one time to the middle-digit arrangement. For instance, if folders were numbered from 764300 through 764399, they would be moved as a block to middle-digit storage in the 43 section.
2. If color is used, misfiling is reduced in the same manner as is true in the terminal-digit storage method.

The disadvantage of the middle-digit storage method is again related to the complexity of the method—people fear it. A period of retraining of filers is necessary since the reading of numbers begins with the middle digits. Then reading moves to the left and then to the right, contrary to normal reading habits.

Block Numeric Storage

Block numeric storage is still another method of nonconsecutive numbering. Briefly, round numbers (100, 200, 300, etc.) are assigned to specific groups (or main subjects). Subdivisions of these subjects are then assigned numbers within the main numbers (110, 120, 130, etc.). As you study this method, the system becomes clearer.

Description. **Block numeric storage** is a numeric storage method based on the assignment of groups of numbers to represent primary and secondary subjects. For example, each department of a business may be assigned a block of numbers to use on its forms as the forms are designed. If the accounting department, for instance, were assigned the numbers 100 to 149 for its exclusive use, the first form designed would be numbered 100, the second form would be 101, the next form would be 102, etc. The purchasing department might be assigned the numbers 150 to 199; sales, 200 to 249; human resources, 250 to 299; and so on.

Advantages and Disadvantages of Block-Numeric Storage. The advantages are:

1. Decentralization of files.
2. Reference numbers are easier to recognize rather than sort long alphabetic filing segments.
3. Closer grouping of files.
4. Changes can be easily made.
5. Infinite expansion.
6. A unique place can be provided for every subject.

The disadvantages are:

1. An index is required.
2. Creating and starting the system is time consuming.
3. Personnel must be trained to use the system.

Chronologic Storage

Records are stored by date.

Chronologic storage is filing records by calendar date. The most recent date is *always* on top. Exact chronologic storage is not well suited to correspondence because of the need for keeping together all records from, to, and about one individual or organization. Chronologic storage is often used for daily reports, deposit tickets, freight bills, statements, and order sheets, which may be best stored by date.

The chronologic principle is followed in all methods of storage as records are placed in their folders. The most current records are at the front of the folder thereby keeping the most recent records in the most accessible place.

Tickler files are another form of chronologic storage. You may want to refer back to the discussion of tickler files in Chapter 5.

Mnemonic Coding

A mnemonic code may be alphabetic, numeric, or a combination.

Mnemonic means to assist the memory. Some numerically filed records are given a specific **mnemonic code** that assists memory. The code may be alphabetic, numeric, or a combination. The placement of the letters and/or digits are consistent and have specific meanings. The specific meaning of each digit is found in the company's manual. Users may be required to memorize the definitions or, more practically, have a table or list made up and kept nearby when classifying or indexing records.

Mnemonic codes may be a combination of alphabetic prefixes (or suffixes) and digits or may be digits alone. The placement of letters and digits must have specific meanings and be consistent in form. For example, a computer printout may be assigned the mnemonic code

BE100F92—the Business Education Department (represented by BE) enrollment figures (represented by the 100) for Fall 1992 (represented by F92). When using mnemonic cords that include letters of the alphabet, avoid using the letter I, O, and Q because they can easily be mistaken for the numbers 1 and 0.

Two general classifications of mnemonic codes are simple and multiple-digit. A short discussion of each follows.

Simple mnemonic codes are used by some state offices. For example, some motor vehicle departments use mnemonic codes to indicate the county in which the vehicle was purchased. Social security and ZIP Code numbers are other examples of simple mnemonic codes. Some utility companies that bill monthly (telephone, electric, etc.) may assign mnemonic customer codes. The customer account number could be divided into groups of digits that may indicate the billing cycle and/or the location within the service area. The hard copy may be filed by middle-digit or terminal-digit order.

Multiple-digit mnemonic codes are longer than simple mnemonic codes and usually have alphabetic characters as well as numeric. The codes are divided into major and minor categories when created. The disadvantage is the necessity of using indexes and definition listings to be consistent with the system's meanings.

Duplex-Numeric Coding

Organizations that use a subject or geographic filing system with the encyclopedia arrangement (with each major category of names subdivided) are often likely to use duplex-numeric coding.

The **duplex-numeric** is a coding system using numbers with two or more parts separated by a dash, space, or comma. An unlimited number of items may be included under any one division or subdivision. For example:

10	*BUDGETS*	
10-1	ACCOUNTING DEPARTMENT	
	10-10	PAST BUDGETS
	10-11	FUTURE NEEDS
	10-12	RECEIPTS
10-2	DATA PROCESSING DEPARTMENT	
	10-20	PAST BUDGETS
	10-21	FUTURE NEEDS
10-3	ENGINEERING DEPARTMENT	
	10-30	PAST BUDGETS
	10-31	FUTURE NEEDS

Note the numbers are separated by a dash.

Decimal-Numeric Coding

The decimal system is used by libraries.

Decimal-numeric is a system for coding records in units of ten. An unlimited number of subdivisions is permitted through the use of digits to the right of the decimal point. This method was first used in 1873 by Dr. Melvil Dewey for classifying library materials. Decimal systems are found in libraries, railroad companies, government offices, public utility companies, and large engineering companies. The system has nine general classes or main divisions (100-900). A tenth division (000) is used for records too general to be placed in any of the nine main divisions. Each main division may be divided into nine or fewer parts (110, 130, to 190). These nine parts can be divided into nine additional groups (111, 112, to 119). Decimals are added for further divisions (111.1, 111.1.1). This method is *not* recommended for correspondence storage.

Alphanumeric Coding

Alphanumeric is a variation of decimal filing where a combination of letters and numbers is used.

Alphanumeric coding is a coding system that combines alphabetic and numeric characters. Main subjects are arranged alphabetically and their subdivisions are assigned a number. After all main subjects are determined, they are given a number (usually in groups of 10 or 100). More elaborate variations of this system can use both letters and numbers and have numerous subdivisions. For example:

BOE:101   Elementary Typing

Section

001	MWF	8:25-9:50
002	MWF	10-11:25
100	MW	7-9:15
210	Day Lab	
250	Evening Lab	

The letters BOE tell what department the course is in (Business and Office Education). The 101 indicates the course (Elementary Typing). The regular class day sections begin with 001; the regular class evening sections begin with 100; the lab classroom day sections begin with 210; and the lab classroom evening sections begin with 250. Therefore, if someone enrolls for BOE:101.100, they have enrolled in the Business and Office Education Elementary Typing course for the evening section on MW from 7-9:15.

IMPORTANT TERMS AND CONCEPTS

accession log	duplex-numeric
alphabetic file	indirect access
alphanumeric	middle-digit storage
block numeric storage	mnemonic code
chronologic storage	nonconsecutive numbering
consecutive numbering method	numeric storage method
decimal-numeric	terminal-digit storage

REVIEW AND DISCUSSION

1. What are the basic features of the consecutive numbering method? Describe each. (Goal 1)
2. What is the procedure for storing records by the consecutive numbering method? (Goal 2)
3. Is the numeric method a direct or an indirect access method? What is the difference between the two? (Goal 2)
4. Why is it recommended that a general alphabetic section of folders be placed at the beginning (not the end) of a consecutively numbered storage arrangement? (Goal 2)
5. Of what value is an alphabetic file in the numeric storage method? (Goal 2)
6. Why is an accession log necessary in numeric storage? (Goal 2)
7. How does the coding step for storing records by numbers differ from the coding step for storing records alphabetically? (Goal 2)
8. Why will some entries in the alphabetic file bear a code of G; some will have a crossed-out G and a number (G 178); and other entries will have only a number (93)? (Goal 2)
9. How do you cross-reference in the consecutive numbering method? Are cross-references numbered? Why or why not? (Goal 2)
10. In converting from an alphabetic arrangement to a consecutively numbered arrangement, you will not assign numbers to the general folders in alphabetic storage. Where will these folders be located in the numeric storage arrangement? Will records in these folders be coded with a number? Why or why not? (Goal 2)
11. List the advantages and disadvantages of consecutive numeric records storage. (Goal 3)

12. What is the difference between the consecutive numbering method and a nonconsecutive numbering method of storing records? (Goal 4)
13. Assume that you are talking with someone who does not know about the nonconsecutive numbering storage methods. Clearly explain two nonconsecutive numbering storage methods, including advantages and disadvantages. (Goal 5)
14. How does the addition of folders in terminal-digit or middle-digit storage differ from the addition of folders in a consecutively numbered storage container? (Goal 5)
15. What is block numeric storage? (Goal 6)
16. Explain chronologic storage and how it is used. (Goal 7)
17. Explain mnemonic coding. Give an example and explain what it means. (Goal 8)
18. Explain the similarities of the duplex-numeric, decimal-numeric, and alphanumeric coding systems. (Goal 9)

APPLICATIONS (APP)

APP 8-1.   Improving the Present Storage Method

You are presently working in a large insurance company at a job requiring you to refer to clients' records many times each day. Records are stored by insurance policy numbers in consecutive order in an open-shelf arrangement. The records of the last 10 years are included in the active storage area.

The records are in excellent condition and are relatively easy to find because all of the employees are very careful about refiling the numbers correctly. Sometimes, however, a record you need will not be in storage, and you have no idea where to look for it. The company charge-out policy (which is closely adhered to) is that any record removed from storage in the morning must be returned to storage that afternoon; any record removed in the afternoon must be returned the next morning. This policy often means you have to wait half a day or overnight to find the record you need.

The folders are in good shape, with typed labels bearing both policy number and client's name. Each January 1, the color of the folders and labels is changed. Last year they were yellow; this year they are pink; next year they will be buff, in keeping with the sequence of five repeated colors: pink, buff, blue, white, yellow. An example of the label is shown below.

A master file containing about 400,000 entries is arranged alphabetically by the names of clients. The card file occupies many drawers, similar to what you see in a library. Congestion at the card file is becoming a problem, and many times several people need to work at the same place in the storage area.

Your supervisor customarily holds a staff meeting each Monday morning. On the agenda for the next meeting is the question of records storage. Your supervisor has asked every employee who uses clients' records to come to the meeting with suggestions of any kind about what to do to make the records more readily accessible. You have been reminded that the company policy is to keep at least 10 years of records together in one area, so transfer at this time is not possible. Also, the company is ready to computerize many of the records.

What suggestions do you have? Be specific. Your supervisor will welcome every suggestion. Offering unusual solutions to a problem often brings out ideas that would not otherwise be advanced, and your supervisor can adapt or change ideas that at first do not seem workable. List your suggestions so that you can not only give them orally but also have them ready to hand to your supervisor at Monday's meeting. (Hints: a better numbering method? color usage expanded? label change? use of computer file?)

APP 8-2. Analyzing a Numeric Method of Storage

Get a copy of your school's class listings. In a short paper analyze what system (or systems) is used to identify the different departments, courses within that department, and the various sections within a course. Include in your paper at least one positive statement about the system used and at least one improvement you would recommend.

APPLYING THE RULES

Job 10, Consecutive Numeric Correspondence Filing; Job 11, Termi-nal-Digit Numeric Correspondence Filing

9 GEOGRAPHIC RECORDS STORAGE

GOALS

After completing this chapter, you will be able to:

1. List advantages and disadvantages of the geographic storage method.
2. List the differences and similarities between the geographic and alphabetic methods of records storage.
3. Describe the kinds of businesses that might use the geographic method of storage.
4. Explain the differences between the location name guide plan and the lettered guide plan of geographic arrangements.
5. Describe the sequence of guides and folders in the most commonly used geographic arrangement, by states and by cities within states—the location name guide plan.
6. Explain the use of an alphabetically arranged index in the geographic method of storage.
7. Describe the difference in labels or captions as they appear on guides and folders used for the geographic method as opposed to those used on guides and folders for the alphabetic method.
8. List the types of cross-references used in the geographic storage method.
9. Give examples of the combination of the geographic method with other storage methods.

The last of the alphabetic methods to be discussed in this text is the **geographic storage method**. This is an alphabetic records storage system arranged by the locations or addresses of the correspondents, followed by their names. Records are stored and retrieved by *place* or *location* as the first filing segment and then by individual or business name. Because you may encounter the geographic storage method where you work, or you may find it needed in your office situation, the method is discussed here. Although limited in use because there is no widespread need to store information by geographic area, its principles and procedures are necessary if you are to have a complete understanding of the four primary methods of records storage. As you study this chapter, you will see again the necessity for using the rules for alphabetic indexing that were presented in Chapters 2 and 3. You will also see the similarities between the alphabetic and geographic methods.

Businesses that may store records by the geographic method include:

1. Multinational companies—those businesses with foreign branches and customers outside the boundaries of the United States, whose records are arranged first by country.

2. Businesses that have many branches (possibly sales branches) at different geographic locations within the country and often a great deal of intracompany correspondence.

3. Businesses that are licensed to operate in some states but not in others (such as insurance companies, franchised operations, investment firms) and whose records are kept according to the states in which business is conducted.

4. Mail-order houses and publishers whose business is conducted through the United States mail and who refer to their customers' records first by geographic location.

5. Companies that direct their advertising promotions to specific geographic areas, such as to the West Coast states.

6. Utility companies (electricity, gas, telephone, water) whose customers are listed by street name and address first.

7. Real estate firms that list their properties by areas. Sometimes the areas may be quite unusual, such as islands, or castles and estates in foreign countries; sometimes the areas are divisions of countries or cities; and sometimes in a metropolitan area, the listings may be grouped by subdivision names or by street boundaries within the city itself.

8. Government agencies whose records might be stored according to geographic areas, such as state, county, township, etc., depending upon the scope of the governmental function.

Several geographic record arrangements will be illustrated and explained. The equipment and supplies needed for geographic arrangement have been discussed in Chapter 5. The advantages and disadvantages of the geographic method will be listed and then the procedures for storing and retrieving records geographically will be discussed.

ADVANTAGES AND DISADVANTAGES OF THE GEOGRAPHIC METHOD

As is true of any storage method, the geographic method has advantages and disadvantages. Human problems (carelessness, inattention to detail, and inexperience) may be added to the specific disadvantages discussed in the following paragraphs.

> Carelessness, inattention to details, and inexperience are disadvantages.

Advantages of the Geographic Method

Speedy reference to specific geographic areas to retrieve information of a geographic nature is the main advantage of geographic storage. All the advantages of alphabetic storage are included in this method also, because this is basically an alphabetic arrangement. Many geographic systems use color as a safeguard to give the filer a check against misfiling.

> All the advantages of alphabetic storage are also advantages in the geographic method.

The number of records generated in various geographic areas can be compared by looking at the space required by the stored records within those areas. An analysis of those records can be used in sales work to note areas with the most complaints; to note aggressive selling effort (or the lack of selling effort); to note areas that need special attention; or to show where territories need to be combined, separated, or subdivided. If territories are changed, geographic guides and folders may be readily rearranged. Each location is a unit or a group, and the shifting of groups is relatively easy because it simply means moving an entire group from one place to another.

Disadvantages of the Geographic Method

One disadvantage of the geographic method may be the complexity of the guides and folder arrangement. Because the nature of the geographic method calls for many subdivisions, a geographic arrangement requires more time to set up than does an alphabetic arrangement. Getting records into and out of storage is time consuming because reference must be made first to an area (such as a state), then to a certain point within that area (such as a city), and finally to a correspondent's address and name.

An alphabetic index of all correspondent names and addresses must be prepared on cards or on an electronic system and kept current. If the location of a correspondent is not remembered and no alphabetic index is kept, much time is lost by the filer in trying to remember the address or in locating the correspondence by chance. Even with the use of an index of alphabetized names, delay occurs because two operations are necessary in order to store material—a quick check of the index to be sure the correspondent's name is stored correctly in it, plus the actual storage of the record in its correct geographic section. Two operations may also be necessary in order to find records—a check of the index, if only the individual correspondent's name is given, to find the address to which reference must be made, and then the actual search in storage for the records of the correspondent.

Misfiling can result because of the similarity of state names (Ohio and Iowa, North Carolina and South Carolina, North Dakota and South Dakota, Vermont and Virginia). If two-letter abbreviations are used, carelessness may confuse CO and CA, NV and NE, SD and SC. The frequency of identical city names within various states can also lead to misfiling. (Springfield is found in at least 18 states!)

ARRANGEMENT OF RECORDS STORED BY THE GEOGRAPHIC METHOD

The geographic arrangement that is used in an office will depend upon:

1. The type of business being operated.
2. The way that records are referred to (by state, by geographic region, by country, and so forth).
3. The geographic areas to which the records are related.

Generally, a geographic arrangement is organized according to one of two plans: (1) the location name guide plan or (2) the lettered guide plan. You will find the location name guide plan used more often than the lettered guide plan. Each of these plans is explained in detail in the following paragraphs. As you study them, refer to the illustrations to help your understanding.

Location Name Guide Plan

A geographic storage arrangement based on the **location name guide plan** uses location names (such as names of countries, provinces, states, counties, or cities) as the filing segments that make up the main divisions. Probably the most frequently found location name guide plan arrangement is that based on state names as the first filing segment.

States. The main divisions in storage are the names of the states. The subdivisions necessary within each state depend on the number of records to be stored behind each state name. For instance, a national pharmaceutical company uses one guide for each state. Behind each state guide are 12 numbered folders corresponding to the 12 months of the year (1 = January, 2 = February, etc.). The color of the folder for each month is different, the same color sequence being used behind each state. In these folders are stored returned goods authorizations and claims and adjustments in random order because the number of records is small.

> The main location name guide plan arrangement is based on the state names.

A national fast food chain, which constructs its buildings according to a master plan throughout the United States, stores its architect's drawings geographically in large flat drawers labeled for each state. City names also appear on the labels in alphabetic order. Within the drawers the drawings are arranged first by city name, then within cities by street address.

Figure 9-1 on the next page shows part of a drawer based on the location name guide plan by states. Illinois is shown here; Indiana will follow it and Idaho will have preceded it. As you study the arrangement, refer frequently to the figure. The circled numbers on the figure correspond to the following numbered paragraphs:

1. The first item in the drawer is the primary guide for the state name, Illinois. Because this arrangement uses the state names as the largest geographic divisions, the guide tab with the state name on it is double width and centered to give the guide prominence. A different color may be used for each of these guides as a further aid in storing and retrieving records. All folder and guide tabs following the color state guide would then bear the same color as the state guide.

2. The second item in the drawer is a city guide for Alton, the first location name guide after the state guide. Because this city guide usually stays in the drawer in its correct position, it does not need the name of the state on it.

3. The third item is a general city folder for Alton. In this folder are stored the records from all correspondents located in Alton for

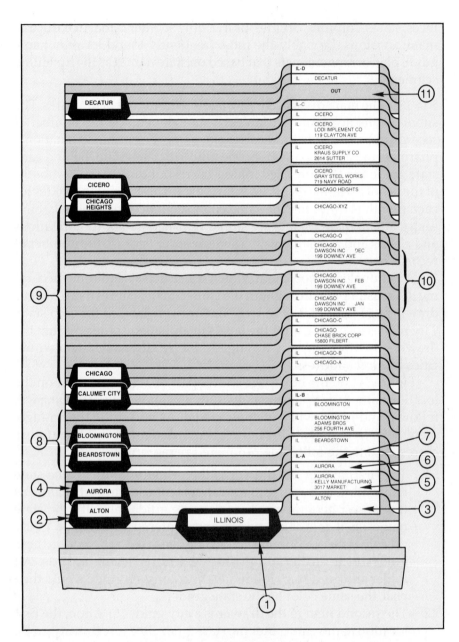

Figure 9-1 ■ Location Name Guide Plan for a State

whom only a few records have accumulated. When their number increases to a predetermined figure (usually five), the records are removed and an individual folder is prepared. Because the Alton folder may be removed from storage, it bears the name of the state to which it belongs (using the two-letter state abbreviation as approved by the Postal Service) in addition to the city name. There are undoubtedly other Altons in the United States, and failure to put the state name on the tab will require the filer to look inside to see to what state the folder belongs when it is to be refiled. This folder is the last folder in the city section.

4. The fourth item is a city guide for Aurora.
5. The fifth item is an individual folder for the Kelly Manufacturing Company in Aurora. The first piece of correspondence from Kelly Manufacturing Company was placed in the IL AURORA general city folder (No. 6 in Figure 9-1). When records of the company increased to a sufficient number (perhaps five), it was necessary to make an individual folder and place it between the Aurora guide and the Aurora general city folder. Note that the caption on the individual folder bears state and city as the first filing segment. Then the name of the correspondent and the address are given.
6. The sixth item is the general city folder for Aurora, in which are stored the records from all correspondents located in Aurora for whom only a few records have accumulated.
7. The last item in the A section of this drawer is a general state folder with the caption IL-A. In this folder are stored records from Illinois correspondents located in cities beginning with the letter A for which there is not yet a city folder (because five records relating to any one city have not yet accumulated).
8. The next six items in the drawer are those that relate to B city names. Study them carefully so that you understand the placement of each one.
9. Because Chicago is the location of so many correspondents, one general city folder is not large enough to contain the records. Therefore, the names of those correspondents whose records will have to be stored in a Chicago general folder are grouped alphabetically. The groups are separated into lettered folders. (See IL CHICAGO-A, IL CHICAGO-B, IL CHICAGO-C, IL CHICAGO-O, and IL CHICAGO-XYZ, the intervening letters having been omitted to conserve space.)

Individual folders for correspondents located in Chicago are placed in alphabetic order among the Chicago alphabetic folders according to the first letter of the key unit of the name filing segment. (See Chase Brick Corp. Its folder is behind the general IL CHICAGO-B folder but in front of the general IL CHICAGO-C folder.) The general folder is the last item in its section.

10.   If the correspondence with one individual or firm is very heavy, monthly individual folders are provided (see Dawson, Inc.). Only January, February, and December show in the illustration; but folders would be in storage for all of the other months, too. Note that all folders are arranged first by state, then by city, then by correspondent's name, and finally by date.

11.   Near the back of the file drawer, an OUT guide is placed in third position.

If a business needs to have a geographic arrangement of states showing counties and cities, the location name guide plan shown in Figure 9-2 can be used. Here, fifth-cut first-position guides show the

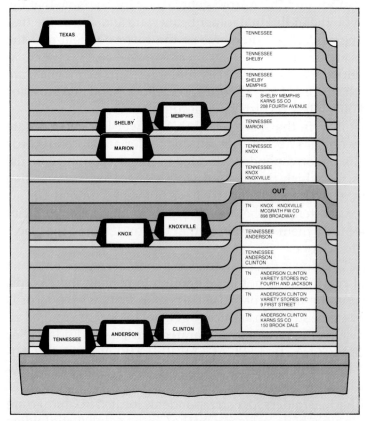

Figure 9-2 ■ Location Name Guide Plan Showing Both Counties and Cities

state names in alphabetic order. Fifth-cut second-position guides show county names alphabetically arranged (Anderson, Knox, Marion, Shelby) with a general folder at the end of the items in each county. Fifth-cut, third-position guides show city names alphabetically arranged within their counties. The corresponding general folders are the last items within their sections. Third-cut and third positions are used for all folders. Note that the state, county, and city names appear on the first line of the captions; correspondents' names appear next in indexing order, followed by their addresses. OUT indicators in third-cut, third position are easy to see.

Districts within States. If the nature of the business requires a breakdown of the states into regions or districts, the storage arrangement can reflect this by means of the captions on the general guides and folders. Figure 9-3 shows how the geographic method is used to

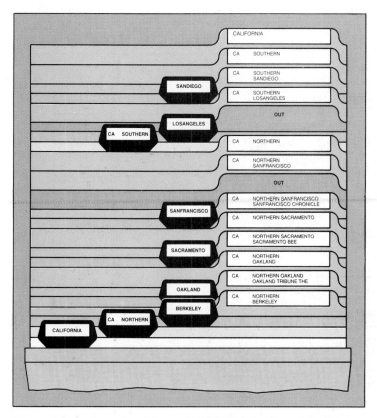

Figure 9-3 ■ Location Name Guide Plan for State Regions

divide the state of California into northern and southern regions. The cities within each region are listed (in alphabetic order) on fifth-cut tabs in third position with their general folders having one-third cut tabs in the third position—the last item within their sections. Individual folders have tabs in the third position, also. The sequence of information on the tabs is state, region, city, and correspondent's name and address. Again, OUT indicators are in third-cut, third position. A map of California must be readily available, showing the boundary between southern and northern California, so that all filers will store records in the correct region.

Local Areas. Some businesses (utility companies, for example) that have customers in a restricted area, such as a city or a county, store records by the street locations of their customers. Such an arrangement may indicate names of suburbs and must show names of streets and names of customers with their house or building numbers (see Figure 9-4). In this arrangement there are no general folders; each

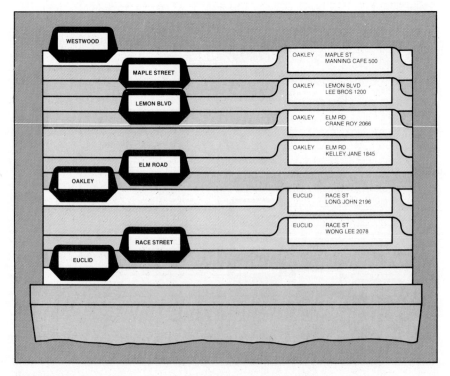

Figure 9-4 ■ Location Name Guide Plan for Local Use

folder is an individual one for one specific location. Guides in first position bear the names of suburbs; second-position guides have the street names on them; individual folders are on the right. No city name is necessary because this business serves only one city.

Many times the required information is too long to fit on the individual folder tabs as easily as that shown in Figure 9-4. If names are long, two lines must be used but the sequence of information is the same: suburb name, street name, customer name in indexing order, and house or building number last. The house or building number takes precedence over the name of the customer in the storage arrangement. This arrangement is needed because reference to the records is made by the location of the customer first; the customer's name is the least important piece of information.

Foreign Countries. The location name guide plan can be readily adapted to the needs of organizations that do business in or with foreign countries. For example, if a business has correspondence with several individuals and firms throughout the world, it might have a storage arrangement similar to that shown in Figure 9-5 on the next page. The word FOREIGN appears on the drawer label, but the label might have read: FOREIGN A-M. The arrangement is alphabetic by country and alphabetic by city within each country. Individual folders are arranged alphabetically by correspondents' names if there are two or more folders within the same country or city (see Montreal in Figure 9-5). The arrangement in Figure 9-5 is as follows (paragraph numbers correspond to circled numbers):

1. The first item in the drawer is the permanent guide for the country name, Canada (fifth cut, first position). If color is used, a different color is assigned to each country as a further aid to storing and retrieving. All folder and guide tabs for a country would then be of one color.

2. The second item in the drawer is the city guide for Calgary Alberta (fifth cut, second position). The name of the province is also given because all Canadian location names include city and province in their addresses. Because this guide is never removed from the drawer in regular storage activity, the name of the country does not need to be written on it.

3. The third item in the drawer is an individual folder for Calgary Wholesalers Ltd (third cut, third position).

4. The fourth item in the drawer is the general folder for Calgary Alberta (third cut, third position).

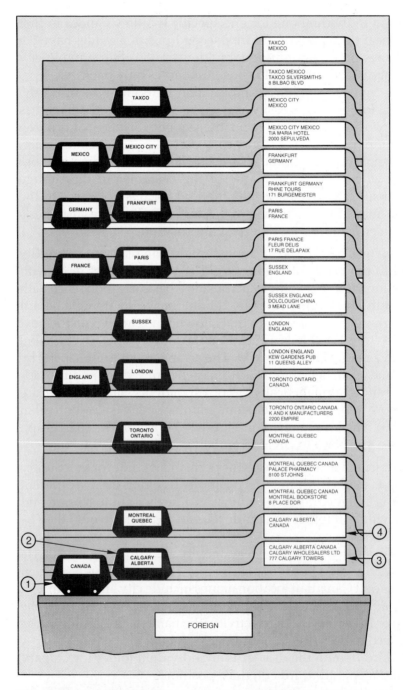

Figure 9-5 ■ Location Name Guide Plan for Foreign Countries

If many Canadian records are to be stored, the arrangement might be slightly different. Guides and folders might be arranged alphabetically first by province and then by city (instead of by city first, as shown in Figure 9-5).

The arrangement of guides and folder tabs is a matter of personal preference. Straight-line arrangement (as is shown in Figure 9-5) is preferred because additions may be made to the drawer contents without disturbing the orderly arrangement of either guides or folders.

Each foreign country has its own unique geographic divisions. The use of a world gazeteer or a world almanac would be very helpful to the filer.

> Reference to a world almanac is helpful in setting up multinational company files.

Special Folder Arrangements. All of the arrangements of folders explained thus far have been in alphabetic order. However, a geographic arrangement may be of more value if the alphabet is disregarded. For instance, sections may be set up for storage according to areas outlined on a map. Records might be arranged in an order as follows: Canada, Northern U.S., Eastern U.S., Southern U.S., Midwestern U.S., Mountain States U.S., Western U.S., Alaska-Hawaii U.S., Mexico. Or the guides and folders might be arranged alphabetically by those regions: Alaska-Hawaii U.S., Canada, Eastern U.S., Mexico, Midwestern U.S., Mountain States U.S., Northern U.S., Southern U.S., and Western U.S. Another special arrangement may be by distance zones from a central point, such as those used in the post office to figure parcel post rates. Any such nonalphabetic arrangement, however, requires the use of a plainly marked map to show the area boundaries. If a map is not used, misfiling results because people guess the location of a correspondent instead of checking the location.

> Not all geographic arrangements are alphabetic.

Lettered Guide Plan

The lettered guide plan can be used in any geographic arrangement. If the volume of records stored geographically is very large, alphabetic guides will cut storage and retrieval time by guiding the eye quickly to the correct alphabetic section of storage. The **lettered guide plan** is a geographic storage method using guides printed with alphabetic letters—sometimes with letters and numbers—in addition to guides with location names printed on them as main divisions.

Figure 9-6 on the next page shows part of a drawer of Michigan records stored by the lettered guide plan. Refer to the figure often as you study the arrangement, where circled numbers are explained by similarly numbered paragraphs below.

1. The first item in the drawer is the guide for the name of the state, Michigan, the largest geographic division in this storage plan. The guide tab is double width and centered to give it prominence.

2. The primary guides are fifth-cut alphabetic guides that divide the state into alphabetic sections. The guides are in first position (A-1, B-2, C-3, D-4). Each guide indicates the section of the alphabet within which are stored records with city names in that section. The guide tabs are numbered consecutively so that they will be kept in correct order.

3. Each primary guide is accompanied by a corresponding general alphabetic folder, which is placed at the end of that alphabetic section. The folder has the same caption as that of the primary guide, and it is placed in the third position, third cut. Each general alphabetic folder contains records from correspondents located in cities with names beginning with the letter of the alphabet on the folder. For instance, the general A 1 folder would contain correspondence from organizations and people in Addison, Adrian, Albion, Allegan, Anchorville, Athens, Auburn Heights, and Avoca, but not from Ann Arbor because that city has its own general folders.

4. In second position appear two types of guides: (a) special city guides to indicate cities for which there is a considerable volume of records (MI ANN ARBOR); and (b) special alphabetic guides that provide a breakdown of correspondents' names in the cities identified by the special city guides (A-M and N-Z).

5. Special general city folders to accompany the special city guides (MI ANN ARBOR A-M; MI ANN ARBOR N-Z; and MI BIRMINGHAM) are in third position, third cut.

6. Individual folders with third-cut tabs appear in third position. The caption for an individual folder contains the name of the state and that of the city in which the correspondent is located as the first line on the label. The second line bears the correspondent's name; the third line, the street address or box number.

7. OUT guides have third cut tabs in third position.

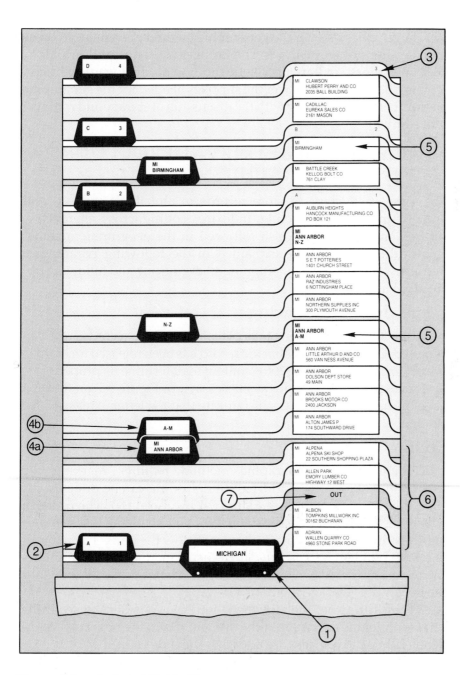

Figure 9-6 ■ Lettered Guide Plan

The supplies used in the geographic method are similar to those used in other storage methods. The supplies consist of guides, folders, OUT indicators, and an alphabetic index. You may want to briefly review Chapter 5 and go over the supplies needed for the geographic method before continuing with the discussion of storage and retrieval procedures.

STORAGE AND RETRIEVAL PROCEDURES FOR THE GEOGRAPHIC METHOD

The same basic steps to store records in alphabetic, subject, and numeric methods (inspecting, indexing, coding, cross-referencing, sorting, and storing) are also followed in the geographic method. Small differences will be explained in the following paragraphs. Retrieval procedures (requisitioning, charging out, and following up) are also basically the same.

Inspecting and Indexing

Inspecting and indexing take place at the time a record is ready to be stored. Checking to see that the record has been released for storage (inspecting) and scanning it for content to determine its proper place in storage (indexing) are always necessary. In Figure 9-7 on the next page the handwritten letters JK indicate that the letter is released for storage.

Coding

Coding in the geographic method requires marking the correspondent's *location* (address) first. Coding can be done by circling the filing segment (see Figure 9-7, Muncie, IN). The order in which the words are to be considered for alphabetizing is sometimes indicated by numbers written above or below the units. The name of the correspondent is then coded in the usual manner (by underlining, checking, starring, etc.). Figure 9-7 shows a letter properly coded for the geographic storage method.

At this time, too, the alphabetic index is consulted to see if the correspondent is currently in the system. If not, the new correspondent's name and address are added to the index.

Cross-Referencing

Cross-referencing is as necessary in the geographic storage method as it is in the alphabetic storage method. In Chapters 2 and 3, types of

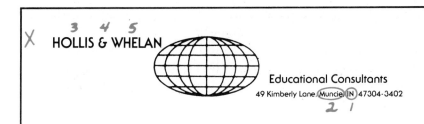

3 4 5

X **HOLLIS & WHELAN**

Educational Consultants
49 Kimberly Lane, Muncie, IN 47304-3402
2 /

𝒿𝓀   May 4, 19--

MAY 5 19-- 9 31 AM

Dr. Ester L. Dawes
School of Business
Yorkshire University
Terre Haute, IN 47805-5410

Dear Dr. Dawes

Your request for 50 brochures explaining in detail the
programmed learning materials we have available for use in
summer workshop programs has been referred to our Pittsburgh
office.

Interest in this exciting and novel material has been
extremely high, and we have been pleased that professors
are finding it so worthwhile. Because of the extraordinary
number of requests we have had for this brochure, it is
temporarily out of stock. We expect a supply within the
next two weeks, however, and will send your 50 copies as
soon as we receive them.

Thank you for letting us provide you with helpful materials
for your workshop.

Sincerely

H. A. Hollis

H. A. Hollis
Educational Consultant

dw

2 /

Branch Office: 2964 Broadway, Pittsburgh, PA 15216-7523 X

Figure 9-7 ■ Letter Coded for Geographic Method

names for which cross-references are customarily prepared are listed. In addition, cross-references should be prepared for names of companies that have more than one address and for companies located at one address and doing business under other names at other locations.

In the geographic method, cross-references are inserted into (1) the alphabetic index, and (2) the storage containers. In the alphabetic index, it is necessary to have an entry for every name by which a correspondent may be known or by which records may be requested. For the letter shown in Figure 9-7, cross-references are indicated because the name is composed of two surnames and a branch office is located in another city.

In the storage containers, three kinds of cross-references may be used: (1) cross-reference sheets that are stored in folders to refer the filer to specific records, (2) cross-reference guides that are placed in storage as permanent cross-references, and (3) SEE ALSO cross-reference notations on sheets or on folder tabs. Each of these cross-references is explained below.

A *cross-reference sheet* is used to call attention to a specific record stored in a folder other than the one in which the filer is searching. The cross-reference sheet in Figure 9-8 is made for the branch office

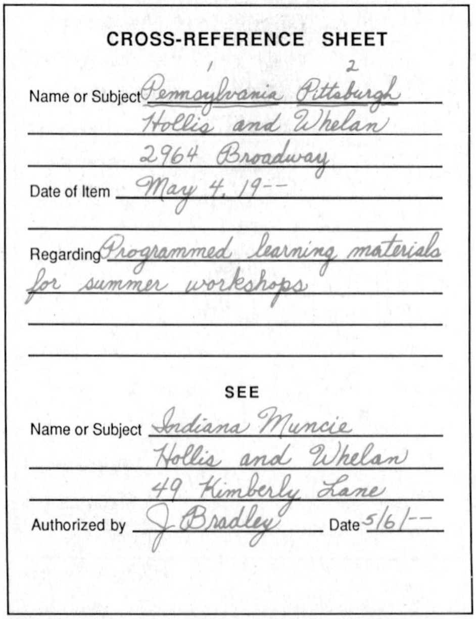

CROSS-REFERENCE SHEET

Name or Subject Pennsylvania   Pittsburgh
Hollis and Whelan
2964 Broadway

Date of Item   May 4, 19--

Regarding Programmed learning materials for summer workshops

SEE

Name or Subject Indiana Muncie
Hollis and Whelan
49 Kimberly Lane

Authorized by   J. Bradley   Date 5/6/--

Figure 9-8 ■ Cross-Reference Sheet for Geographic Method

indicated on the letter shown in Figure 9-7. The letter itself would be stored in the I section of the geographic storage (for Indiana), but the cross-reference sheet would be stored in the P section (for Pennsylvania). Another cross-reference sheet or a copy of the letter would be stored in the I section under Whelan and Hollis.

A *cross-reference guide* (see Figure 9-9) may be placed in storage to indicate to the filer that all records pertaining to a company that has several branches, for instance, are stored under the home office address. If the home office of Mortenson, Incorporated, is in San Francisco, and if a branch office is in Monterey, CA, all the correspondence may be stored under the home office location. A cross-reference guide would be placed in storage at the proper place for Monterey, CA—the guide shown in Figure 9-9. This cross-reference indicates that all records are stored under the San Francisco address even though the record bears a Monterey address. The words *San Francisco* must be written on each record when it is coded. The cross-reference guide is stored according to the location on the top line of its caption, in alphabetic sequence with other geographically labeled guides and folders.

Figure 9-9 ■ Cross-Reference Guide for Geographic Method

SEE ALSO cross-references are used to direct the filer to sources of related information. If a company has two addresses and records are stored under both addresses, two SEE ALSO cross-references would be used (for instance, Wills Supply Company, Inc., in Chicago, IL, and also in Peoria, IL). The references would indicate that information is to be found in both places in storage. If these SEE ALSO cross-references are sheets of paper, they would always be kept as the first items in their respective folders so that they would not be overlooked (see Figure 9-10 on the next page). Instead of being written on separate cross-reference sheets, this SEE ALSO information may be typed on the tabs of the two folders for the Wills Supply Company, Inc. (see Figure 9-11 on the next page).

SEE ALSO cross-references are kept in front of the folder to avoid being overlooked.

CROSS-REFERENCE SHEET	CROSS-REFERENCE SHEET
Name or Subject _Illinois Chicago_ _Wills Supply Company Inc_ _1313 North Sixth Street_	Name or Subject _Illinois Peoria_ _Wills Supply Company Inc_ _2264 Evanston Avenue_
Date of Item _____	Date of Item _____
Regarding _____	Regarding _____
SEE ALSO	**SEE ALSO**
Name or Subject _Illinois Peoria_ _Wills Supply Company Inc_ _2264 Evanston Avenue_ Authorized by _C Collins_ Date _2/4/--_	Name or Subject _Illinois Chicago_ _Wills Supply Company Inc_ _1313 North Sixth Street_ Authorized by _C Collins_ Date _2/4/--_

Figure 9-10 ■ Cross-Reference Sheets for SEE ALSO References

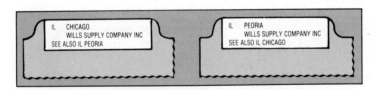

Figure 9-11 ■ SEE ALSO References on Folder Tabs

Sorting

Records are sorted by location, the distinctive feature of the geographic method. Sorting is accomplished in the following order: (1) by the largest geographic unit (perhaps a state), (2) by the first subdivision (such as a city), and (3) by the names of the correspondents, in alphabetic arrangement.

Storing

Because of the complexity of a geographic arrangement — individual correspondents' folders, special city folders, alphabetic subdivisions of cities with their corresponding general folders, general folders for alphabetic groupings of cities, and general state or regional folders — the filer must be extremely careful when storing. It is easy to place a record in the wrong folder!

Location Name Guide Arrangement.   Assuming the arrangement is by state and city, the filer first finds the state, then looks for the correct city name. If a city guide is found, the filer then searches for an individual correspondent's folder. And if one is found, the record is stored according to date.

If there is no individual folder, the record is stored in the correct general city folder according to the geographic location of the correspondent and then by name, in alphabetic order with the other records within the folder. If more than one record is stored for a correspondent, the records are arranged chronologically with the most recent date on top.

If there is no general city folder, the record is placed in the general state folder, first according to the alphabetic order of the city name and then by correspondent's name and street address (if necessary), according to the rules for alphabetic indexing.

Lettered Guide Arrangement. Again, assuming the arrangement is by state and city, the filer finds the state. The lettered guides are then used to locate the alphabetic state section within which the city name falls. After finding that section, the filer looks for an individual correspondent's folder. If one is found, the record is stored in that folder in chronologic order.

If there is no individual folder, the filer must look for a general city folder. If it is found, the record is stored according to the correspondent's name in the same manner as in an alphabetic arrangement. If there is no general city folder, the record is stored in the general alphabetic folder within which the city name falls. Again, arrangement is by city name according to the rules for alphabetic indexing.

Within a city, the names of correspondents are arranged alphabetically; the records of one correspondent are grouped together with the most recent date on top. If there are identically named correspondents in one city, the rules for identical names are followed (see Chapters 2 and 3 for review).

When enough correspondence has accumulated to warrant making a separate folder for a certain city, a certain geographic section, or an individual correspondent, the filer removes the records from the general folder and prepares a new folder with the geographic location on its tab as the first item of information. The filer then prepares a similarly labeled guide, if one is needed, for the folder. The folder and guide are then placed in their correct positions in storage.

While the practice varies on the requirements for preparing a separate folder for a specific geographic location, a good rule of thumb is: *When five or more records accumulate that pertain to one specific geographic location (such as a state, a city, or a region), a separate folder should be made for that location.*

Retrieving

Retrieval of a record from the geographic arrangement involves these four steps: (1) asking for (requisitioning) the record, (2) searching in the storage containers to find it, (3) charging it out by some means, and (4) following up to see that the record is returned to storage within a specified time.

Requisitioning. When a record is requested from a geographic arrangement, it may be asked for by location or by correspondent's name. If the request is made by location, finding the record should be simple. If the request is made by name, however, reference to the alphabetic index is necessary in order to locate the address by which the record was originally stored (unless the filer's memory is superb and can supply this information without reference to the index!).

Charging Out Records. Once the record is located, the process of charging it out from a geographic arrangement is the same as that for charging out records from any other method of storage. An OUT indicator is inserted where a folder or record is removed.

Follow-Up Procedures. The follow-up procedures used with the geographic method, to secure the return of borrowed records, are the same as those used with any other storage method. A tickler file or other reminder system is used to make sure that records are returned to storage at designated times and to remind the filer of records that need to be brought to someone's attention in the future.

COMBINATIONS OF THE GEOGRAPHIC METHOD AND OTHER STORAGE METHODS

Geographic arrangements are often found in an otherwise alphabetic arrangement. For instance, correspondence with a company may accumulate to such volume that one folder becomes overcrowded. Inspection of the contents reveals that the correspondence concerns the same company in two or three different states or cities. By separating the correspondence into folders arranged geographically by state or by city, the overcrowding will be eliminated. Such an arrangement is found in Figure 9-12. The ILM Products folders are arranged geographically (in alphabetic order by location) by state names. A distinctively colored guide precedes this arrangement to help the filer locate that section of storage easily.

The basic rules for alphabetic indexing determine the placement in each of the storage methods (or combination of methods).

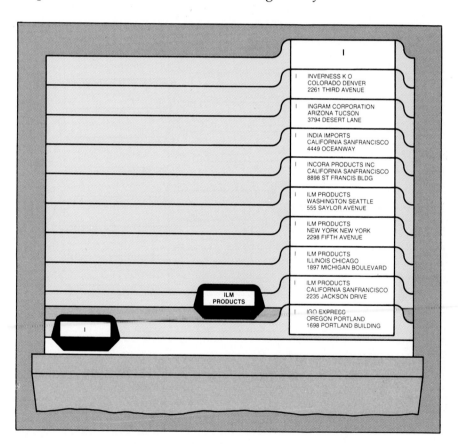

Figure 9-12 ■ Combination of Geographic and Alphabetic Methods—Arranged by State Names

Another geographic arrangement within an alphabetic arrangement might be helpful if correspondence were received from and sent to several officers of one organization that has, for instance, a vice president in each of several different districts. Because their terms of office are for only one year, the names of the vice presidents are not important. The districts in which vice presidents are located are the important filing segments. Figure 9-13 shows the five district folders of the National Office Workers, in which correspondence with the five vice presidents is stored. The five folders are alphabetically arranged with other N folders and are also arranged alphabetically by their location names (Great Lakes, Northeast, etc.).

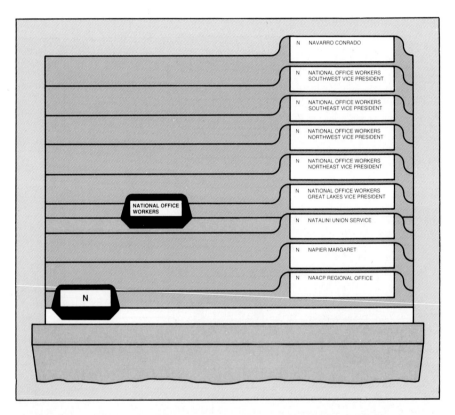

Figure 9-13 ■ Combination of Geographic and Alphabetic Methods—Arranged by Region Names

Geographic arrangements can also be combined with numeric designations. For example, a large manufacturer with branches in hundreds of cities may combine geographic storage with the numeric arrangement. The home office assigned numbers to the names of the cities in which the branches are located. Correspondence from each branch office is stored in numbered folders. Because remembering the numbers assigned to all the cities is impossible, a list of the cities arranged alphabetically is necessary, with the assigned number appearing beside each city name as shown below. If there are identically named cities, they are arranged alphabetically by state.

GREENSBORO	67
GREENVILLE NC	107
GREENVILLE SC	93
GREENWICH	41

Unless city names are identical, state names are not used in the alphabetic listing. Within these cities, another subdivision occurs if there is more than one salesperson in the office. For instance, the number of Research Triangle Park (a city) is 235 and there are three salespeople in that office. A numbered geographic arrangement, with alphabetic order according to salespersons' names is used. Labels on folders for that location would read as follows:

235	TAN TITA
235	DIAZ A
235	ADAMS BILL

(Front of file)

The combinations of alphabetic, subject, numeric, and geographic arrangements are many. Yet the basic rules for alphabetic indexing determine placement in each of the storage methods or combinations.

IMPORTANT TERMS AND CONCEPTS

geographic storage method
lettered guide plan
location name guide plan

REVIEW AND DISCUSSION

1. What are the advantages and disadvantages of the geographic storage method? (Goal 1)
2. How does the geographic storage method differ from the alphabetic storage method? How does it resemble the alphabetic method? (Goal 2)
3. What types of businesses might use the geographic storage method rather than the alphabetic name storage method? (Goal 3)

4. How does the location name guide plan differ from the lettered guide plan? (Goal 4)
5. What is the sequence of guides and folders in a geographic arrangement where the names of states are the major divisions, with subdivisions by city and by location within the city? Use a state of your choosing to explain your answer. (Goal 5)
6. Why is an alphabetic index a necessity in geographic storage? (Goal 6)
7. How do the labels on individual folders used in geographic storage differ from the labels used in alphabetic storage for a customer name? (Goal 7)
8. What types of cross-references are used in the geographic method? Where are they stored? (Goal 8)
9. Give two examples of the combination of the geographic method with either the numeric or the alphabetic methods. (Goal 9)

APPLICATIONS (APP)

APP 9-1.   Selecting the Most Efficient Geographic Arrangement

Refer to Figures 9-1 through 9-6 as you complete this application. For each of the situations listed below, recommend a geographic arrangement and explain your choice. Be prepared to sketch a rough picture of the arrangement you recommend.

1. A large oil company has its home office in Texas. It stores correspondence and records to and from stations, refineries, suppliers, and branch offices in cities in all 50 states as well as in foreign countries.
2. The French tire manufacturer Michelin has its U.S. headquarters in New York City. Its sales department records in NYC include distributors in many parts of the United States and Canada.
3. A professional organization has its headquarters in Boulder, CO. Its organizational structure is such that each one of its many chapters belongs to one of five geographic areas in the United States. It also has Canadian chapters and Mexican chapters as well as affiliate chapters in other foreign countries. Correspondence and other records are stored by chapter. Because much of the organization's business is done by computer, each chapter has been assigned a number.

APP 9-2.   Geographic Filing Steps

Prepare 3" x 5" cards (or key and print out a list) for the following list of names. After preparing the cards, go through the indexing, coding, cross-referencing, sorting, and storing steps for geographic filing. Assume that the main filing segments are city, state, and correspondent's name or organization, in that order. Circle the first two units of the filing segment and place corresponding numbers above the rest of the filing units. Indicate any cross-references that may be needed by placing an X beside the name.

Indian River Community College
3209 Virginia Ave.
Fort Pierce, FL 33482-3209

Lincoln Land Community College
Shepherd Rd.
Springfield, IL 62708-0101

Portland Community College
12000 SW 49th Dr.
Portland, OR 97219-0123

University of South Florida—
Sarasota Campus
5700 N. Tamiami Trail
Sarasota, FL 34243-5709

Delaware Tech Community College
400 Stanton Christiana Rd.
Newark, DE 19713-0401

Springfield College in Illinois
1500 N. 5th St.
Springfield, IL 62702-1509

Southwest Missouri State Univ.
901 S. National Ave.
Springfield, MO 65804-0901

Penn Valley Community College
3201 Southwest Traffic Way
Kansas City, MO 64111-3201

Monroe Community College
1000 Henrietta Rd. E.
Rochester, NY 14623-1089

Kansas City, Kansas, Community
Junior College
7250 State Ave.
Kansas City, KS 66112-7255

Chapman
333 N. Glassell St.
Ontario, CA 92666-1333

Rutgers
175 University Ave.
Newark, NJ 07102-1175

Oakland University
Rochester, MI 66112-0698

Armstrong State College
11935 Abercorn St.
Savannah, GA 31419-0193

El Camino College
16007 Crenshaw Blvd.
Torrance, CA 90506-0163

Pioneer Community College
560 Westport Rd.
Kansas City, MO 64lll-0568

Hawaii Community College
874 Dillingham Blvd.
Honolulu, HI 96817-8743

Jackson State University Rochester Community College
1325 Lynch St. Highway 14 E
Jackson, MS 39203-1325 Rochester, MN 55904-1415

Jackson Community College
2111 Emmons Rd.
Jackson, MI 49201-2111

APP 9-3. Planning, Organizing, and Implementing a Records Program for a Small Business Operation

You and two friends have decided to start a small service business. You will work during nonschool hours and on weekends, as you can, doing all sorts of jobs. You'll repair small appliances; help with moving; clean out basements, garages, and attics; do yard work; do small paint jobs and minor carpentry; and provide bookkeeping or accounting services to other small businesses. Your customers will provide all painting, cleaning, repairing, and other materials and supplies needed.

You plan to advertise in a neighborhood newspaper, *The Village Advocate*, and distribute flyers door-to-door. You have no office but work out of one of your rooms where there is a telephone, a typewriter, a two-drawer file cabinet, and a desk (at which you also study). You have no letterhead stationery or business cards but your business will be known as A-1 HELP!

Each of you has a special task to help get your business under way. One of you is taking care of setting up the books or financial records you must have. One of you is preparing the flyers and contacting the newspaper. You have volunteered to set up the nonfinancial office records.

Your task is to plan the type of paper records that you will be generating and will need to keep for reference and for keeping track of jobs (future, in progress, and completed). Then you must organize your thinking by doing the following:

1. List the supplies you believe to be absolutely necessary, in addition to the two-drawer file cabinet you already have. Keep your list short, as the three of you have very little money to spend.
2. Determine what method(s) of storage (filing) you believe your business should use—alphabetic, subject, numeric, or geographic. Write the reasons for your choice(s) and also why the other method(s) may not be as suitable as is/are your choice(s).

3. List the guide captions you believe will be necessary. Assume that the following customers noted on your calendar have already given you jobs:

   (1)   Diaz Nissan Motors, 100 West Main—Basement cleaning
   (2)   Dameron Tax Service, 151 Front Street—Painting
   (3)   Ms. Dorine George, 3918 Stone Park Blvd.—Toaster repair
   (4)   Navarro Asphalt Co., 118 East Main—Bookkeeping
   (5)   Donald R. Ambler & Brothers, 412 West Main—Bookkeeping
   (6)   Mrs. Denise Neuman, 3900 Stone Park Blvd.—Carpentry
   (7)   Newman & Dorris, Attorneys, 235 Front Street—Painting
   (8)   Dock and Doris De Angelo, 4200 Erwin Road—Moving help
   (9)   Deborah DeAngelo-Newman, 4318 Erwin Road—Sweeper repair
   (10) D & D Office Supply, 357 Front Street—Bookkeeping
   (11) Dorton Arena Copy Center, 6900 Stone Park Blvd.—Cleaning
   (12) David L. Camp, 1400 Warren Avenue—Carpentry
   (13) C. A. M. Parts Co., 533 East Main—Painting
   (14) CAMP Costumes, Ltd., 600 Front Street—Bookkeeping
   (15) Don R. Ambler, 4208 Erwin Road—Yard work
   (16) Mrs. Daisy Newman, 1543 Warren Avenue—Yard work
   (17) Noriko Nozaki, 4301 Erwin Road—Moving help
   (18) D. J. Newmann, Chickory Downs #3—Cleaning
   (19) Mary Chan, 3906 Stone Park Blvd.—Yard work
   (20) Dr. Roger Rodriguez, 4200 Stone Park Blvd.—Yard work

4. List the order of your guides (and folders) as they will appear in your storage drawer.
5. Record the arrangement you have made for transferring inactive records—or will you have any in the near future?
6. As a conclusion to this case, list the evaluation steps you will take after you have been in business for a few months, to see if your records needs are being met.

APPLYING THE RULES

Job 12, Correspondence Filing—Geographic

4

Records Management Technology

Part 4 introduces you to basic systems concepts and the information technology that is applied to the operation of records systems. The first half of the Part discusses in detail the nature and purpose of computers and shows you how they are employed in automated records systems. The second half of the Part focuses on the use of microfilm (or microimage) systems, many of which are used with computers to speed the storage, use, and retrieval of records.

10 AUTOMATED RECORDS SYSTEMS

GOALS

After completing this chapter, you will be able to:

1. Describe the makeup of a basic system and its role in the automation of records.
2. Identify the key elements of a technology-based records system.
3. List the main features of computers and the purpose of each in the processing of information.
4. Describe the main phases in a computer system and the equipment needed for operating each phase in the system.
5. Describe the various magnetic media used by computers to store automated records.
6. Define a word processing system and explain how records are created, stored, and retrieved in a word processing system.
7. Define *optical digital data disk* and describe the main advantages of its use in a records system.
8. Discuss office automation and explain how the various automated records systems are combined into a network of records systems.
9. Summarize the safety and security procedures for computer records

Speed, cost, and efficiency—three reasons for moving from manual to automated record systems.

Even in the Age of Computers, manual systems still comprise the most commonly used method of records storage. As discussed in Chapter 1, in manual systems records are created, indexed, coded, sorted, and stored by hand; and when needed for use, retrieved by hand. These manual operations are slow, expensive, and inefficient— three reasons why modern businesses turn more and more often to higher-level technology to operate their records systems. Databases, discussed in Chapter 4, represent an effective use of computers to store and retrieve information.

In this chapter we will (1) briefly examine the nature of systems; (2) show how the computer and related equipment affect the creation, use, storage and retrieval of records in automated systems; (3) discuss word processing systems and optical disk systems; (4) introduce you to the concept of an office automation network; and (5) identify ways to provide safety and security for automated records. Each of these topics is discussed in nontechnical language in keeping with their use in the modern office.

TECHNOLOGY AND RECORDS SYSTEMS

How often we use the word *system* in our ordinary conversations! In today's world people frequently discuss circulatory systems, road systems, educational systems, economic and political systems, and many other systems relating to their lives. In records management, our primary concerns are *records systems* and the *information systems* of which they are a part. To understand records systems and the automated methods of processing, storing, and retrieving records, you must first understand several basic systems concepts, as discussed in the following paragraphs.

Basic Systems Concepts

As a direct result of using computers, records managers and other information specialists now have a much broader—and clearer—view of the organization and how its parts work together. Early in the history of computers, managers discovered the great power of this machine for creating, processing, storing, retrieving, and distributing information to all functions in a firm, and not just to payroll and billing, the first application areas. Top-level managers who formerly fixed their attention on one or two divisions of their firms, such as accounting and finance, soon saw that the computer had great value in each of the main functions in the total organization (such as marketing, human resources, production, accounting, finance, purchasing, and general administration). The phrase *seeing the whole picture* stems from the broad, company-wide view of a firm's operation made possible by studies for using the computer. Thus, a new way of thinking about problem solving, often called the *systems approach*, was born. Basic systems concepts as tools of the problem solver and useful to the records manager are summarized in this section.[1]

Systems thinking provides a broad view of business firms.

---

[1]For more detailed information on systems, consult Norman F. Kallaus and B. Lewis Keeling, *Administrative Office Management*, 10th ed., South-Western Publishing Co., Cincinnati, 1991, Chapters 4 and 21.

First, several systems terms need to be defined. A **system** is a *set of related elements* that are *combined* to achieve a *planned objective* or *goal*. Note the words in italics that indicate the terms to be emphasized. Of these, the general phrase "related elements" needs to be defined in specific systems terms, for it affects our understanding of all systems. *Related elements* refer to systems resources—people, space, equipment, forms and related records, procedures for performing work, and data to be processed that work together to achieve the system's goal. Examples of these elements are typewriters, computers, clerks, office space, sales order forms, procedures for filling out such forms, and data obtained from surveys. Records managers use all these elements to provide records services. Furthermore, these elements are found in *every system* and *every level of system* in the firm. For example, the purchasing function is considered a major information system in the firm.

A records system may be thought of as a major system within the firm; and within the records system there are lower levels of systems—which are smaller in scope—to handle all phases of the record

Subsystems have the same makeup as the main systems.

life cycle. Each lower level of a system is called a **subsystem** because it is a part of the broader records management system. Examples of records subsystems are records creation, records distribution, records use, records maintenance (including storage and retrieval), and records disposition—which you will recognize as the five phases in the record life cycle. However, regardless of their nature, *all systems have the same set of phases or steps necessary for their operation*.

In each system a set of sequential steps or *phases* is followed for the system to achieve its goal. (Figure 10-1 on the next page shows these phases and their interrelationships in general form.) Thus, keeping in mind the goal, or desired *output* of the system (Phase 3), a system's operation begins with the *input* (bringing in) of resources (Phase 1) that are to be *processed* (Phase 2). This processing is done according

All phases of a system must be controlled.

to certain *controls* or standards by which the system's output will be measured (Phase 5), operating within a certain *environment*. (Keep in mind that the environment is *not* a phase but rather the setting in which all the phases operate.) After the processing has been completed, it is compared with the desired standards to determine if any correction (change in the system's operation) must be made. At this

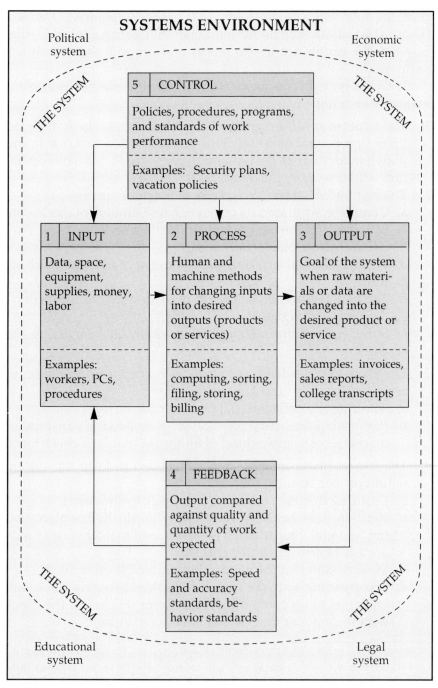

Figure 10-1 ■ Systems Environment and Phases

point the output may be sent to *storage* (Phase 4) as required.[2] *Feedback* (Phase 4) occurs after all the systems operations are completed—that is, when the results are in—to report on how well the system has performed.

Let's see how this basic system works with a simple example—manually creating a new record, a bank check:

1. The *output* or goal is a completely legible, accurate check recorded on the proper check form. (This phase is listed first, for if you understand the goal, the remaining phases in the system's operation will have more meaning.)
2. The *input* necessary to produce such output requires:
    a. Complete, accurate data on payee name, amount of check, date of check, and the reason for writing the check.
    b. An acceptable blank check form.
    c. The human skill and labor time necessary to fill out the check form.
    d. The pen, typewriter, or printer needed to fill out the form.
    e. An approved signature.
    f. Sufficient resources (space, desk, chair, etc.) for doing the work.

3. The *process(es)* needed to produce such output using the input resources listed in Step 2 above include:
    a. Selecting the necessary data to enter on the form.
    b. Performing the actual physical steps (following a manual or machine-based procedure) of filling out the blank check form.

4. The *control* phase refers to actions needed to keep the system within proper bounds, such as:
    a. Ensuring that the correct type of check form is used.
    b. Verifying that the check should be written in the first place, that the "amount" information is correct, and that adequate funds are available to cover the check.
    c. Making sure that the handwriting is legible or verified.
    d. Proofreading to make sure the check is properly filled out, which includes comparing the amount written on the check with the amount that should have been written.

---

[2]It is customary to show sorting and filing/storing operations in the processing phase of the general systems model, for these are processing (doing) activities in the system. However, in the computer and word processing systems shown later in this chapter, it is a common practice to show storage as a separate systems phase.

5. The *environment* within which the check-writing system operates includes:
    a. The rules of the banking system for writing checks.
    b. Similar rules developed by the legal system.
    c. The procedures for dispensing funds within the business.
    d. The attitudes and morale of the firm's employees.
    e. The quality and style of the managers and supervisors.

6. The *feedback* phase results in such activities as:
    a. Recording the information obtained by step 4d in the appropriate accounting papers—indicating that the check has been written, new account balances prepared, and so on.
    b. Notifying the appropriate person(s) that new checks must be written and why, in case errors are found in checks.

Remember that all of the elements of a system are interdependent—they must work together as intermeshed gears. Also, keep in mind that each of the phases in a system (input, process, etc.) uses all the resources at hand to achieve the system's goal. Consequently, actually solving the problems that arise in finding records or writing a computer program to sort or retrieve records requires that the records manager consider all of these phases and elements and how well they work together to achieve the final result.

> All elements of a system are interdependent.

The entire records management program may, under these circumstances, be considered as the *total records system*. In discussing any of the subsystems in the total records system, such as those dealing with storage and retrieval, we make repeated use of systems concepts. The more you understand such basic systems concepts, the better you will be able to recognize and solve records management problems in all records systems, but especially in the automated systems discussed in this chapter.

Automated Records Systems

The word *automated* comes from **automation**, which means a self-operating process that regulates or controls itself. The computer is the central machine in an automated system, along with other equipment, or *hardware*, that works with it. Thus, we can define an **automated records system** as an information system in which all or most of the records functions are controlled by the computer or related equipment.

Two main areas of automation have been developed: (1) computer systems emphasizing the processing of numbers and related information, and (2) word processing systems. Our discussion of automated records systems that follows explores how the main steps in the record life cycle are affected by the computer in today's offices.

Technology Used in Records Systems

Technology refers to the machines (hardware) and procedures and programs (software) needed to operate records systems. As a rule, hardware used in automated systems is much more expensive and complex than is the equipment used in manual systems, although recent breakthroughs in technology have lowered the cost of automated hardware. However, technology-based systems are much faster and more accurate than manual systems, but more difficult to set up and operate. For these reasons, the records manager or office manager must study carefully the basic systems elements required for a successful automated records system. Such a study must include information on the:

1. *Volume of records* at present and expected in the future.
2. *Uses of records* and by what departments.
3. *Equipment available* and the *equipment required.*
4. *Physical form of records* entering the system, and the form of records desired as output of the system.
5. *Activity of records* (how often the records are used and how often the information on records changes).
6. *Speed* and *accuracy* expected for records retrieval.
7. *Cost of the machine system* compared with benefits expected from its use.

A system's most important goal is to provide the right information at the right time.

Of all these elements, the most important is the ability of the system to provide the *right information* at the *right time* (the purpose of item 6 above) as desired by the users. If the requested information is not available when needed, managers will be forced to wait for information and delay their operations, which adds to operating costs.

The systems discussed in this chapter use various types of media for storing and retrieving records. Automated systems use microfilm, as discussed in Chapter 11, as well as magnetic, optical, and paper records, as explained later in this chapter.

COMPUTER SYSTEMS

The main purpose of a computer is to convert numbers into meaningful information. And a computer system, like all systems, is composed of inputs, processes, outputs, and controls to regulate the system. Emphasis in this section centers on how the computer assists in creating, storing, and retrieving records.

Main Characteristics of Computers

Computers are often classified by size. The largest type of computer is a **mainframe** which is capable of controlling hundreds of terminals and storage devices and is commonly used in large organizations. Smaller in size is the **minicomputer**, which provides less processing and operating power than a mainframe and is used in smaller firms or within departments of large organizations. The **microcomputer**—known widely as the *personal computer (PC)*—is the smallest computer in size and capability and is the least expensive. PCs are widely used in homes and schools as well as in offices by administrative support personnel and management. For this reason the PC is emphasized in this textbook because it is the type of machine that you will most likely use on the job.

In this textbook the PC is emphasized for its widespread use in automated records systems.

All computers share these common features:

1. *Electronic circuits*, the electronic channels for moving data as electronic pulses into, within, and out of the computer.
2. *Internal memory* for storing the instructions (the computer program) and the data to be processed. With a program stored in memory, the computer remembers the details of the program and follows automatically one instruction after another to completion.
3. *Ability to perform arithmetic operations* (addition, subtraction, multiplication, and division) and to make comparisons between two or more data items. On the basis of such comparisons, the computer can sort, store, or retrieve information.
4. *Automated control of input, processing, and output activities*. The computer regulates the flow of instructions in its internally stored program and performs many other operations, such as storing or printing the results of its processing operations at very fast operating speeds.

Computer Systems Phases

As the center of power in an automated system, the computer directs the completion of a set of sequential phases that ensures that the system meets its goals. Figure 10-2 outlines the main phases of the system, all of which have important roles to play in the operation of an automated records system.

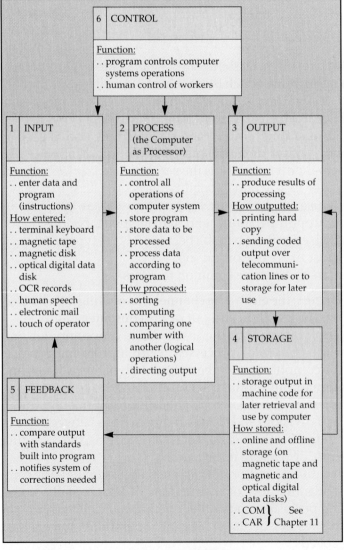

Figure 10-2 ■ Computer Systems Phases

Input. Both the data (words, numbers, and other symbols) and the program (software) for processing the data must be entered into the computer. The most common method of entering input into the system is by manually keying data into the computer. The typical method of *reentering* computer-coded information into a PC is for the operator to reinsert into the computer the disk on which the data are stored.

> A keyboard is the most common method of inputting data into a computer system.

Information preprinted on documents, such as the account number and check amounts printed at the bottom of your bank checks, can be entered into a computer through the use of *scanning devices* or **optical-character recognition (OCR) equipment**. OCR readers eliminate the need for human operators to manually keyboard data.

Other forms of computer input have also emerged. A computer **voice-recognition system** "understands" the human voice as input and performs operations based on this input. Simple voice systems require short pauses between words; in larger systems, the words are spoken—and interpreted by the computer—in a natural, connected speech pattern. (The computer program Sphinx illustrates this latter system.) The human voice must be converted into the digital (numeric) code of the computer before any processing or storage can occur. An **audio-response system** uses a computer-activated voice to answer questions using a vocabulary stored in the system. Such systems are used to supply information on a 24-hour-a-day schedule. Time-of-day and temperature-reporting systems provide such input to customers, and banks commonly provide account-inquiry information to their patrons with a mechanical voice response.

> The human voice must be converted to a numeric computer code before processing can occur.

Graphics and image devices also furnish input to computers. For example, the *mouse* is a device used to move the cursor around on the display screen and carry out operations. By moving the mouse around on a flat surface such as a desk, the operator directs the movement of the cursor on the screen for creating or editing graphic records. Another input device—the **light pen**—is used for writing or sketching on the display screen. As the pen reacts to the light from the screen, the image written or sketched is digitized (converted to a numeric code) by the computer for processing, storing, and printing in the system (see Figure 10-3). The number of such input devices continues to grow as increasing breakthroughs in technology occur.

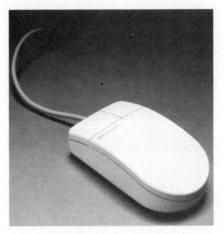

Figure 10-3B ■ Light Pen
Courtesy of International Business
Machines Corporation

Figure 10-3A ■ Microsoft Mouse

Processing. Once entered (inputted) into the system, the data are
ready for the computer operations required by the program. Examples of such operations are performing arithmetic computations
and sorting numbers and alphabetic lists. Figure 10-4 shows the
computer filenames for four major customers of a manufacturing
plant randomly created when the accounts were opened. The four
files can be rapidly sorted by the computer into new sequences—by
ZIP Code, by customer name, and by customer number—as needed
in a sales manager's office. A sort command to the computer results

---

A. Random (Unsorted) Order of Files as Files Were Created:

Cust No.	Cust Name	Address	ZIP	Credit Rating
1234	JANES SOC SERV	Box 126, Perkinsville, NY	14990-2486	1
3652	CHAIRTOWN LUMBER	Box 845, Gardner, MA	01440-3879	2
0078	FARMERS SAV BK	Box 125, Richmond, IA	52247-1019	1
2691	BERTAS SEW SUPP	40 E Lee, Tempe, AZ	85001-9105	3

B. Terminal Displays of Customer File Sorts:

(1) Sorted by ZIP Code	(2) Sorted by customer name	(3) Sorted by customer number
01440-3879 CHAIRTOWN LUMBER 14990-2486 JANES SOC SERV 52247-1019 FARMERS SAV BK 85001-9105 BERTAS SEW SUPP	BERTAS SEW SUPP CHAIRTOWN LUMBER FARMERS SAV BK JANES SOC SERV	0078 FARMERS SAV BK 1234 JANES SOC SERV 2691 BERTAS SEW SUPP 3652 CHAIRTOWN LUMBER

Figure 10-4 ■ A Customer File Computer-Sorted into Three Categories

in the files being placed in a desired order according to the data item specified (ZIP Code, customer name, etc.).

Output. As the end result of processing, output involves making printouts (hard copy) of processed information in readable form; or the output may be stored for long periods of time in computer-coded form on magnetic tape, magnetic disks, and microfilm (computer output microfilm). Temporarily, computer output is stored in the internal memory of the computer and can be displayed on the terminal screen.

> Internal memory can serve as temporary storage for a computer's output.

Storage. The computer does not store internally the results of its processing because this space is limited and must be used for storing the program and the data to be processed. Therefore, a computer system needs storage for output outside the computer. **Offline storage** refers to the storage equipment that is not directly connected to the computer, and **online storage** refers to the storage equipment directly connected to the computer. As shown in Figure 10-2, tape drives and disk drives are used to store output on magnetic tape and magnetic disk, respectively, used in mainframe systems; and small disks store output from the PC. Because of the extreme importance of the storage function to an understanding of automated records systems, we explain computer storage concepts in a separate section of this chapter.

Feedback. Computers can be programmed to send messages to other computers or other devices that are connected to the computer system. The basic notion of sending messages—let's consider them as records—is discussed briefly in the section, "Office Automation and Records Systems," which appears later in this chapter.

Control. In any system where the computer is used, controls must be present so that the machines and people involved operate according to the system's plan. Two types of control are required: (1) the set of *human controls* that regulate the performance of managers, supervisors, and workers in the data processing system; and (2) *technological controls* that regulate the performance of the equipment. Of these two types of control, human controls are the most important. People must control the preparation and input of data into the computer so that transcription errors and inaccurate input do not occur. In addition, people must maintain reasonable turnaround time sched-

> People maintain the most important control in the computer system.

ules by working in an efficient manner. Finally, people must keep tight control over the information stored in the files, such as protecting the confidentiality of social security numbers.

From a technological standpoint, control is maintained over the computer's operations by a well-written and properly tested program. In addition, internal controls are built into the circuitry of the computer to ensure the reliability of the computer's operations.

Creating Computer Records

Within the computer system, records may be created in several ways. Usually this is done at the input phase of the system, as explained earlier. Also, new paper records are created when the computer's output is printed. In order to control a company-wide records system, the records manager must understand the reasons why records are created in the automated system just as much as the creation of records must be understood in the manual system.

Indexing and Coding Computer Records

Indexing and coding processes are needed to prepare records for computer systems. The following types of codes, as assigned by records personnel, are most commonly used: Alphabetic (Class AAA), numeric (50-99), and alphanumeric (1A, 4F, 5EEE).

Figure 10-4 shows three examples of numeric codes, the most frequently used codes in business computer applications: customer number, ZIP Code, and credit rating. The instructions in the computer program determine how the coded information is to be arranged in the printout.

Indexing and coding have been given additional meanings in automated records systems. In computer systems, as in systems using microfilm discussed on page 271, *indexing* refers to the process of assigning some type of identification or address to each record location in the computer's files. Also in computer systems, the term *index* is used to describe a list or table of computer files. Therefore, within computer storage as well as in a hard-copy file available to the computer operator, an index may be created by the computer program to show the complete list of accounts receivable for a business firm arranged alphabetically by customer name. For example, the short list of accounts shown in Figure 10-4 could be expanded as a full-fledged alphabetic index to show the entire file of 4,000 accounts. A portion of such a computer index is shown in Figure 10-5 with the printout appearing in typically concise (abbreviated) computer form.

Customer Name	Customer Number	Record Address*
Adams Realty	0402	0001
Berta's Sew Supp	2691	0002
Chairtown Lumber	3652	0003
Dave's Crafts	0222	0004
Farmers Sav Bk	0078	0005
Garner's Jewelry	0402	0006
Jane's Soc Serv	1234	0007
. . . .	. . . .	. . . .
Zale & Yoder	0328	4000

*May be used as the filename on a disk.

Figure 10-5 ■ Printout of a Portion of a Computer Index of Accounts

Coding in computer systems is usually restricted to programming operations in which the steps for solving a problem on the computer are converted into a programming language. The coded program then consists of a set of commands or instructions that the computer recognizes and follows.

Storing and Retrieving Computer Records

The most common ways to store computer information are on (1) magnetic records and (2) computer printouts, each of which is discussed in this section.

Magnetic Records. The term *magnetic records* refers to the various types of records on which the computer has electronically stored its output. Examples of such storage media are magnetic tapes, disk packs, and disks.

Magnetic Tapes. Information is stored on magnetic tape in the form of magnetized spots. The actual records are stored *sequentially* (in numeric and/or alphabetic order) by an identifying code number, such as employee number, customer number, or stock number, that accompanies each record on the tape; such records can be updated on tape. Because many records can be stored in a small amount of space, magnetic tape provides low-cost records storage. However, in a tape file it is impossible to access individual records without reading all preceding records on the tape. The sequential nature of magnetic tape

Magnetic tape records are filed in sequential order.

records is shown in Figure 10-6; its use is confined to large computer systems and for storing backup copies of records created on microcomputers.

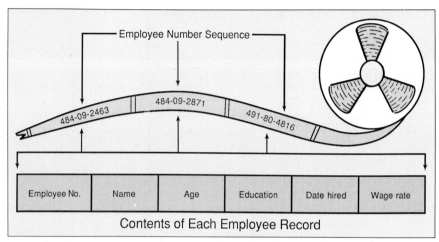

Figure 10-6 ■ Sequential Organization of Records on Magnetic Tape

Magnetic tape is stored on reels in round metal boxes that rest either on a backward-slanting shelf, in a holder attached to the bottom of a shelf, or are inserted into slotted hangers attached to the tops of shelving (see Figure 10-7). Tape reel containers are usually assigned

Figure 10-7 ■ Magnetic Tape Storage

numbers and filed in numeric sequence. These numbers are often color coded to speed storage and retrieval of the containers, both of which are done manually.

Magnetic Disk Packs. *Magnetic disk packs* are similar in appearance to phonograph records arranged in groups or packs for mainframes. Each track on the disk has an address that can serve as the key for locating information immediately, even though the records may not be stored in sequential order.

Because the mechanical arm for reading into and out of a disk storage location can go directly to the desired record, disk records are often stored *randomly* (rather than in sequential order) with an address or code number. For this reason, retrieval of disk pack records is often called *random-access* or *direct-access*. An index or directory is maintained for all records stored on disks. The terminal operator often displays this directory on the screen in order to see the entire set of files.

Disk records are usually filed in random (nonsequential) order.

Magnetic Disks. Microcomputers store information on small disks. They are popularly called *floppies* because of the thin, fragile quality of the 5-1/4-inch disk itself (see Figure 10-8A). The even

Figure 10-8A ■ 5-1/4-inch Disk and 3-1/2-inch Disk

PCs commonly use 3-1/2- and 5-1/4-inch disks for storage.

smaller 3-1/2-inch disk is encased in a hardshell plastic case for use in personal computerss. These small 3-1/2-inch disks, which usually store information on both sides, provide double-density (closely packed) storage capacity of approximately 800,000 characters, or about 300 pages of text per side. A *hard disk* is a rigid aluminum platter usually encased within the computer (see Figure 10-8B). Data are stored more closely on a hard disk, which saves storage space. Also, hard disks rotate at higher speeds, which makes faster retrieval (up to ten times faster than floppies) possible.

Hard Disk

Figure 10-8B ■ Cutaway View of A Hard Disk
Courtesy of International Business Machines Corporation

Each disk is assigned a filename that reflects the contents of the record. The filename is used for both storage and retrieval. A label with identification and any special instructions for manually retrieving a record may be attached to each disk, as shown in Figure 10-9 on the next page. Such disks are filed according to the label: (1) alphabetically by title (subject or name); (2) chronologically by date of creation; or (3) coded numerically by sequential numbers, or by a decimal system keyed to departments within an organization. In addition, hardware and software used to create the disk files may be added to the label to assist in storing and retrieving the files.

Figure 10-9 ■ Disk Label

Disks are stored in various types of containers, depending on the intended use of the record. Figure 10-10 shows two types of equipment for storing disks on the desktop where they are convenient for the operator's use.

Figure 10-10B ■ Rotary Disk Storage Stand
Ring King Visibles, Inc.

Figure 10-10A ■ Disk Storage Tray

Computer Printouts. Frequently the output of the computer is stored on paper and in a variety of arrangements including business forms. College transcripts and grade reports as well as statements to customers are examples. Many times, however, the output appears on printout sheets that are kept in binders. These binders may be labeled by subject, by date, by account numbers, and the like, and are usually stored on printout carts, shelves, or cabinets as shown in Figure 10-11, or in file drawers.

Figure 10-11 ■ Cart and Shelf Computer Printout Storage Equipment
Wright Line, Inc.

WORD PROCESSING SYSTEMS

Word processing systems operate in every size office.

Word processing systems are directly involved in the operation of records systems in *every* office. For this reason, it is important for you to understand basic word processing concepts. High-level skills and technical knowledge relating to hardware and software, on the other hand, remain the responsibility of automation systems specialists.

A **word processing system** combines the use of people, equipment, and procedures for changing the words originated by a person into a final product—communication or *text*—and forwarding it to a user. This definition applies to the traditional office system—a handwritten letter recorded on a yellow pad and transcribed into mailable form by using a typewriter is also word processing. However, the main use of the term *word processing (WP)* is to describe an automated way of creating, producing, editing, storing, retrieving, and distributing such communications. This section reviews the creation of records in an automated word processing system and discusses briefly how such records are stored and retrieved.

Creating Word Processing Records

Word processing systems, like other automated systems, require hardware and software for creating records. The hardware needed includes *standalone word processing equipment* (electronic typewriters and word processors that operate as independent units) and computers. Word processing has become a common application of the microcomputer using special software such as WORDSTAR, WORDPERFECT, and DISPLAYWRITER. The main function of WP software is to record (that is create), add, delete, change, correct, and move or relocate copy (sentences, paragraphs, graphics, and tables) rapidly. (With the exception of the recording function, all of these automated activities are usually referred to as *text-editing* functions.) Figure 10-12 illustrates the main equipment required to operate a word processing system based on a microcomputer.

Word processing represents a very common application of microcomputers.

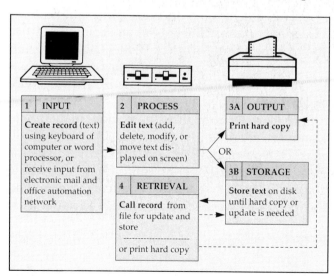

Figure 10-12 ■ Automated Word Processing System

The records management staff must understand records-creation methods and assist the office employees in choosing the most efficient, least expensive methods. We discuss cost control in Chapter 12.

Storing Word Processing Records

In the microcomputer, records are stored temporarily in internal memory during the period of time the machine is in operation. To keep the record in its present form or for updating, the information is stored on the disk for a time and then printed out. A careful operator usually creates a backup disk stored in another location. Figure 10-12 shows a typical method of storing text in a WP system.

Retrieving Word Processing Records

In order to find anything—from wearing apparel at home to records at the office—our memory or an index (or directory) of items stored must be consulted. With an index of each of the files or contents of a WP disk shown on a terminal screen, the operator can quickly select the desired records to be displayed on the screen for updating, re-storing, or printing hard copy.

Desktop Publishing

Desktop publishing (DTP) is a word processing software package that provides for writing, assembling, and designing publications through the use of microcomputers. Businesses most commonly use DTP to create annual reports, newsletters, flyers, bulletins, and brochures. Each of these publications usually has text, graphics (drawings and charts), and other illustrations requiring a variety of typefaces. Usually DTP uses a PC with page layout software and a laser printer to produce a master copy that is very close in quality to that produced by commercial printers — and at a fraction of the cost. The copy produced is "camera-ready" because DTP software, such as Ventura and PageMaker, allows the operator to combine at one time the word input and graphics input needed for producing a document. Prior to DTP, these operations were separate tasks, and some were manually produced.

Desktop publishing often eliminates the need for commercial printing.

Many types of word processing systems are available, each having its own set of procedures for use. The procedures explained in this section include the basic concepts needed to understand records automation in the modern office. More detailed information is readily available—in school and community libraries, on the magazine racks of retail stores, and from equipment and supplies manufacturers.

OPTICAL DISK SYSTEMS

An **optical digital data disk** (often shortened to *optical disk*) is an information storage medium that resembles a phonograph record. In an optical disk system, a laser beam burns or etches holes called *picture elements* to form a dot pattern of the letters, numbers, lines, and drawings as it copies from the original onto the disk (see Figure 10-13). Information is retrieved or read back from the disk by using the same laser device. Optical disks can store alphanumeric data, pictures, graphs, and drawings in a very compact manner.

A laser beam creates records on an optical disk.

Figure 10-13 ■ Optical Digital Data Disks--3M Optical Recording

Optical disks are available in several sizes, such as 5-1/4", 8", 12", and 14"; with larger sizes, more storage capacity is provided. It is estimated that the storage capacity of one double-sided, 5-1/4-inch optical disk is 16,000 pages—equal to the storage capacity of 160, 5-1/4-inch magnetic disks. A single 12-inch optical disk stores as much as 80 file cabinets or 60 reels of standard magnetic tape. In addition, the cost of storing information on optical disks is incredibly low. For example, the annual cost of storing one billion characters on a 12-inch optical disk is estimated to be about 12 cents; and on a small magnetic disk, $2. Data stored on erasable optical disks can be changed or rerecorded as magnetic media allow. Because optical disks are similar in shape to magnetic disks, both types of disks can be stored in the same manner. Often, large-scale optical disk storage is arranged in the form of a "jukebox," which is similar to the disk pack arrangement of magnetic disks discussed earlier.

The most common method for entering information on an optical disk is by using scanners or optical readers that can activate the information-recording code on the disk. For providing hard-copy output of images (such as charts and pictures) and text from one disk, laser printers are available that produce output at extremely high speeds.

OFFICE AUTOMATION AND RECORDS SYSTEMS

In addition to creating, storing, and retrieving records in automated systems, the computer also plays a leading role in performing other information systems activities. With each new development in information technology, the office becomes more automated. Also, *in each case, records are involved*. Thus, each new application of automation to the field of records management expands the responsibilities of the records management staff. Several of the most widely recognized office automation methods as they affect records systems are explained here.

Standalone Automated Records Systems

When automated systems first emerged, each piece of equipment operated as a separate, standalone system. Thus, a computer and its related equipment operated on an individual basis. If a firm had two computers, neither was connected to the other. Most of the PCs used in the home and in small offices are standalone systems and thus are not connected to any other system for creating records. However, the strong trend exists for automated equipment to be interconnected into larger systems, as discussed next.

The Office Automation Network

Because the computer can be connected to the telephone system, a new and more powerful "super" system is created. This new system, called a **telecommunication system**, sends words, numbers, graphics, and voice messages (in effect, records) within a firm as well as to all parts of the world.

Telecommunication has made the office automation network possible.

Within a firm, a **local area network (LAN)** transmits computerized records of business operations over telephone lines under the direction of the computer and its software. Outside the firm, **widearea networks (WAN)** carry messages all over the globe. This process of linking together a series of varied information systems activities—including the transmission of records—is called **networking**. Thus, an *office automation network* combines the transmitting (message sending) function with the processing of numbers, words, and graphics; microfilming; and reprographics (the reproduction of information discussed in Chapter 12).[3]

By studying Figure 10-14 on the next page, the entry of information at various locations in the office network within the firm can be traced. In this figure, the jagged, lightning-shaped arrow represents a telephone line connection in the office network; the solid line, on the other hand, represents an electrical (cable) connection. Both are illustrations of online systems. New automated records are created at the telephone, at a video display terminal keyboard, and at various word processing terminals. Also, optical character recognition (OCR) machines scan documents and convert the contents into computer code, thereby creating computer records. In this last method of records creation, the keyboarding operation is not required to enter data into the automated system.

Other forms of automated records creation technology is available. **Electronic mail** transmits records—words and images, such as drawings and blueprints—over telephone lines or relays them via satellite network. The most popular form of electronic mail is **facsimile** (or *fax*). In the sending office, a fax machine connected to the telephone line sends the message to its destination (a fax receiving/sending machine). Because of the widespread use of fax, many firms print

Electronic mail sends words and graphics over telecommunication channels.

---

[3]More detailed information on office automation can be found in Kallaus and Keeling, *Administrative Office Management*, Chapter 16, as well as in other office management and records management references found in school and city libraries.

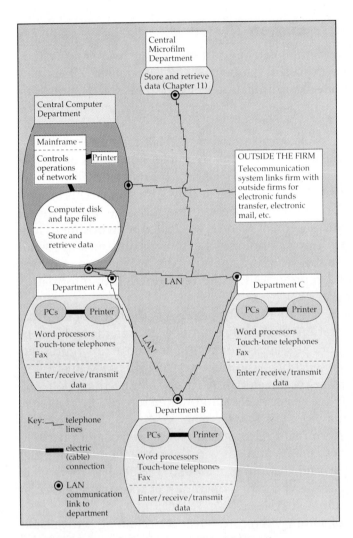

Figure 10-14 ■ Office Automation Network

their fax number alongside their main telephone number on their letterhead stationery to assist in sending messages. Another form of electronic mail is produced by a **communicating word processor**, which is an advanced type of word processor capable of keyboarding, editing, and transmitting its output over telephone lines. Also, a **computer-based message system (CBMS)** sends and receives voice messages electronically. (The term **voice mail** is often used to describe such a system, which eliminates the need for written records because one-way voice messages are stored in the computer mailbox and reconnected to the caller's voice as necessary.) In a CBMS, each user is assigned an **electronic mailbox** (identified by a location code or a special user-name code) as the storage location where an incoming voice message is "filed" in computer-code form. At the receiving end, the user keys in an identification code, after which the computer displays the list of stored messages. The user may then decide which messages to print out.

An electronic mail system permits many types and large numbers of records to be swiftly and inexpensively transmitted worldwide. At the same time, the system may reduce the amount of paperwork, including internal and external mail, that is required in the office. But we should not forget: *Electronic mail creates many new records that must be controlled.*

In the banking industry, an **electronic funds transfer system (EFTS)** allows customers to request information about their checking and savings accounts as well as withdraw money and make deposits. Computer terminals located in convenient places, such as supermarkets and shopping malls, permit banking transactions without the inconvenience of physically going to the bank. Little paperwork is performed by the customer although the customer receives a statement of the EFTS activity at the end of each reporting period. However, a large reduction in the records work within the bank has resulted in fewer teller-window procedures and a decrease in bookkeeping functions (deposits, withdrawals, and file maintenance of accounts).

The computer also creates automated records at a retail store's checkout counter using the data contained in the bar code appearing on the product label. The store's computer file is updated after each transaction, and the customer's printout receipt shows the name and price of each item purchased.

Other applications of the computer to everyday information processing tasks continue to grow. Such topics are covered in detail in data processing, word processing, and general systems references.

SAFETY AND SECURITY OF AUTOMATED RECORDS

Magnetic records, like paper records, must be protected from all types of conditions that could interfere with their proper use and control. To provide such protection, automation specialists recommend that both safety and security measures be put in place over automated records, as we discuss next.

Records Safety

Safety refers to protecting the records from the many physical hazards existing in the office environment. Following are five procedures to consider for controlling records in the physical environment:

1. *Adopt special protective measures for the hardware and software.* These measures include protecting magnetic records from changes (surges) in electric voltage, physically locking up computer files and equipment, and separating computer equipment and personnel from other employees. Also, dust screens and protective envelopes for PC disks should be used to protect against damage from dust, scratches, and fingerprints during handling and storage. The relative humidity of the workplace should be carefully controlled by using a humidistat to prevent equipment operating problems.

2. *Take inventory and test hardware regularly, and attach personal computers to furniture.* Portable computers and printers should be given special attention because of their light weight and ease of access.

3. *Regularly convert the records stored on magnetic media to hard copy if the records are to be kept for long periods of time.* This suggestion is made because some automated records may have a limited shelf life, depending on storage conditions.

Copy computer files to avoid loss of information.

4. *Protect against loss of files* with a policy of copying computer files for use as backup in case of systems problems and storing the copies in fireproof cabinets or in an offsite location. Duplicating automated records is done quickly and inexpensively and provides good insurance that the records will always be available when needed.

5. *Take special measures to fight the computer "virus,"* a special computer program—created for illicit reasons—that may be used to distort or erase automated records. The use of virus detectors, making backup copies of each software package as soon as it is opened, and making copies once a month along with the data entered into the system each month are effective means of avoiding this "plague" that could "infect" automated records.

Records Security

Security is the protection from unauthorized access to the information stored on the records. Security practices in widespread use include:

1. *Developing a security policy to ensure the safe, reliable operation of the records system.* Such a policy is based on a detailed study of equipment used, records functions performed, information contained in the principal records, employees having access to the records, and current security devices.

   > Automated records protection starts with a sound security policy.

2. *Conducting security checks, and if necessary, bond personnel using the hardware and software in the system.* The automated records security policy should include close supervision of the work plus holding employees personally accountable for the proper maintenance of company equipment and information.
3. *Providing deterrents to crime.* Some firms have a security warning programmed into the computer for display on the terminal screen. An effective method of controlling access to a computer room is a card reader/combination lock system into which employees must insert their cards and punch in a personal code.
4. *Protecting the data stored on the disk or tape.* Safeguards to protect company data from unauthorized use include:
   a. *Passwords* that employees must use to retrieve data.
   b. *Encryption systems* that scramble data in a predetermined manner at the sending point in order to protect confidential records. The scrambled data must then be decoded at the destination.
   c. *Call-back*, a records protection procedure that requires the individual requesting data from the computer system to hang up after a telephone request is made and wait for the computer to call back. In call-back systems, telephone numbers can be checked by the computer before information is released to the requesting party to be sure that only authorized persons have access to the requested information.

IMPORTANT TERMS

audio-response system	communicating word processor
automated records system	computer-based message system
automation	(CBMS)

desktop publishing (DTP)
electronic funds transfer systems
     (EFTS)
electronic mail
electronic mailbox
facsimile
light pen
local area network (LAN)
mainframe
microcomputer
minicomputer
networking
offline storage

online storage
optical-character recognition
     (OCR) equipment
optical digital data disk
subsystem
system
technology
telecommunication system
voice mail
voice-recognition system
wide-area network (WAN)
word processing system

REVIEW AND DISCUSSION

1. Let's consider your class in records management as a system. Describe the makeup of this system and the points where the record life cycle is involved. (Goal 1)
2. Most of us pay our utility bills in a system that is only partially automated. As a class group,identify each of the phases in the bill-paying system (from input on), and indicate which phases are automated and which are not. Explain reasons for the automation conditions you find. (Goal 2)
3. Describe the characteristics that all computers have in common. What is the purpose of each? (Goal 3)
4. By knowing the phases in a computer system, you understand how information flows through a computer to create records. Trace the flow of information needed to prepare your semester/ quarter course grades. Also, indicate the types of computer systems equipment needed to produce these records. (Goal 4)
5. How does offline storage differ from online storage? What types of equipment are used for these types of storage? (Goal 4)
6. What forms of storage are used to file computer records? (Goal 5)
7. What are the principal phases in an automated word processing system? Trace the path of information through this system and show how records are created, processed, and stored in this system. (Goal 6)
8. Explain what desktop publishing is and how it works. (Goal 6)
9. How is an optical digital data disk record created? (Goal 7)

10. What is an office automation network, and how does it affect the creation and use of records in a records system? (Goal 8)

11. Special care must be given to protecting computer records. List the main methods recommended for ensuring such care. (Goal 9)

APPLICATIONS (APP)

APP 10-1. Identifying Systems Activities in a Part-Time Office Job

You are employed part-time in an office job to help pay your school expenses. On the job your main tasks involve (1) using the telephone, (2) keying letters to customers using a PC, and (3) filing records—mostly correspondence and paid invoices. In order that you can relate basic systems concepts to the real world, complete the following steps:

1. List typical activities or procedures found in each of the three main tasks mentioned above.

2. Fit each of these main tasks into an overall office system that helps to explain the interdependence of these tasks in your office. (A chart similar to that shown in Figure 10-2 may be used to simplify this part of the problem solution.)

3. Indicate (using a simple code) whether the activities are completed by manual or automated methods. (Goals 1 and 2)

APP 10-2. Understanding the Basics of an Automated Records System

In order to understand how automated records systems are created, used, stored, retrieved, and protected, you are asked to consider the system that you as students use to register for classes in your school. In most cases, the system will be partially or completely computerized; in others, all or a large portion of the system may be manual.

To assist you in completing this Application, consider the role of each of the systems phases discussed in this chapter. In addition, review the makeup of your school's registration system and the major users of the information produced by this system. (Keep in mind that various administrative offices in your school need the registration information created in the system.) Present your solution to this case problem in nontechnical, user terms by answering these two questions:

1. What are the main phases of the registration system and who are the users of the information created in this system?
2. What records are needed and created in this system? (Show whether these records are prepared by (a) manual and/or (b) automated methods.) (Goals 2, 4, 9, 11)

11 MICROIMAGE RECORDS

GOALS

After completing this chapter, you will be able to:

1. Define *micrographics*, *microimage*, *microrecord*, and *microform*.
2. Identify the four requirements for ensuring microfilm quality.
3. List the most common microforms and their uses.
4. Explain the steps required to produce computer output microfilm (COM) and computer input microfilm (CIM).
5. Outline the general steps involved in filming, processing, and duplicating a microrecord.
6. List ways of protecting microrecords from the hazards found in storage and usage environments.
7. Describe the types of procedures and equipment used in storing and retrieving microrecords.
8. State the differences between offline and online computer-assisted retrieval (CAR).
9. Outline important management considerations regarding when to use microrecords, how to determine the legality of microrecords, and how to evaluate microrecord systems.
10. Describe microrecord applications in large and small firms.

Even in the computer age, paper records discussed in earlier chapters continue to grow at an increasing rate, causing major problems for the records manager. To save space and increase efficiency, many companies are microfilming their records, an important process that is discussed in nontechnical terms in this chapter.

Microfilming is a process that involves photographing documents and reducing them in size to create **microimages** of records. Such very small records are also known as *microrecords*. The full range of services for creating, storing, retrieving, using, and protecting microrecords is known as **micrographics**. These records, in turn, may

What are the basic concepts in the field of microfilming?

be packaged in a variety of convenient and easy-to-use forms—
microforms—of which the most common varieties are roll film,
microfiche, microfilm jackets, and aperture cards.

In this chapter we will discuss the microfilming process and the
microforms used in this process. In addition, we will discuss the
procedures and equipment commonly used in microrecord systems.
Finally, we will explain when to use microimage systems and how to
determine the legality of such systems—information of primary
importance to management. Common applications of the microfilming process are also discussed.

MICROFILMING

To be used, the microrecord must be enlarged to the original record
size and projected on a viewing screen using special procedures and
equipment. In addition, special types of film must be used and a high
level of microrecord quality must be maintained if the microrecord
system is to achieve its purposes.

Sizes of Film

Microfilm comes in various widths measured in millimeters (mm)
of which the three most common are 16mm, 35mm, and 105mm. The
narrowest film (16mm) is most frequently used for filming small
documents, such as checks and standard- and legal-size records.
When larger records such as newspapers, maps, and engineering
drawings, are filmed, 35mm microfilm is used; 105mm microfilm is
commonly used in the preparation of microfiche.

The size of microfilm
selected depends
upon the size of the
original record.

Microfilm is also available in various lengths and thicknesses. The
length of microfilm varies from 100 feet to over 200 feet. The thickness
may vary from .06mm to .175mm. Consequently, the thinner the film,
the greater the number of feet of film that can be stored on a standard
reel (spool).

Microfilm Quality

Microrecords must be carefully prepared, filmed, processed, and
protected during storage and retrieval to represent a true copy of the
original record. Four factors relating to the filming process are (1)
resolution, (2) density, (3) reduction ratio, and (4) magnification ratio.

Resolution. **Resolution** refers to the sharpness of lines or fine detail on a microrecord. To ensure good resolution, a high quality of film and a camera with a good lens are required. Resolution is an important factor, for there must be good, clear images on the microrecord so that when it is enlarged, clarity of detail is not lost.

Density. **Density** is a numeric measure of the contrast between the dark and light areas of the film as determined by a device called a **densitometer**. A high-quality microrecord has a wide variation in the dark and light areas of the film. The higher the contrast, the easier it is to read the images on the microrecord.

Reduction Ratio. The **reduction ratio** is the size of the microimage as compared to the original document. A ratio stated as 24 to 1 (usually shortened to 24X) means that the image on the film is 1/24th the dimensional size of the original record, both horizontally and vertically. (A document microfilmed at 24X is 1/24 x 1/24, or 1/576th its original size.) Reduction ratios range from 5X up to 2400X, although the most common reduction is 24X. The higher the reduction ratio, the smaller the images, and the greater the number of images that can be photographed on one square inch of film. For example, 8,100 regular-size bank checks can be photographed on 100 feet of microfilm at 24X reduction and 16,600 such checks at 50X. An interesting example of the reduction ratio is shown in Figure 11-1 in which all 773,746 words in the Bible are reduced to this incredibly small space. This microrecord can be read with appropriate reading equipment.

> The most common reduction ratio is 24 to 1.

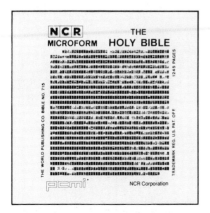

Figure 11-1 ■ The Bible in Microform
NCR Corporation

Magnification Ratio. In order to be read by the user, a microrecord must be enlarged or magnified. The **magnification ratio** describes the relationship between the size of the microrecord and the enlarged record on a microfilm reader screen. For example, a one-inch square microrecord that is magnified ten times (a magnification ratio of 10X) appears in its enlarged form as ten square inches.

MICROFORMS

Early usage of microrecords was on rolls of film. As time passed, manufacturers developed a wide variety of other forms on which filmed records are made, stored, and used.

Each microform shown in Figure 11-2 has a wide range of applications to meet the special needs of an office. In this chapter we discuss in detail roll film, microfiche, jackets, and aperture cards, because these microforms are the most commonly used.

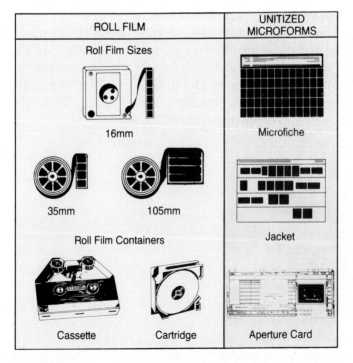

Figure 11-2 ■ Common Microforms

Roll Film

The most inexpensive and most widely used microform is **roll film**, which is a length of microfilm containing a series of images much like a movie film. Roll film is normally used for information that needs to be stored in sequence, such as employee records. A typical length 100-foot roll can hold more than 2,000 images. These images may be either positive (black characters on a clear background) or negative (white characters on a black background).

Records are stored in sequence on roll film.

Typically, roll film is used to photograph records that are not used frequently or records that do not require changes. Large volumes of information can be stored on film in very little space at low cost. If changes in records do not occur often, such changes can be made by cutting out the old information and splicing in the new film. However, such changes in the film are expensive and may weaken the film as well as make it inadmissible as legal evidence in a court of law.

Reels of 16mm microfilm are used primarily for storing correspondence, checks, invoices, and purchase orders. The wider 35mm reels of film are used for storing larger documents, such as maps, X rays, engineering drawings, and newspapers.

Microfilm cartridges, as shown in Figure 11-2, serve as convenient packages for rolls of microfilm and permit automatic threading of the film into the viewer. Cartridges are plastic cases that protect the film from fingerprints and other possible sources of damage. **Microfilm cassettes** provide even greater convenience for the handling of a continuous length of roll film. Each cassette contains two film reels — the feed and the take-up — that eliminate the need for rewinding the cassette when it is removed from a viewer.

Microfiche

Microfiche, usually shortened to *fiche* and pronounced "feesh," is the French word for *index card*. Fiche is a sheet of film containing a series of microrecords arranged in rows and columns. As such, fiche is called a **unitized microform** because it contains *one unit* of information such as a section from an employee manual. Fiche permits direct access to any record without having to advance a roll of film to the appropriate location. Although fiche is available in a variety of sizes, the 6" x 4" fiche is most commonly used and has been designated by the microfilm industry as the standard-size sheet. The maximum number of images that can be contained on a fiche depends on the

Fiche permits direct access to any record.

amount of reduction. At a typical 24X reduction, 98 original documents can be stored on one microfiche, arranged in a grid of seven rows and fourteen columns.

Most commonly, 16mm film is used in the preparation of standard microfiche. Recent product developments enable microfiche to be updated so as to provide a current record for use in the office. *Updatable microfiche* permits changes to be made in the records stored on microfiche.

In Figure 11-3, notice the arrangement of pages (labeled "Pa") in each section (labeled "Sec") in an employee handbook. Another common method of arranging records on microfiche is to film documents in a continuous series by rows. Because the title (header) at the top of the fiche is eye-readable by the user, fiche can easily be stored and retrieved manually, similar to index cards. Microfiche on 105mm film may also be imaged directly from computer tape, as discussed later in this chapter.

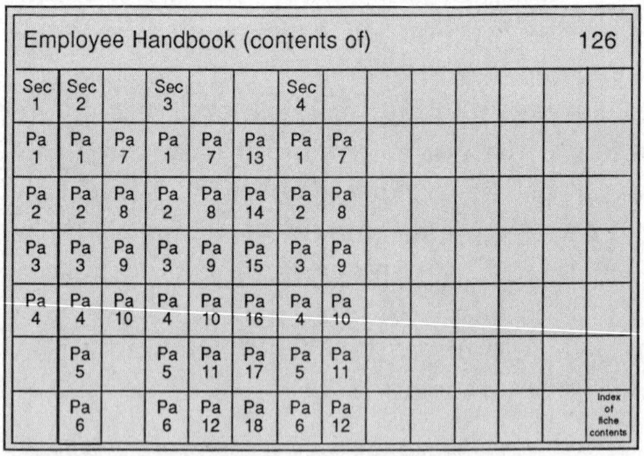

Employee Handbook (contents of)							126						
Sec 1	Sec 2		Sec 3			Sec 4							
Pa 1	Pa 1	Pa 7	Pa 1	Pa 7	Pa 13	Pa 1	Pa 7						
Pa 2	Pa 2	Pa 8	Pa 2	Pa 8	Pa 14	Pa 2	Pa 8						
Pa 3	Pa 3	Pa 9	Pa 3	Pa 9	Pa 15	Pa 3	Pa 9						
Pa 4	Pa 4	Pa 10	Pa 4	Pa 10	Pa 16	Pa 4	Pa 10						
	Pa 5		Pa 5	Pa 11	Pa 17	Pa 5	Pa 11						
	Pa 6		Pa 6	Pa 12	Pa 18	Pa 6	Pa 12						Index of fiche contents

Figure 11-3 ■ Layout of Images on a Microfiche

Fiche can be mailed easily and economically, just as can any 6" x 4" cards. With developments in color photography, fiche can be produced in colors closely resembling the colors on the original records. Color fiche can be viewed longer without eyestrain than can black and white pictures. The surface and elevation of maps filmed in color hold more information for the user. With advertising brochures and sales kits filmed on color microfiche, sales representatives do not have to carry heavy sample cases. Other uses of colored microfiche continue to grow.

Jackets

A **jacket**, a second unitized microform sometimes called a *microfilm jacket*, is a transparent plastic carrier with single or multiple horizontal channels into which strips of 16mm or 35mm microfilm— cut from roll film—are inserted (see Figure 11-4). The most commonly used format is 6" x 4" with four channels holding 12 images each. With the use of a jacket, strips of film are protected and are easily organized into units of information similar to microfiche. The jacketed film may be duplicated without removal from the jacket. In addition, new microrecords may be inserted into the jacket, and a header identifying the jacketed strips can easily be placed at the top of the microform for easy storage and retrieval. Jackets are widely used for microrecords of personnel and medical records, as well as for correspondence, legal, customer, and policyholder files.

> Jacketed film is organized into units of information similar to microfiche.

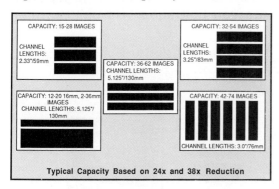

Figure 11-4A ■ Standard Microfilm Jacket Layouts

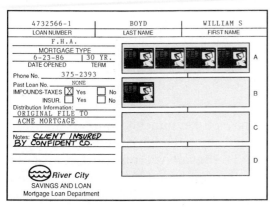

Figure 11-4B ■ Card Jacket Ready for Use

Card jackets are also used. Figure 11-4A illustrates the layout of microrecords for storage in standard card jackets approximately 6" x 4" in size. Figure 11-4B shows an example of a jacket that combines microrecords with identifying information about the insured client in a savings and loan institution.

Aperture Cards

A third unitized microform, the **aperture card**, is a standard data processing punched card (7-3/8" x 3-1/4") with a precut opening (aperture) for mounting microfilm. The most commonly used aperture card contains a single 35mm engineering drawing or blueprint (see Figure 11-5). Aperture cards for storing 16mm film hold up to eight images. Four letter-size (8-1/2" x 11") pages can be included within the aperture at a reduction ratio of 16X; and up to 400 pages can be contained in an aperture at a reduction ratio of 160X on 16mm film.

Figure 11-5 ■ Aperture Card

Adding or updating aperture cards is done simply and quickly.

Identifying information may be keypunched into an aperture card and at the same time printed along the top edge as a heading to serve as an index for storage and retrieval. Aperture cards are easy to update since they require only the removal of the obsolete card and the substitution of a new one. Interfiling new cards or replacing cards within a file of cards can be accomplished quickly.

Many large businesses and government agencies use aperture cards to store maps and other drawings, X rays, and business records. Firms have found that the principal disadvantage of using aperture cards is cost. The expense of card supplies, mounting, and the fact that fewer images can be stored on each aperture card than on microfiche, makes the costs of using aperture cards higher than the costs of other microforms. Filing space requirements for aperture cards are estimated to be at least five times greater than those of a file of records maintained on roll film.[1]

Computer-Based Microrecords

Two processes assist the computer in the production and use of microrecords. They are computer output microfilm and computer input microfilm.

Computer Output Microfilm.   **Computer output microfilm (COM)** eliminates the need to print hard copies of paper records before filming the records. With the use of a special tape-to-film photographic device called a **recorder**, computer output stored in digital (binary) form on magnetic tape is converted to a microimage on 105mm roll film or microfiche. (When the computer output is stored on microfiche, the result is *computer output microfiche*.) Less than four ounces of microfiche can store the equivalent of 60 pounds of hard copy. By eliminating the need for hard copy output, COM greatly reduces the cost and space needed for records storage.

COM creates microrecords directly from the computer.

Figure 11-6 shows the steps involved in an *offline* operation in which the filming is not directly connected to the computer. Rather,

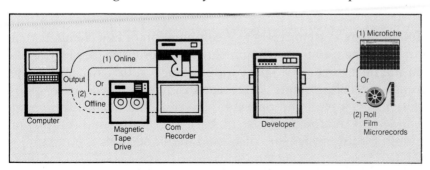

Figure 11-6 ■ The Computer Output Microfilm Process Showing Online and Offline Operations

[1]Katherine Aschner, ed., *Taking Control of Your Office Records*, Knowledge Industry Publications, Inc., White Plains, NY, 1983, p. 75.

the computer generates a magnetic tape that contains all the data to be put on microfilm. This tape serves as input to the COM recorder. In addition, Figure 11-6 also shows how COM can also be performed *online*—that is, directly connected to the computer and run as an automatic photographing operation. In the latest COM systems, digital input to the COM device controls a laser beam that burns the computer record directly into the microfilm.

The production and storage costs of COM are much lower than the equivalent paper costs. And when a high number of copies are needed, COM usage can save from 80 to 90 percent of the cost of hard copies. Also, COM systems replace the generation of huge amounts of computer output, such as operations records and routine documents.

Computer Input Microfilm. The computer can also be used with records already on microfilm. **Computer input microfilm (CIM)** takes plain language (uncoded) data on microrecords and translates such information into computer-language code for storage on magnetic tape as input to a computer. As a result, CIM makes the powerful storage and retrieval capabilities of the computer available to microimage systems. Often COM and CIM are combined in one system to exchange both input and output between the computer and the microimage system.

PROCEDURES AND EQUIPMENT FOR MICROIMAGE SYSTEMS

An efficient system is needed to use records in microform.

A **microimage system** refers to a combination of key elements that form an efficient unit for using records in microform (see Figure 11-7 on the next page). Of special importance in this system are the several levels of personnel, discussed in Chapter 1, who are responsible for developing and operating the procedures and equipment needed in the microrecord system. Basic procedures and equipment required for this system are discussed in this section.

Preparing Documents for Microfilming

Documents must be carefully checked before filming to ensure that the camera will function properly. This means that all paper clips and staples must be removed. Records to be filmed may need mending; attachments to records, such as envelopes, routing slips, and duplicate copies of records should be removed. Records should also be batched and placed in sequential order before filming.

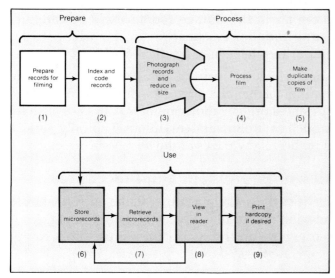

Figure 11-7 ■ Microimage System

Maintaining a Controlled Environment

With constant handling, microrecords are subject to dirt, abrasion, oily fingerprints, contamination by foreign materials, and exposure to excessive light and temperatures. Records managers should be alert to the following needs for protecting the environment in which microrecords are stored and used:

1. *Microrecords require the same preservation and protection measures observed for other types of records.* The term *file security* is often used in this regard when microfilm is relied upon for duplicating irreplaceable records as assurance against the loss or destruction of the original documents. Other detailed measures for preserving and protecting records appear in the next chapter.

2. *Because of the unique chemical properties of film, special precautions need to be taken to control the storage environment.* Most important are temperature and humidity. Microrecords that have a permanent retention period should be stored under controlled conditions that include a maximum temperature of 70 degrees and relative humidity that stays within a range of 30 to 40 percent.

The chemical properties in film require special preservation and protection measures for microrecords.

3. *Film reels and paper enclosures or attachments to the film should be constructed from special materials that are free from acids and other contaminants* that can cause destructive chemical reactions on film.
4. *If possible, film should be stored in sealed containers.* If this is not possible, then the air in the storage room should be carefully controlled by an air-filtration system to remove abrasive particles and gaseous impurities that can harm the records.

Service bureaus, which are private firms specializing in the storage and preservation of microrecords, are available in most large cities, in case the business organization cannot, or does not wish to, provide such controlled environmental conditions. Typically, service bureaus are listed in the yellow pages of the telephone directory.

Providing Efficient Equipment and Procedures

Figure 11-7 identifies the main procedures in the microimage life cycle—filming, indexing and coding, processing, duplicating, reading, storing, and retrieving—and for each of these procedures, equipment is needed to operate the system.

Filming Equipment. For filming large-volume records, such as checks and invoices, a **rotary camera** is frequently used, primarily because it is the least expensive method of filming records. Rotary cameras use rotating belts to carry documents through the camera and make images on 16mm film at speeds exceeding 500 documents per minute.

A **planetary camera** uses 35mm film to microfilm oversize engineering drawings, hardbound books, and other large documents placed upon a plane (flat) surface. Filming with this type of camera is much slower than with a rotary camera since the original documents must remain stationary during filming and are photographed one by one. Hence, filming is more expensive than with the rotary camera, but a higher quality image is produced.

The **step and repeat camera** is used to film microfiche. This camera films images directly onto a 4"-wide film, which, when cut into 6" lengths, produces a standard-size master microfiche of 6" x 4" each.

In systems requiring frequent changes in the records—as in maintaining spare parts inventory records—an **updatable microfiche camera** (a modification of the step and repeat camera) is available. With such a camera, additional images can be added to a microfiche at any time if unexposed space exists on the fiche. Also, such a camera can alter existing images by overprinting such words as VOID and PAID.

Indexing Procedures. The indexing or coding process takes on an additional meaning in microfilming just as in the automated record systems discussed in Chapter 10. In such nonpaper record systems, indexing refers to the process of assigning some type of identification, such as an address, to each microimage. The film address may also include the film roll number, the microrecord frame number, or other type of identification for locating the microimage. Microrecord indexing is accomplished either at the time of filming when a terminal operator, stationed adjacent to the microfilm camera, assigns identifiers during the filming process. Or, the index may be prepared after filming. In this case an operator places a roll of microfilm into a retrieval terminal, views each image, and assigns an identifier by keying into the computer memory the identifier and the sequential number assigned to the microimage.

> Indexing is the key to locating records in the microfile.

The term *index* may also refer to the list of microrecords on roll film, on a microfiche, or in an aperture card file. In this sense, an index operates like a telephone directory, which can be considered an index (list) of all telephone subscribers in the community.

Finding a microimage is rather easy if its address, as provided by the location index, is known. Several common methods of indexing are shown in Figure 11-8 and discussed in the following paragraphs.

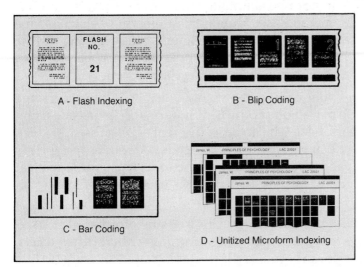

A - Flash Indexing   B - Blip Coding

C - Bar Coding   D - Unitized Microform Indexing

Figure 11-8 ■ Common Methods of Indexing Microrecords

Flash Indexing. **Flash indexing** is used on roll film (see Figure 11-8A). Each 100-foot length of film is divided into sections or groups of records in the same way that divider tabs are used to separate the sections of information in a notebook or that guides are used with folders in a file drawer. Usually the arrangement of records is predetermined, that is, based on the original order of paper records in the file. An example is employee records in a personnel office arranged consecutively by employee number. Prior to filming the records, a **flash card** (a kind of tab or guide for a microfilm record file) with identifying information is placed in front of the group of records. In a human resources employee file, a section of information might be the records for 50 employees. The records of 1,200 employees would have 24 sections requiring 24 flash cards in the file. The container in which the film is housed is then marked to show the section position and the contents of each section.

The key to flash indexing is the use of a well-placed flash card.

Blip Coding. The fully automated system for retrieving microrecords discussed later in this chapter uses image-count blip coding to retrieve microrecords from roll film. During filming, a **blip** or rectangular mark is placed below or above each microimage and each blip is given a sequential number (starting with 0001 to the maximum number of images on the film) (see Figure 11-8B). To retrieve a document, the operator consults the index prepared during filming and enters the image number. The retrieval device then counts the blips at high speed until the requested record is found. A related indexing method uses sequential numbering, which is done by manually stamping numbers on documents before filming. Or, the camera can automatically number each document. An operator then looks for such a number when retrieving the microrecord.

Bar Coding. **Bar coding** shown in Figure 11-8C uses the same type of bar code placed on products in supermarkets—a code using from 13 to 21 bars. Each bar can be *on* (present) or *off* (absent), which accounts for its being called a binary code. A special terminal is required to advance the film, interpret the code, and stop the film at the desired group of images. Bar coding is used on roll film and on microfiche.

Unitized Microform Indexing. Unitized microforms are indexed in various ways to speed up the retrieval process. Microfiche, jackets, and aperture cards can be indexed by including an easily readable title at the top of the microform created by the camera or added manually.

Unitized microforms are indexed at the top of the record.

(The title usually includes the name of the document and the microrecord sequence number as shown in Figure 11-8D.) Also, fiche can be color coded by adding a band of color to the title or heading area of the microform. Such a color code is attached to a batch of records or to an entire file to identify a selected type of record. Misfiled microrecords can be readily identified if they are placed in the wrong batch. Other methods of indexing microimages are discussed in advanced records management and microimage systems publications.

Processing Equipment. After the images of the original document have been recorded on film, the film must be processed in a darkroom. Some film can be developed in regular light and therefore requires no special processing room or equipment. Inexpensive processors are available for in-house processing. More complex film processing is usually performed by commercial microfilming companies.

Duplicating Equipment. Frequently several copies of microforms are needed. Small organizations send original microforms to commercial micrographic service bureaus for duplication; larger firms may produce duplicate copies within the firm on special duplicating equipment. A simpler method of duplication is accomplished by simultaneously exposing two rolls of film in the camera.

Reading/Viewing Equipment. To read information stored on a microrecord, special equipment is needed. A **reader**—sometimes called a *viewer*—is a device that displays the enlarged microimage on a screen so that the record can be read. Two types of readers are available: stationary (or desktop) readers and portable readers.

> Readers are needed to use microrecords.

A *stationary reader* provides a larger screen for viewing and a wider choice of optional features (such as a hood for reducing glare) than portable readers. Some desktop readers permit the simultaneous viewing of two pages. Other readers accept only one kind of microform while still others allow a number of different microforms (film, fiche, aperture cards) to be used. An example of a typical stationary reader is shown in Figure 11-9A on the next page.

A *portable reader* weighs less than a stationary reader, usually less than 10 pounds. One version of portable reader, the *lap reader*, is often used with microfiche in cars, on outdoor job sites, or in service vans. Such a reader can be powered by dry cells, by automobile battery, or operated from the cigarette lighter of a vehicle. Small hand-held

Figure 11-9A ■ Stationary Microrecord Reader

Photo Courtesy of Bell & Howell Document Management Company

Figure 11-9B ■ Portable Microrecord Reader

Photo Courtesy of Bell & Howell Document Management Company

viewers are also available for browsing microfiche rather than for intensive reading (see Figure 11-9B).

Another type of reader, called a *reader-printer*, serves dual purposes—for reading and for printing a hard copy. With such equipment, users can make a hard copy of the microimage seen on the viewing screen. The hard copies generally range in size from 8-1/2" x 11" to as large as 18" x 24". When larger sizes are desired, an enlarger-printer must be used.

Storage Equipment. For each type of microform, various storage containers are available. Typical examples of such storage equipment are shown in Figure 11-10.

Records photographed on 16mm or 35mm film are stored on reels or in cartridges or cassettes, as shown in Figure 11-2. In turn, these containers are stored in boxes on shelves or in cabinets partitioned to fit the boxes. Carousel arrangements of partitioned shelves are also common, and small desktop units or floor units are also available. Figures 11-10A and 11-10B show a conventional microfilm drawer cabinet and a carousel-type unit, for the storage of roll film, cartridges, and cassettes, respectively.

Many microforms are stored manually, like paper records.

Figure 11-10A ■ Microfilm Storage
Wright Line, Inc.

Figure 11-10B ■ Cartridge
Carousel Unit
Business Efficiency Aids, Inc.

An even wider variety of equipment is available for storing microfiche. Common examples of such equipment, as shown in Figures 11-10C and 11-10D on the next page, are desktop trays and rotating stands for the use of fiche records at the workstation. In addition, fiche are frequently stored in three-ring binders and in drawer cabinets.

Figure 11-10C ■ Microfiche Desktop Storage Tray
Fellowes Manufacturing Co.

Figure 11-10D ■ Microfiche Rotating Desktop Stand
Ring King Visibles, Inc.

Because aperture cards are stored vertically, the equipment to house them is the same as for other vertical cards discussed in Appendix B. Usually aperture cards are stored in drawers the size of the cards, as shown in Figure 11-10E on the next page.

Plastic jackets and card jackets can be stored in the same type of housing equipment as microfiche. Desktop trays or visible filing equipment similar to the equipment discussed on page 342, Appendix B, are commonly used.

Retrieval Equipment and Procedures. In the manual systems for handling microforms, the main piece of equipment is the reader. Thus, for finding microrecords on reels, cartridges, or cassettes, no extra equipment is required. Nor is any special equipment required

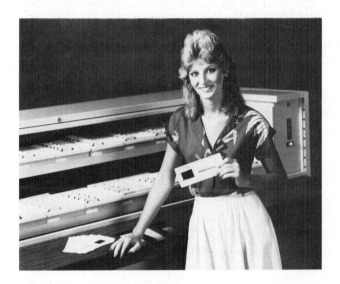

Figure 11-10E ■ Aperture Card Drawer Storage
Kardex Systems, Inc.

for retrieving fiche and jackets in the manual system. Aperture cards, on the other hand, may be retrieved by hand, or more quickly by a mechanical sorter that reads (decodes) the record-storage information that is punched into the cards.

In addition to manual methods of retrieval, the computer is also used to retrieve microrecords. **Computer-assisted retrieval (CAR)** is the process of merging the computer (for great speed in storing and searching data) with microimage systems. Such storage is estimated to be 500 times less expensive than the storage of data on computerized magnetic tape. Using CAR, incoming paper records are microfilmed, usually in random sequence since precise sorting of records is not required. During filming each paper record is assigned a sequential location number (address) that corresponds to the location of its microfilmed image. Next, the microrecord address and keywords, such as record title or subject, are entered into the computer. This information becomes the computer index to the microfilmed records. A typical record request (Find all records relating to the Jameson Bankruptcy.) uses keywords (the two underlined words) by which the search is made. To find the desired records, the computer compares the record numbers/keywords entered on the terminal screen with the corresponding record numbers/keywords in the file index.

Computers greatly speed up the retrieval of microrecords.

When a match of such identifiers is made, the records found are listed on the VDT screen. The operator can then decide which, if any, microimages to access.

Two types of CAR systems are in use. An *offline CAR system* stores microrecords in regular storage equipment according to the location code index stored in the computer. To retrieve a microrecord from this CAR system, the user enters the appropriate record identification into the keyboard. Next, the computer searches its memory to find the location code of the microrecord. The computer terminal screen then displays the location number (page and frame numbers of microfiche, for example) or the frame number and cartridge or roll number of the microfilm record. With this information available, the user manually retrieves the microrecord container from the file for use in the reader.

Online CAR systems retrieve microrecords faster than offline systems.

In an *online CAR system*, records retrieval is connected directly to the computer. To request a record, the computer searches its online index and directs its micrographic retrieval device to locate and display the internally stored microimage on the terminal screen, or if desired, printed. COM-prepared microrecords may also be retrieved in this way. Figure 11-11 shows a CAR system using a minicomputer.

Figure 11-11 ■ Computer-Assisted Retrieval Using a Minicomputer

Eastman Kodak Company

MANAGEMENT CONSIDERATIONS

Three critical questions must be answered by managers who are considering the use of microfilmed records:

1. When should microfilm be used?
2. Are microrecords legal instruments in courts of law?
3. What factors should be considered in evaluating a microimage system?

What information is needed before deciding on the use of microrecords?

In this section, we briefly discuss answers to these questions.

When to Use Microrecords

There are no cut-and-dried situations for recommending the use of microrecords. Instead, most experienced users of microrecords suggest that paper documents should probably be converted to microrecords when these conditions are found:

1. *Considerable space can be saved.* Great savings in space can be achieved when microfilming is used, with the actual amount depending upon the reduction ratio used. As many as 3,000 standard-size 8-1/2 x 11" letters or 40,000 bank checks can be placed on 100 feet of 16mm film with obvious savings in storage and floor space.
2. *The records system can be made more efficient.* Microfilming large bulky materials, such as engineering or architectural drawings, eliminates serious storage and mailing problems. And with greater use of the computer in microimage systems, much faster retrieval of microrecords can be achieved compared with the retrieval of paper documents.
3. *Microfilmed records can be preserved as long as paper records.* In a carefully controlled environment, records stored on microfilm can be protected and preserved for decades with estimates extending to hundreds of years. When the other advantages of microrecords over paper records are considered, this additional fact strengthens the case for film.
4. *The costs of microfilming, storing, and using microrecords are lower than the costs of using paper records.* The main microfilming costs include cameras to film the original records, or having the records filmed by an outside service agency; processors, duplicators, and

necessary supplies; readers; storage and retrieval equipment; space for the preparation, storage, retrieval, transportation, and use of microrecords; overhead costs, such as climate control, telephones, and insurance; and labor for operators, supervisors, and managers. Rules of thumb suggest the following:

   a. Records kept for three years or less cost less to keep on paper than on microfilm. In some cases, records kept from four to seven years may also be less expensive on paper than on film.
   b. Records kept from 7 to 15 years should be considered for microfilming if the records are accessible and a cost benefit resulting from saved storage space is likely.
   c. Records kept on a permanent basis need to be microfilmed. Typical paper records yellow and show other signs of deterioration after a number of years.

5. *The document can be microfilmed successfully.* Remember that:
   a. Blurred copies do not microfilm well.
   b. Colors on original documents may not microfilm.
   c. Defects on the original documents may be magnified on the microrecord.

Microrecords have many advantages over paper documents. Because of their very small size, microrecords cost less to mail than paper copies of the same records, and all types of records may be microfilmed. With technological advances, new equipment costs less but produces better images and permits speedy computerized storage and retrieval. However, users find several disadvantages that need to be studied. Special equipment is needed to read microrecords as opposed to paper records. Continuous or prolonged use of microrecords requiring a reader may cause eyestrain for the operator and is difficult for groups or conferences; only one person at a time can view the record on the reader. Comparing microrecords with related paper documents (such as purchase requisitions with related purchase orders) is difficult as problems often arise in getting the related records together. The indexing of microrecords presents another problem as the indexing may not be accurate or understood by a user trying to locate a record. Under such conditions, finding specific microrecords is time consuming. Often, too, the fixed location of readers is a problem since the user must go to the reader, which wastes time.

Legality of Microrecords

The most important piece of legislation on whether microrecords are fully admissible as evidence in a court of law is the Uniform Photographic Copies of Business and Public Records as Evidence Act of 1951. As passed by the Congress, this act allows microfilmed business documents to be admitted as evidence in courts of law if the following conditions are met: (1) if the microrecord was made from an original document in the regular course of business; (2) if the microrecord was photographed from an entire record to make identification of the original document easy; and (3) if the microrecord is legible enough to constitute an accurate representation of the original record.

Three conditions must be met before microrecords can be used in courts of law.

Federal and state agencies often have their own regulations concerning the substitution of microfilmed records for hard copies. The Securities and Exchange Commission, for example, allows filming, provided a duplicate of each microrecord is stored separately from the original document. (Note that here the original document is retained.) Thus, to ensure the legality of all business records on film, attorneys recommend that records managers maintain logs to verify the accuracy of the microfilming process. Also, they should prepare certificates that verify the authenticity of each set of microrecords. A form available from the American National Standards Institute (ANSI) can be filmed and added to the beginning or other designated place in each set of microrecords. In addition, specific state legislation should also be checked. Many states consider microrecords inadmissible in court when the record involved is a negotiable instrument, such as a stock or bond.

Optical disks, which are now serving a growing number of offices as alternatives to microrecords, have only a short history of use and are not yet admissible as evidence in court. To ensure that the data on optical disks may be used in court, backup files should be created on microfilm.

Evaluation of Microimage Systems

Adequate records are needed to confirm how much money is spent on the program as well as on the volume of records created, maintained, and destroyed. Records managers also need information from all departments on how frequently they have used microfiles and how much they plan to use such files in the future. Procedures,

Microimage systems must be evaluated regularly to determine their effectiveness.

too, must be studied. For example, records managers or office managers should know how well the procedures for converting paper records to microform are functioning; how well the equipment meets the needs of the office; and how efficient is the space devoted to the microrecords operations.

The general guidelines for evaluating records management programs, discussed in Chapter 12, can help lay the groundwork for evaluating a microimage system. And in offices where the physical facilities and specialized staff do not permit in-house filming or storage of microrecords, a service bureau needs to be considered. The choice of such a facility can best be made by considering its reputation for service, its turnaround time, the safety (security) of the storage facilities, the ease of storing and retrieving the records, and the cost of using these services.

MICROIMAGE APPLICATIONS

Microrecords have proved to be valuable tools for managing information in all business fields. Applications common to most industries are accounts receivable, accounts payable, and personnel records. In addition, each industry has developed applications to fit its own special needs, as discussed briefly in the following paragraphs.

1. *Government Applications.* The Social Security Administration handles several hundred million payroll earnings items a year on 100-foot film cartridges, each containing the complete files of 1,000 individuals. The U.S. Patent Office has converted more than 20 million patent records to microfilm which it uses to process more than 25,000 daily requests for paper copies of the patent records.
2. *Insurance Applications.* Applications in the insurance industry range from the indexing of policy numbers on CAR systems for immediate retrieval of microrecords to payment histories and policy status records.
3. *Consumer Services Applications.* Many retail stores maintain inventory records on microfiche. Oil and credit card companies keep their customer accounts on microfilm with retrieval time for providing customer service information at 20 seconds.
4. *Scientific Applications.* Hospitals place patients' histories on microfilm to provide reductions in space requirements and savings in

retrieval time. The engineering profession finds many applications for large engineering drawings on aperture cards.

5. *Emerging Integrated Applications.* With ever-expanding breakthroughs in information technology, increasing opportunities exist for integrating or merging information functions in one "super" system. Two examples cited are microfacsimile and micropublishing. **Microfacsimile** or *microfax* is a cross between facsimile and micrographics. A microfax system takes a microfilmed record, digitizes it (converts it to numeric form), and transmits it over telecommunication lines to a hard-copy fax machine's output device. The output is printed on standard letter-size paper or on 18-inch-wide paper for engineering drawings.

Micropublishing is the process of substituting microfilm for paper publications. Specially designed micrographics equipment is used to store and retrieve in an efficient manner book manuscripts, reports, conference proceedings, and telephone directories of major cities. Private firms, too, are turning to micropublishing to produce catalogs, parts lists, instruction manuals, internal telephone directories, and other documents. The cost is low and the high speed of publications eliminates the lag time involved in the production of hard copy. This is true because a computer can update a manual, convert it to fiche, and duplicate a large number of copies overnight. And the weight of eight fiche holding 3,360 pages of information is one ounce. To mail the equivalent information printed on 8-1/2 x 11" paper would cost over $30.[2]

In addition to these applications in large firms, many examples of the use of microfilm are found in small firms and in small towns. In each local courthouse, the county clerk searches microrecords for titles of properties owned; when the records are found, hard copies can be quickly printed. More and more, libraries purchase microfiche that index important items of information. In fact, many libraries have converted their card catalogs of holdings to microform—some with computer indexing capabilities. With such microrecords available, students can quickly locate the names of books and outlines of their contents, trade papers, abstracts, and similar publications. The only equipment needed in these cases is the inexpensive reader.

---

[2]David Barcomb, *Office Automation: A Survey of Tools and Technology*, 2d ed., Digital Press, Bedford, MA, 1989, pp. 235-236.

IMPORTANT TERMS

aperture card
bar coding
blip
computer-assisted retrieval (CAR)
computer input microfilm (CIM)
computer output microfilm (COM)
densitometer
density
flash card
flash indexing
jacket
magnification ratio
microfacsimile
microfiche
microfilming
microfilm cartridges
microfilm cassettes

microforms
micrographics
microimages
microimage system
micropublishing
planetary camera
reader
recorder
reduction ratio
resolution
roll film
rotary camera
service bureau
step and repeat camera
unitized microform
updatable microfiche camera

REVIEW AND DISCUSSION

1. How are micrographics, microimages, microrecords, and micro-forms related? (Goal 1)
2. What four factors are required to ensure that a microrecord is of high quality? Explain the role that each plays in achieving quality. (Goal 2)
3. List the most common microforms and the principal uses and advantages of each. (Goal 3)
4. Describe how computer output microfilm (COM) and computer input microfilm (CIM) are produced. Explain how each saves paper in the office. (Goal 4)
5. In nontechnical words, explain how paper records are filmed. Once filmed, how are copies of the filmed records processed and duplicated? (Goal 5)
6. Describe several common conditions in an office that may prove hazardous to microrecords. What control practices may be considered to overcome these conditions? (Goal 6)
7. Explain the purpose of indexing microrecords. How do indexing methods vary from one type of microform to another? (Goal 7)
8. Explain the various types of equipment required to store and retrieve microrecords. (Goal 7)

9. How does the computer assist in finding microrecords? (Goal 8)
10. If you were responsible for deciding whether to continue using paper records or to convert them to microfilm instead, what points would you consider and why? (Goal 10)
11. Can microrecords of business documents be used as legal evidence? Discuss. (Goal 9)
12. Assume you were assigned to evaluate your firm's microrecord system. How would you proceed? (Goal 9)
13. Cite three uses of microrecords in large businesses and industries in the United States. Can you think of any types of firms that would not use microrecords? Explain. (Goal 10)
14. What role, if any, does microfilm play in the operation of small offices? (Goal 10)

APPLICATIONS (APP)

APP 11-1. Surveying Your Community to Learn More about "Real-World" Microimage Systems

After completing this chapter on microimage systems, your instructor makes this announcement:

Class, if you really want to tie together everything you've studied about microrecords, you need to see a good microimaging system in action right here in our own community. But first, we need to locate such a firm and let it know what information we "newcomers" to microfilming would like the firm to provide.

Think about it and then one week from today I'd like each of you to bring to class a list of questions that we can use to prepare a questionnaire from the class. Also, bring an outline of procedures that we should follow to complete the survey and arrange a visit to a microfilm installation. Any questions?

Comply with your instructor's request. (Goals 4, 5, 6, 7, 9, 10)

APP 11-2. Answering the Question, "Should I Microfilm?"

Five years ago your neighbor, Robin Stiers, opened a small craft shop. Through hard work and good management her business prospered and expanded into many new lines (most recently quilting, woodworking, and metal crafts), each requiring hundreds of small merchandise items. Thus, her inventory numbers in the thousands, which seems to Stiers impossible to control, even though she has five full-time employees and six students who work part-time for her.

During a recent backyard barbecue, Stiers discussed her concerns about maintaining good inventory records. She also asked you about the possibility of considering, in her words, "some kind of microfilm." Her questions to you were very straightforward:

1. Would a microfilm system help me in my business?
2. If so, how would I go about converting my records?
3. What types of equipment and training would be needed? Assume you wish to be a good neighbor and provide answers to Stiers' questions. In order to answer such practical questions, it is necessary to review systems concepts in records management (Chapters 1 and 10) and special records storage (Appendix B). If this assignment is subdivided into major topics as suggested by your review, you should be able to answer the questions asked in a concise manner, such as in outline form.

Specific instructions for completing this Application will be provided by your instructor, either as a group or individual project. (Goals 5, 7, 9, and 10)

5

Records Control

12 ■ Controlling the Records
   Management Program

Part 5 provides a comprehensive picture of the most essential phase of
a records system—control. In this Part, the coverage includes the role
of standards in achieving control in a records system and practical
procedures for controlling paperwork problems in large and small
offices.

12 CONTROLLING THE RECORDS MANAGEMENT PROGRAM

GOALS

After completing this chapter, you will be able to:

1. Define *control* as a process in records management and give examples of two types of control.
2. Explain how the records retention schedule, the records audit, and the records management manual help to provide control in a records system.
3. Identify the two main types of standards in a records system and provide two specific examples of each.
4. List the principal evaluation guidelines used in a records system, and describe how each guideline assists in the control of records.
5. Describe the role of efficiency ratios in controlling records.
6. Identify the major costs involved in a paperwork system and ways of controlling these costs.
7. State the objectives of a forms control program.
8. Understand the main objective in forms design and how each design guideline helps to achieve this objective.
9. Identify principal costs involved in producing correspondence and suggest methods of reducing such costs.
10. Explain the main reprographic process for making record copies and how costs of copymaking are successfully controlled.
11. Describe how a small office can control its records system.

An expert in records management has made this astounding statement: *An average company today doubles its volume of records every ten years.* Assuming this is true, in such companies, records are largely out of control.

We often use the word *control* in society as well as in business where it has important implications for management. In this chapter, control is discussed as a means of evaluating the performance of a records management program.

THE CONTROL PROCESS IN RECORDS MANAGEMENT

As we mentioned in Chapter 1, **control** means measuring how well one's goals have been met. If they have been met, then our system is "under control." Usually we think of *evaluation* as the main element in control because we evaluate a system in order to find out "how we're doing"; that is, how well our controls are working. The control process in records systems is discussed in this section.

Evaluation is the main element in control.

Types of Control

For control reasons, society tells each of us what we can and cannot do. For example, we are not allowed to steal the property of others, harm another person, or avoid paying our bills. To make sure that these controls are maintained, federal and state legislation has been created, the court system has been developed, and law-enforcement agencies have been set up. The Internal Revenue Service controls our income tax behavior; the Federal Communication Commission, our telephone usage; and the Interstate Commerce Commission, many of our business operations. The state departments of education help to regulate the public school systems in each state. Figure 12-1 outlines in broad terms the role that control plays in a system.

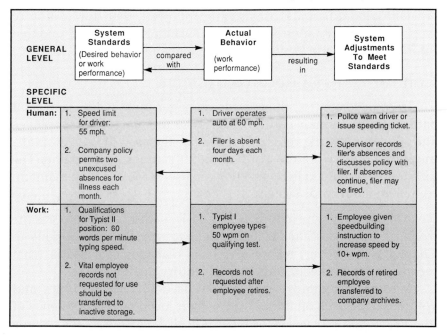

Figure 12-1 ■ Role of Control in a System

In effective records systems, controls are used widely. At the outset, records managers develop policies or broad guidelines for operating their programs. From that point, all of the main elements in the records system are involved with control, as we see in the following list:

All the systems elements involve control.

Systems Element	Control Examples
1. Personnel	Attendance and work performance records; personnel evaluation
2. Space	Janitorial services and records space assignment guidelines
3. Equipment	Machine maintenance inspections and operator training programs
4. Procedures	Rules for storing and retrieving records and for gaining access to files; charge-out and cross-reference procedures; and use of control numbers and passwords in automated systems

These specific controls are designed to keep the system within reasonable bounds. In turn, the records manager must make sure that efficient procedures are consistently followed, that duplication of work and of information stored in the system is minimized, and that information is made available in complete and low-cost form.

Control Tools in Records Systems

To achieve control, the records manager must wage a constant battle against human nature—resistance to change, lax employee attitudes about work, refusal to recognize the need to keep costs at a minimum, and a whole host of "I-couldn't-care-less" viewpoints. The techniques discussed in this section are useful tools to help maintain control in the records system.

First, find out how many records you have; then, schedule how long to keep them.

Records Retention Schedule.
A basic records control tool is the *records retention schedule*, which is defined and discussed briefly in Chapter 6. However, before a records manager can decide what records to retain (keep), a records inventory must be taken.

A **records inventory** is a survey used to find the types and volumes of records on file as well as their location and frequency of use. From such a survey of the records in all departments, the records or office manager hopes to (1) locate duplications in records, (2) determine how long to keep records, (3) decide when to transfer records to less expensive storage, (4) place a value on each record, and (5) decide when to destroy such records. A simple form that combines inventory and records retention information is shown in Figure 12-2.

RECORD TITLE CORRESPONDENCE, PURCHASING					
INVENTORY			**RETENTION**		
DEPARTMENT PURCHASING			APPROVALS		YEARS
RECORD COPY [X] DUPLICATE COPY [ ]			RECOMMENDED (SPECIFY SOURCE) *July 1986 article in Purchasing magazine*		5
VOLUME			ADMINISTRATIVE		
INCLUSIVE DATES	LOCATION	QUANTITY	BY *Jean Mills, Mgr.* DATE *2/12/87*		
			no requirement LEGAL COUNSEL		
1/1/84 – 12/31/86	OFFICE	*118 cu. ft.*	BY *Kevin Norris* DATE *3/10/87*		
			EXECUTIVE		
1/1/79 – 12/31/83	STORAGE	*165 cu. ft.*	BY *K. T. Lee, V.P.* DATE *3/30/87*		
REMARKS *We can reduce total files from 8 years to 7 years holdings and reduce files in office from 3 years to 2 years; 7 file cabinets to be released.*			FINALIZED SCHEDULE		
			IN OFFICE 2 years	IN STORAGE 5 years	DESTROY after 7 years
			BY *Parris Mason* DATE *4/14/87*		
COUNTED BY *James Finch*	DATE *1/16/87*		SPECIAL INSTRUCTIONS *Watch activity of last 2 yrs. in storage. Further reduction of files in storage may be possible.*		
RECORDS INVENTORY AND RETENTION CONTROL CARD					FELLOWES MANUFACTURING CO.
FORM 4797					

Figure 12-2 ■ Records Inventory/Retention Control Card

Courtesy of Fellowes Manufacturing Co.

Combining these two types of information is convenient because the inventory will often uncover duplicate titles of files and records no longer used. Also, information collected during the records inventory helps the records staff, in cooperation with the department or departments in which the records are used, to place a value on each record. The importance of the records retention decision can be noted in this figure by the three signatures of approval (administrative or department, legal counsel, and executive) that are required.

As discussed in Chapter 1, records are used—and retained for reuse—because they have the following values to the firm: *administrative value, fiscal value, legal value,* and *historical value.* Using this set of values as the basis for making retention decisions, the records staff analyzes each record to determine its worth to the information system of the business. From this records analysis, as shown in Chapter 6, the records staff has developed a practical records classification that includes (1) records that are not worth keeping, (2) records to keep for short-term storage (up to three years), (3) records to keep for long-term storage (seven to ten years), and (4) records to keep permanently. Depending upon its use in the office, each record falls into one of the four values classifications and is shown with its approved classification on the retention schedule. A portion of a retention schedule showing the various types of records and the recommended periods for keeping each record is shown in Figure 12-3.

Type of Record	Retention Period in Years	Type of Record	Retention Period in Years
Accounting/Fiscal		Corporate	
Accounts		Annual reports	P
receivable	10	Contract,	
Balance sheets	5	employee	P
Budget work		Stockholders'	
sheets	3	minutes	P
Cash books	25		
Cash sales slips	3	Insurance	
Checks, payroll	7	Accident reports	11
General journal	10	Claims,	
Profit and loss		automobile	10
statements	P*		
		Legal	
Administrative		Charters	P
Correspondence,		Mortgages	5
accounting	5	Personnel	
Correspondence,		Applications	3
general	3	Attendance	
Correspondence,		records	6
purchase	5	Disability and	
Correspondence,		benefits records	8
tax	20	Worker's	
Requisitions	3	compensation	
Telephone records	3	reports	10
*Permanently filed			

Figure 12-3 ■ Part of a Suggested Retention Schedule for Business

PC software, such as InfoStruct, is available for automating records retention schedules, which reduces the administrative time in maintaining and using such schedules. Information for creating and keeping such schedules up-to-date can be obtained from the Superintendent of Documents, U.S. Government Printing Office, which periodically publishes the *Guide to Records Retention Requirements*, and from each of the 50 states. State publications specify, in their statutes of limitations, the time after which legal rights cannot be enforced by civil action in the courts. Once a record reaches an age beyond which the statute of limitations applies, the record has no value as evidence in a court of law.

Records Audit. The records retention schedule serves as one of the main methods used in a records audit. A **records audit** is a regular examination of the records management program to determine how well the program is functioning. From the audit, managers hope to find ways of improving the program's performance. Large organizations may use their own technically trained staff to undertake such an audit, or they may hire outside consultants (usually having more objectivity) for this purpose. Small firms commonly use the services of outside auditors because of the lack of qualified persons within the organization.

A records audit helps to determine how well the records controls are working.

The records audit provides three kinds of information about the records management program:

1. *Information about the present operations,* such as how well the objectives of the program are being achieved; whether written policies and procedures are available and followed by all personnel; and the extent of records management activities as well as the main problems associated with them.
2. *Analysis of the present system and its needs,* such as the layout of the files; the effectiveness of the procedures; the qualifications of the staff; the uses of the available equipment; active and inactive storage systems; and security measures taken for preserving and protecting records.
3. *Recommended solutions for improving the records management program* and estimates of the cost of putting the recommendations into practice.

Records Management Manual. The most important control reference for a records management staff is the **records management manual**, which is the official handbook of approved policies and procedures for operating the records management program. Such a manual also establishes responsibility for the various phases of the program, standardizes operating procedures, and aids in training employees.[1]

The records management manual is the official handbook for maintaining records control.

---

[1] For excellent, detailed coverage of manuals, see Betty R. Ricks, Ann J. Swafford, and Kay F. Gow, *Information and Image Management: A Records Systems Approach*, 3d Ed., South-Western Publishing Co., Cincinnati, 1992, Chapter 19.

The contents of a typical records management manual established by a large firm are listed as follows:

Main Sections	Section Contents
1. The records program	Definition, goals, policies, and personnel responsibilities
2. Main phases of the records program	Records classifications, alphabetic index, records retention schedules
3. Record codes	Records classification codes, retention and disposition codes
4. Types of files in the records system	Subject files, case/project files, special files
5. Retention schedule	Permanent records, semi-permanent records, and short-term storage records
6. Records storage	Department sites, central sites, off-site locations
7. Annual program evaluation	Purposes and requirements of each program evaluation

8. Storage procedures for
   a. paper records
   b. microimage records
   c. automated records
	Preparing records for storage; what to store and when; classifying and coding; preparing cross-references; sorting records; placing records in files; restricting access to records; retrieval suggestions; charge-out system; folders and drawer maintenance.

9. Records disposition	Disposition functions; implementing retention schedules; packing records and labeling boxes; retrieving inactive records from storage; destroying records in inactive storage
10. Records manual: distribution, maintenance, and use	General policies and procedures; records classifications, records schedules, and administrative responsibilities

Other more specific control tools are discussed later in this chapter.

GUIDELINES FOR EVALUATING RECORDS MANAGEMENT PROGRAMS

Much of our everyday life involves evaluation—deciding on the quality of something. In order to evaluate, we use standards that have a direct bearing on the ways our world is controlled. In the office, we find standard sizes of desks, chairs, and paper records as well as typewriter/printer ribbons; and we also find standards applied to human behavior and the performance of employees. In this section, standards are explained and illustrated, with special attention given to the use of standards in evaluating records systems.

> We need standards in order to evaluate records.

Standards in the Control Process

A **standard** is a measure or yardstick by which the performance of a system is rated. Such measures have long been used by industrial engineers to evaluate the *quantity* and *quality* of factory and office work. Professional organizations, such as the Association of Records Managers and Administrators, Inc., the Association for Systems Management, the American National Standards Institute, and the manufacturers of office equipment and supplies have developed a large number of standards, many of which have considerable value for controlling records systems.

Quantity Standards.
A **quantity standard** is a common measure that involves simply counting how many products, sales, or hours of labor have been created in factory and office operations for use in deciding how many quantities *should* be produced. The Consumer Price Index is a quantitative standard for measuring economic conditions; miles per gallon, a measure of automobile performance; amount of employee turnover, an evaluation of a firm's new hires and fires or quitting employees; and par 72, a golfer's performance measure. In the office, the number of letters that *should be* filed, words or keystrokes per minute that *should be* typed/keyed or the number of invoice totals that *should be* verified—all are examples of quantity standards.

Although the development of quantity standards is a complex process, basically it involves selecting a typical (average) worker with the experience needed for performing the task to be standardized. Next, the worker's performance is observed and the amount of work accomplished is measured. After the observations have been repeated a reasonable number of times and a typical work pattern is clearly observed, a quantity standard is created. This standard is then used to evaluate the work of similar employees working under the same type of conditions.

Quality Standards.   A **quality standard** measures how good or how bad the work or the worker's performance is. Developing quality standards requires the use of subjective judgment about intangible characteristics of people and their work. Under such conditions, human bias may enter into the control process, a situation that can be held in check by free and open discussions between managers and workers who share the common goals of performing to the best of their ability for the good of their employers.

Developing quality standards requires the use of subjective judgment.

Quality standards are found in all areas of work and society. Examples include courteous behavior to customers, good taste in dress, the persuasiveness of a sales letter, the neatness of a business report, and the expectations of dependability and cooperation of an employee. Clearly these qualities are not measurable in themselves but are nevertheless important factors to consider in evaluating a worker's productivity.

In order to be sure that fairness is maintained in developing standards, office systems analysts frequently measure the time and motions of office workers and develop tables of standard times for basic tasks to be performed in the office. Standard times have been developed for typing standard-size letters, for the number of keystrokes produced per hour, for line or page counts used in word processing systems, and for records storage and retrieval operations. However, few standards are set for supervisors or managers because their work combines both quality and quantity features. In fact, relatively few standards have been developed for offices compared to factories because factory work comprises a greater number of countable operations and the office is composed of a wider variety of tasks, many of which are management oriented.

Benefits of Standards

Standards provide many benefits to employers and employees. These benefits include:

1. Evaluating employees' performance because the employees know the goals expected of them in terms of volume, quality, and time.
2. Enabling the immediate supervisor to measure the effectiveness of a new employee and the rate of learning that takes place.
3. Evaluating the need for improving records systems and procedures and determining the practicality of installing new machines and equipment.
4. Installing wage-incentive systems in which the earnings of employees are based upon how much the employees produce.
5. Measuring the effectiveness of departmental operations by comparing the work completed with the work standards.
6. Identifying high and low performers.

A review of the benefits of using standards leads to one conclusion: *As a result of properly using standards in the office, better control is exercised over the scheduling, performance, and completion of office work, and costs of office systems can be more effectively controlled.* An additional benefit is improved service to customers or clients by reducing the time needed for processing office work. A discussion of specific standards in the records system follows.

> Sound standards can lead to better records control and, in turn, to lower office costs.

Efficiency Guidelines in the Records System

Even though automation has continued to take over more and more office operations, a vast number of records tasks are manual. In offices where terminals and other automated equipment such as word processors are used, the speed and accuracy of operators are measured and standards are developed from such measurements. More information on such automated systems standards can be found in textbooks on office systems, office management, computer systems, and word processing.

In order to develop practical standards for storing and retrieving records, three main questions must be answered: (1) How long does it take to store a record from the time such storage is authorized; (2) how long does it take to retrieve a record from storage; and (3) what is the expected **turnaround time** (the amount of time required to find and deliver a record to the requester after the request for the record has been made)? Turnaround time standards are largely the concern of automated records systems depending on the speeds of computer storage systems. The other two questions can be more directly related to the published standards for manual storage and retrieval systems,

> The typical records requester wants to know the turnaround time.

such as those outlined in Figure 12-4, which have been developed by large firms and standards associations.

TASK	TIME UNIT (h = hour; m = minute)
Manual Systems	
Code typical one-page letter	200/h
Type folder labels	100/h
Sort 5" x 3" cards	300/h
Sort invoices into 3-digit numeric sequence	1,500/h
Sort coded letters	250/h
Place cards in alphabetic file	300/h
Place records in subject file	150/h
Place vouchers in numeric file	250/h
Retrieve record from color-coded file	2.5/m
Retrieve daily report	.5/m
Retrieve 5" x 3" cards	180/h
Retrieve correspondence and prepare charge-out records	70/h
Automated Systems	
Store and retrieve files: Depends on <u>access time</u> (the number of microseconds of time required of a specific computer to store and retrieve data).	

Figure 12-4 ■ Records Storage and Retrieval Standards

Effectiveness Measures. *The most important test of any records system is the speed with which the stored information can be located.* Effectiveness standards that are used to measure the ability of a records system to locate such information include:

1. *The number of misfiles,* usually about 3 percent of the total records filed.
2. *The number of "can't find" items,* which one authority suggests is excessive at a 1 percent level.
3. *The time required to find items,* which should never exceed two to three minutes.

At least once a year an office or records manager should check the effectiveness of the records system. In addition to the three effectiveness standards mentioned above, other topics to be included in such a check are the number of records employees compared to the total cubic feet of stored records; the number of records received (in number of records or in cubic feet of space occupied); the amount of space being used for records compared to the total square feet of floor space; how much unused space is available; how often records are requested from the files; how much equipment is (or is not) being used; and how many records have been destroyed or transferred from active to inactive storage.

Efficiency Ratios. In addition to measuring the work of records personnel using the standards similar to those shown in Figure 12-4, office managers and records managers use efficiency ratios to evaluate their records systems. An **efficiency ratio** is a guideline for measuring several aspects of records systems (see Figure 12-5). The

Efficiency ratios give specific information about the records operations.

TYPE OF RATIO	HOW RATIO IS COMPUTED
1. Activity ratio (measures the frequency of records use)	$\dfrac{\text{number of records requested}}{\text{number of records filed}}$ Example: 500 records requested, 5,000 records filed or a 10% activity ratio. (When the ratio is below 5%, all records in the file that fall below 5% should be transferred to inactive storage or destroyed.)
2. Accuracy ratio (measures the ability of records personnel to find requested records)	$\dfrac{\text{number of records found}}{\text{number of records requested}}$ Example: 5,950 records found, 6,000 records requested, or a 99.17% accuracy ratio. (When the ratio falls below 97%, the records system needs immediate attention.)
3. Retrieval efficiency ratio (measures the speed with which records are found and verifies how files personnel spend their time)	$\dfrac{\text{time to locate records}}{\text{number of records retrieved}}$ Example: A ratio of .75 (retrieving 80 records in 60 minutes) suggests an efficient records system and a productive files operator, depending on the type of files and filing conditions.

Figure 12-5 ■ Guidelines for Evaluating a Records System's Efficiency

most useful ratios relate to (1) the **activity ratio**, (2) the **accuracy ratio**, and (3) the **retrieval efficiency ratio**. These ratios are explained in Figure 12-5.

Evaluating Costs

The size of the paperwork problem pointed out in Chapter 1 carries with it tremendous costs. These costs are estimated as follows:

70% Salaries of managers, supervisors, and operating personnel working directly with records
15% Space occupied by records systems, including personnel
10% Equipment used in the records system
 5% Supplies

People's performance has the geatest potential for controlling records costs.

Labor costs represent about three-fourths of each records dollar. Therefore, the greatest potential for controlling costs is through controlling people costs. This cost category includes managerial, supervisory, and operating personnel salaries along with the employee benefits—pensions, social security contributions, and insurance, to name a few.

Records systems studies point out many opportunities for identifying and reducing costs. The steps commonly taken to reduce costs include:

1. *Identifying all the elements in the four cost categories mentioned earlier.*
2. *Assigning cost figures to the elements in the records system*, such as per-hour pay rates for all records personnel and costs of all file equipment and space occupied by the files. Thus, the costs of maintaining typical files (such as five-drawer vertical cabinet files) can be computed and used in many cost-reduction studies.
3. *Comparing the labor costs of storing and retrieving records in the organization with estimated costs of alternate systems.* Thus, we find, for example, that a seven-shelf movable aisle file requires the least space cost, when compared to four-drawer vertical, five-drawer lateral, and open-shelf files.

    Also, studies show that among all the types of file equipment, a 10-foot mechanized (power) file realizes the most labor time savings, when compared to the other types of equipment mentioned earlier.

Costs of equipment, space, and supplies can be controlled by eliminating unnecessary records, carefully supervising the use of equipment and supplies, and by selecting equipment that requires smaller amounts of space. The greatest opportunity for reducing costs of labor can be realized by putting performance standards into operation. The performance of employees can then be measured against these standards.

Evaluating Performance

The attitudes that each records employee brings to the job also affect control. In addition to the time standards discussed earlier, each of the following aspects of human behavior needs to be controlled in the records system:

1. Poor attendance records of workers (frequent tardiness and absences)
2. Excessive overtime work
3. Numbers and patterns of errors in the work of each employee
4. Slow response to work assignments
5. Low morale and lack of interest in the work assigned
6. Lack of concern for, or inability to follow, budget limits
7. Repeated failure to meet performance standards

Supervisors should discuss these performance problems with their employees. By working together in this way, solutions can be developed for increasing productivity in the records system.

METHODS OF CONTROLLING PAPERWORK

From your study of records management up to this time, one point should stand out—*all work in the office centers around records, most of which are paper*. The main point then is that records control systems must be based on methods of controlling paperwork, the subject of this section.

> Records control must be based on controlling paperwork.

At this point, we need to review the causes of paperwork problems as well as to consider suggestions for solving such problems.

With this information in mind, you can better understand why the records manager selects "first things first"—forms, correspondence, and copymaking—in order to control paper records in the office. These areas of paperwork are chosen for discussion because they represent the largest volume and most expensive systems in the records management program.

Controlling Business Forms

The **business form** is a paper record used to record and transmit information in a standardized manner; it is used within or among departments or between organizations. The records manager's responsibilities include controlling business forms since forms are commonly used in every office.

Two types of data are found on a form: (1) **constant data** that are printed on the form and thus do not require rewriting each time by the person filling in the form (such as the word "date" and the phrase "Pay to the order of" on a bank check); and (2) **variable data** that change each time the form is filled in. Examples of variable data on a bank check are the filled-in date, the name of the person to whom the sum of money stipulated on the check is to be paid, the amount of money, and the signature.

Goals of Forms Control Programs.

In large firms thousands of forms are used for recording information. To ensure that these forms are efficiently and economically used, company-wide programs to control all phases of forms work are developed. The goals of such programs are:

1. *To determine the number of forms in each department and how each form is used*. This step occurs as a part of the records inventory.
2. *To eliminate as many forms as possible*. This goal includes locating forms that overlap or duplicate each other, which often makes it possible to combine forms or copies of forms.
3. *To standardize form size and paper quality*, which results in lower form costs.
4. *To ensure efficient design of forms in all types of systems*. Note that forms designed in manual as well as automated systems must be designed by people who apply sound design principles as discussed in the following paragraphs.

5. *To establish efficient, economical procedures for printing, storing, and distributing forms to users.* These procedures should include charging costs to those departments using the forms.
6. *To set up both numeric and functional controls over forms* (discussed later in this chapter in the section "Evaluating the Use of Forms").

Kinds of Forms. Forms come in many sizes and colors and are used for many purposes. *Single-copy forms,* such as telephone message blanks, are used within one department for its own needs. *Multiple-copy forms,* such as a four-copy purchase order set, are used to transmit information outside the "creating" department. Frequently these multiple-copy forms are preassembled packages called *unit sets* that are perforated for easy removal of each copy. *Specialty forms* (such as the continuous forms with punched holes in the left and right margins for use in computer printers) require special equipment for their use. In automated records systems, *soft-copy forms* created by special forms design software appear on terminal screens for the input of data from the keyboard.

Design of Forms. Efficiency in the design of forms is just as important as the efficient design of a house, an office building, or an automobile. In each case, well-tested design guidelines must be applied. In the case of a business form, the designer must understand (1) how the form is to be used; (2) the items to be filled in on the form along with their sequence; (3) the size, color, and weight of the form's paper stock; and (4) the amount of space for each item of "fill-in." This information is obtained from a thorough study of the purpose and use of the form in the office system.

> What's the most basic question to ask before designing a form?

The main objectives in forms design are to make the form easy to fill in, easy to read and understand, and easy to store and retrieve. These objectives can be met by applying the design guidelines shown in Figure 12-6 on the next page. Study carefully the application of each guideline that appears in the right column.

Figure 12-7A (page 305) shows an inefficient forms design that violates most of the design guidelines while Figure 12-7B shows how the design guidelines have been effectively applied. Note that the circled numbers appearing in both figures refer to corresponding design guidelines explained in Figure 12-6. The redesigned form is much easier to fill in and read, as well as much easier to store in and retrieve from a standard records storage cabinet.

GUIDELINES	APPLICATIONS OF GUIDELINES
GUIDELINE 1: Design the form with the user in mind.	**1.1** Use a different color for each department receiving its own copy of the form. **1.2** Use heavy card stock for forms to be used out of doors or subject to large-volume indoor use.
GUIDELINE 2: Keep the design simple by eliminating ruled lines and unnecessary or unlawful information.	**2.1** Don't ask for age <u>and</u> date of birth even when this information must be obtained. **2.2** Place instructions for filling in the form at the top and instructions for its distribution at the bottom. **2.3** Don't request information that may be personal or used for illegal purposes (religion, ethnic background, etc.) **2.4** Don't use horizontal ruled lines when the fill-in is to be typewritten or printed by computer.
GUIDELINE 3: For proper identification, give each form a name (that designates its function) and a number (that shows its sequence within the creating department). Date of form's printing may also be included in the number.	**3.1** Name: Sales Invoice (<u>not</u> Sales Invoice Form). **3.2** Number: S-15(11/91)—to identify the 15th form in the Sales Department last printed 11/91.
GUIDELINE 4: Use standard paper stock size and standard typefaces.	**4.1** Use card/paper sizes that may be cut from standard 17" x 22" mill-size stock without waste. Standard paper sizes, such as 5" x 3", 6" x 4", 8" x 5", 8 1/2" x 11" are economical to buy, use, and store.
GUIDELINE 5: Arrange items on the form in the same order in which data will be filled in or extracted from the form.	**5.1** Information on purchase orders is usually copied directly from approved purchase requisitions. In designing purchase order forms, use the same order of data as the order shown on the purchase requisition.
GUIDELINE 6: Preprint constant data to keep fill-in (variable data) to a minimum and allow fill-in to stand out clearly.	**6.1** Use brown or blue printing on a form to be filled in with black printing, which emphasizes the fill-in. **6.2** Use print size smaller than elite spacing on a standard typewriter or printer, which draws the reader's attention to the fill-in.
GUIDELINE 7: Adapt spacing to the method of fill-in (handwritten or machine) allowing sufficient space. (Computer software controls the spacing on computer forms.)	**7.1** For handwriting, use 1/4" spacing. **7.2** For typewriting or machine fill-in, allow double spacing (1/3"). **7.3** For handwriting or machine fill-in, use double spacing.
GUIDELINE 8: Use the box design for filling in variable data, if possible; and do not require writing if a check mark can be used.	**8.1** Poor design: Married? <u>yes</u> Sex? <u>male</u> **8.2** Good design: Marital Status — single ☐ married ☑ widowed ☐ divorced ☐ / Sex — female ☐ male ☑
GUIDELINE 9: Locate filing or routing information properly to speed retrieval of the form.	**9.1** For visible files, place filing information on the bottom of the form. **9.2** For vertical files, place file number in upper right corner.

Figure 12-6 ■ Forms Design Guidelines

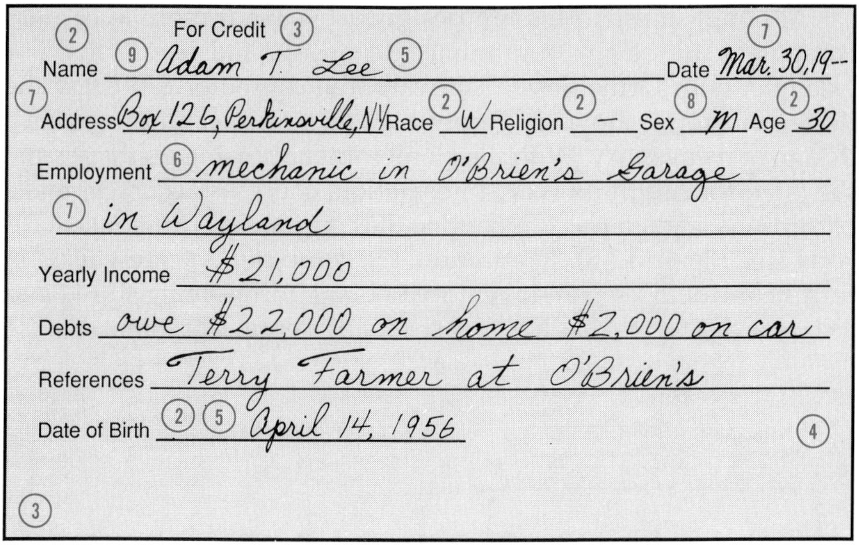

(2) For Credit (3) (7)
Name (9) Adam T. Lee (5) Date Mar. 30, 19--
(7) Address Box 126, Perkinsville, NY (2) Race W (2) Religion — Sex (8) M (2) Age 30
Employment (6) mechanic in O'Brien's Garage
(7) in Wayland
Yearly Income $21,000
Debts owe $22,000 on home $2,000 on car
References Terry Farmer at O'Brien's
Date of Birth (2) (5) April 14, 1956 (4)
(3)

Figure 12-7A ■ Credit Application Form Violating the Forms Design Guidelines

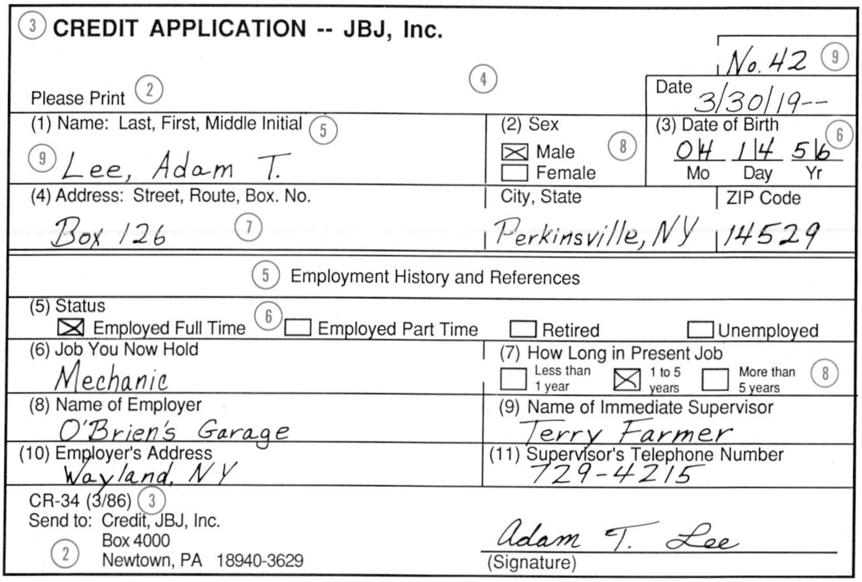

(3) **CREDIT APPLICATION -- JBJ, Inc.**
No. 42 (9)
Please Print (2) (4)
Date 3/30/19--

(1) Name: Last, First, Middle Initial (5)	(2) Sex (8)	(3) Date of Birth (6)
(9) Lee, Adam T.	☒ Male ☐ Female	04 (Mo) 14 (Day) 56 (Yr)
(4) Address: Street, Route, Box. No.	City, State	ZIP Code
Box 126 (7)	Perkinsville, NY	14529

(5) Employment History and References

(5) Status
☒ Employed Full Time (6) ☐ Employed Part Time ☐ Retired ☐ Unemployed

(6) Job You Now Hold: Mechanic	(7) How Long in Present Job: ☐ Less than 1 year ☒ 1 to 5 years ☐ More than 5 years (8)
(8) Name of Employer: O'Brien's Garage	(9) Name of Immediate Supervisor: Terry Farmer
(10) Employer's Address: Wayland, NY	(11) Supervisor's Telephone Number: 729-4215

CR-34 (3/86) (3)
Send to: Credit, JBJ, Inc.
Box 4000
(2) Newtown, PA 18940-3629

Adam T. Lee
(Signature)

Figure 12-7B ■ Credit Application Form Applying the Forms Design Guidelines

Although most forms are designed by hand, more and more computers are being programmed to design and use forms. For example, with forms design software, the computer can draw the design of a form, shown in Figure 12-8, on a screen and store such a design in its memory. With the blank form appearing on the screen, the operator can fill in (key) information, check its accuracy, make corrections, and give a command to the computer to print out a hard copy (see Figure 12-8). In addition, the computer is widely used in forms control to keep an inventory of blank forms being stored and also to order forms that have reached a preset reorder point.

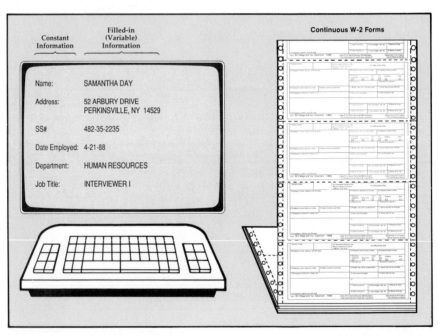

Figure 12-8 ■ Soft Copy Form on a Computer Screen and Continuous Forms for Producing Hard Copies

Evaluating the Use of Forms.   Because the cost of the paper and ink used to print the forms are tangible (physical) items, these costs often receive top priority in studies of records systems. Actually, however, the *cost of using the forms* is much more important and is often estimated to be as high as 40 times the physical costs. Such costs include users' handling and supervisory costs, and costs of acquiring, storing, retrieving, and distributing the form. Each of these costs is

The cost of using forms is much greater than the physical costs.

mainly the cost of various types of labor. Two methods of controlling such costs are (1) *numeric control*, in which a number is assigned to each authorized form; and (2) *functional control*, in which all approved forms are classified by the functions they perform. Such controls are usually centralized in a company; and where duplication of number or function occurs, forms can be quickly eliminated.

Labor costs involved in processing or using the form comprise the largest portion of forms costs, and are obviously where the greatest savings can be achieved. An example of such savings is furnished by a corporation that combined into one form four sets of forms previously written separately as a mailing label, an invoice, an acknowledgment of an order, and a production record. Hundreds of dollars in processing time were saved each year, even though the one newly designed form set cost more than the four individual forms. The new set also required a slight change in office procedures but permitted a reduction of three workers on the office staff.

Purchasing Forms. When new forms are needed, they may be purchased from office supplies stores. Examples of such forms are statements or invoices, telephone message forms, purchase requisitions, and sales receipts. Buying standard forms is less expensive than custom-designed forms provided a standard form meets the needs of the office. If not, then new forms must be designed and produced on special word processing software for internal production or obtained from commercial printers.

Controlling Correspondence

Correspondence represents an important portion of office records. Usually correspondence refers to two types of records—letters that are written to persons outside the organization and memorandums or interoffice memos that convey written messages among departments within the firm. The total system of producing correspondence includes composing the message (dictating, handwriting, or composing at the keyboard), transcribing, and transmitting or mailing the correspondence.

Labor costs of dictating and transcribing correspondence comprise a major portion of correspondence costs and will contribute to the expected increase in the cost of producing letters as inflationary conditions, including higher salaries, continue. To illustrate this steady trend, the Dartnell Corporation of Chicago provides annual reports of business-letter costs showing that the cost of producing a letter dictated face to face in 1960 was $1.83. By 1970 this cost had risen to $3.05, and due to continuous inflation, to $10.85 in 1990.[2]

A recent Dartnell Report shows this cost breakdown:

Cost Factor	Average Cost	Percentage of Total Cost
Salary and time of dictator	$3.07	28.29%
Salary and time of secretary taking dictation and transcribing letter	2.97	27.37%
Nonproductive labor (waiting time, interruptions, etc.)	.91	8.39%
Fixed costs (rent, taxes, overhead, fringe benefits, etc.)	3.14	28.94%
Materials cost (stationery, envelopes, ribbons)	.29	2.67%
Mailing costs (postage, gathering, sealing, stamping, sorting)	.47	4.33%
Total Costs	$10.85	100.00%

Labor represents more than 60 percent of the cost of writing business letters.

In this breakdown, labor costs play the major part as the first three cost factors represent over 60 percent of total cost alone. However, when the same letter is dictated to a machine, thus reducing the amount of labor time, the total cost is reduced to $8.41.[3] Additional labor time and fringe benefits are partially "hidden" in the costs of mailing and sorting.

Reducing Correspondence Costs in the Manual System. The cost breakdown outlined above refers to an average letter, typically 180 to 185 words in length and dictated to a secretary. However, there are many other ways of composing and producing letters, each of which will affect the cost of letter production. With such a wide variety of alternatives, it is important to find the most economical methods of producing correspondence, such as the six effective methods outlined on the following page:

---

[2]Dartnell Target Survey, 1990, The Dartnell Institute of Business Research, Chicago, IL.
[3]Ibid.

1. *Reduce writing time* by using fewer handwritten letters, more form letters, more dictating machines, more telephones and informal replies that are handwritten in the margin of a letter received and returned to the sender, and more routing slips.
2. *Reduce keying time* by using memory equipment; using simple letter styles (the Administrative Management Society states that its simplified-style letter saves 10.7 percent of typing time on a 96-word letter); using window envelopes, which eliminate addressing, editing and proofreading, and retyping; and eliminating retyping of letters requiring corrections by making neatly typed or handwritten insertions.
3. *Reduce rough drafting and reviewing time* for all routine correspondence by devoting more care to preparing the original copy to be printed.
4. *Reduce delivery time* by keeping accurate address lists, including the 9-digit ZIP Code, having routine letters composed by administrative assistants or executive secretaries rather than by their supervisors; and having efficient messenger routes for delivery of mail within and outside the firm.
5. *Reduce reading time* by ensuring that letters are clearly written (to write or call the author asking for clarification means delay and extra costs).
6. *Reduce storing time* by limiting the number of copies of correspondence prepared and later thrown away. Costs are also reduced by eliminating file copies of routine correspondence, transmittal letters, and information-only copies that are seldom required. One study of stored correspondence over a six-month period showed that over 30 percent of incoming correspondence was so routine that it could have been thrown away after it was answered.

Reducing Correspondence Costs in the Automated System. Many of the automatic features of word processing equipment save valuable time for the office staff, such as automatic centering, decimal alignment, indentation, the detection and correction of spelling errors, and the substitution of one word for another throughout the entire stored message.

Automated word processing systems offer many advantages to cost-conscious managers. First, they save the time of dictators or word originators by storing form letters. Rather than compose a new letter each time, these managers can dictate a letter, revise it, store it, and then have it printed. These form letters can be produced quickly by citing key paragraph numbers stored on the magnetic media and listed by number on an index available to each employee. Most important, perhaps, is the cost savings that can result from automated word processing because it represents a more efficient way of employing labor. Word originators can concentrate on producing the ideas while the word processing machines can specialize in producing fast, accurate correspondence stored in memory.

Controlling Copying of Records

A leading reason why so many records are stored in the office is that records are so easy to make. Easy-to-use copiers turn out records by the millions, many of which are unnecessary, adding to the ever-growing cost of running the office.

Reprographics is a term that describes the personnel, equipment, and procedures involved in copymaking. A *copy* of a record is a duplicate of the original record that is made by one of three reprographic processes—carbon copies and duplicating (slow manual processes that are largely obsolete) and copying. Another method of making copies is printing, a highly specialized, technical process that is not covered in this textbook.

Copying machines, or copiers, reproduce records by a photographic process. This process, illustrated by the xerographic method of copying (now commonly referred to as "Xerox"), is often more expensive than duplicating processes; however, the ease and speed of office copier operations make the task of using carbon paper and preassembled carbon form sets less attractive.

Decisions on choosing reprographic machines are based on the following needs of the user:

1. The number of copies needed
2. The need for a certain quality of copy and various colors of copies
3. The ease of making copies
4. The speed of copymaking required
5. Per-copy costs
6. The need for, and availability of, trained operators

For every office cost, there must be an equal- or greater-value benefit.

To control the costs of copymaking, records managers stress the need to be aware of one overriding point: *For every cost originated in the office, there should be an equal or greater benefit.* This means that records employees need to identify all costs of making records (personnel, equipment, supplies, space, and so on) already mentioned. In addition, they should uncover hidden costs, including the costs of ordering supplies and equipment, costs of shelving for storing records, and mailing costs.

Many simple ideas have been developed to control copymaking costs. Examples include selecting the most suitable—and least expensive—method for the copymaking jobs; standardizing equipment, methods and supplies so as to eliminate an unnecessary variety of machine models, which adds to maintenance costs; regularly computing per-copy costs; and charging all copymaking costs to the department involved. Tighter controls over copiers include securing the approval of a supervisor before making copies and installing copiers that require the use of a key or access card to unlock and use the machine. Such a machine may also record the job number, the number of copies made, and a reference for charging the copy costs to the using department. Usage reports can then be regularly processed by the computer.

CONTROLLING RECORDS IN THE SMALL OFFICE

Full-fledged programs to control records, as emphasized in this chapter, originated in large organizations such as state and federal government and major business firms. And it is in these firms that such programs are expanding. However, keep in mind that over 90 percent of all private businesses in the country are small business firms (the local insurance, bank, legal, and medical offices, for example). If we assume that each of these small businesses has one or more offices, then the size of the office group whose records need to be controlled is an important responsibility of records management as a profession. What, then, can the manager of a small office do to maintain control over the records in such an office setting? How can such a person emphasize to all employees the importance of current, accurate information and how essential records are for providing needed information?

All managers of small offices are also records managers.

Typically such questions are answered when the following practices are put into effect:

1. *Assigning the responsibility for managing records to one or two persons who have the greatest knowledge of the firm's information needs* as well as the best aptitude (accuracy, patience, and knowledge of filing procedures) for this type of work. Others in the office should be discouraged from direct use of the files.

2. *Placing the approval for creating all records in a designated person who can analyze the need for such records.* Assistance on forms design, production, and storage can be obtained from printing firms and business forms sales representatives. Usually this service is provided without charge.

3. *Storing centrally a copy of all records and a list of records management practices approved by the office manager.* Such a control set of records is frequently stored in a three-ring notebook. The need for a time-consuming records survey is, therefore, eliminated, but continuous follow-up is necessary. A special section of this notebook needs to be devoted to a chronologic listing of records by time periods showing when they can be destroyed, or where such records are permanently stored.

4. *Classifying all records on the following bases*: (a) their principal use, (b) the frequency of their use, and (c) legal and government requirements for retaining them. At least once a year during a slack work period, the office staff should work its way through the files in an effort to remove all unneeded records.

5. *Cautiously disposing of records so that all records destroyed have been so authorized* and keeping a list of the records and the dates on which they were destroyed.

6. *Using microcomputers wherever possible to help control all aspects of the records management program* and especially making sure that only authorized personnel use the computer files.

To advance, small-office personnel should participate actively in professional associations.

7. *Encouraging small-office filers to participate in professional programs* to increase their understanding of modern storage and retrieval systems. Regular workshops provided by the Professional Secretaries International and the Association of Records Managers and Administrators, Inc., are examples of such programs.

By following the guidelines discussed in this chapter, office managers in small offices will be assured that their records problems can be kept under control. An effective records system should be the result.

IMPORTANT TERMS

accuracy ratio	records audit
activity ratio	records inventory
business form	records management manual
constant data	reprographics
control	retrieval efficiency ratio
efficiency ratio	standard
quality standard	turnaround time
quantity standard	variable data

REVIEW AND DISCUSSION

1. What is the purpose of control in a records system? Cite two examples of records management control and lack of control in your personal and business lives. (Goal 1)
2. How do a records retention schedule and a records audit serve as control tools in a records management program? (Goal 2)
3. Identify the main types of content in a records management manual. How does a manual help a records manager to control records? (Goal 2)
4. What are two basic types of standards used to control a records system? Give two common examples of each type of standard and describe how it "controls" records work. (Goal 3)
5. List five evaluation guidelines that have been developed for controlling records storage and retrieval. How would you, as a records manager, use these guidelines to bring about control over records? (Goal 4)
6. What part does time (minutes or hours of work) play in measuring the effectiveness of storage and retrieval systems? (Goal 4)
7. Of what value are the three efficiency ratios (activity, accuracy, and records retrieval)? How is each ratio computed? (Goal 5)
8. What are the major costs involved in paperwork systems? How does each cost compare with the other costs in terms of its proportionate share of total costs? (Goal 6)
9. How are paperwork systems costs controlled? (Goal 6)
10. Why is forms control a necessary part of a records management program? What specific purposes does such a control program have? (Goal 7)

11. Why is forms design so important in achieving control in a records system? How have computers affected forms design? (Goal 8)
12. What are the principal costs involved in producing correspondence? What methods are available for reducing such costs? (Goal 9)
13. How does the copying process reproduce records? What suggestions do you have for holding copymaking costs in line? (Goal 10)
14. "Even though a small office does not have the specialization needed to bring about strong control over its records, control can still be maintained." Comment on this statement by a well-known records analyst. (Goal 11)

APPLICATIONS (APP)

APP 12-1. Designing a New Money Receipt Form

You work as a part-time employee of your city's recreation center. Yesterday you were asked to design a new form that will serve as a record of all moneys received by the center. The form will be filled in by hand and must include the following information: (1) name, (2) date, (3) address, (4) telephone number, (5) group using the center's facilities, (6) revenue code—a three-digit number to be filled in by the accounting office, (7) amount paid to the center, (8) receptionist's initials, (9) receipt number, and (10) amount of refund, if applicable.

Applying the forms design guidelines presented in this chapter, design a form that meets the needs of the center staff. Be prepared to defend your design as directed by your instructor. (Goals 7 and 8)

APP 12-2. Improving Control in a Records System

You are assistant office manager in a law office involving the legal practice of three attorneys. Over the past month you have carefully observed your records operations, noting especially the following typical conditions:

1. Each of the three typists uses a different style of letter when correspondence is typed.
2. Re-sorting an alphabetized clients file of 500 cards into numeric order by ZIP Code required five hours of clerical time.

3. Over a one-week period, 20 of the last 75 records requested could not be found quickly or were not found at all.
4. Two of the 25 four-drawer file cabinets have not been "consulted" for retrieval purposes for the past two weeks.
5. Each of the six office employees designs his or her own forms and orders them from outside firms on an individual basis.
6. Each employee has free access to the office copier at all times.
7. The most common problems found in examining the files were:
    a. Few guides were used in the file drawers.
    b. Many sizes and types of folders were found with varying tab sizes.
    c. Most of the labels were handwritten, and often hidden from view because of overcrowded file drawers.
    d. Many folders were overcrowded (some contained five inches of filed materials).

Analyze the problem areas cited. What specific control problems do you see? What can be done in this small office to eliminate, or at least improve on, these conditions? (Goal 11)

APPENDIX A

When you were introduced to the field of records management in Chapter 1, you were briefly exposed to the three job levels and job titles in the records management field. At this point, whether it be for supplemental reading following Chapter 1 or for additional information as you complete the last chapter, a more in-depth look at career opportunities in records management and related areas is in order.

Appendix A offers (1) a concise overview of the growth of the information profession of which records management is a part, (2) a discussion of career opportunities and job descriptions at the various job levels in records management, and (3) a look at professional development programs to enhance advancement in the records management field. Special attention is given to jobs and opportunities to advance for students who are entering the world of office work.

THE GROWTH OF INFORMATION PROFESSIONS

By following the daily news reports updating the world economy, you find that one point, among all others, stands out: *The United States is rapidly moving from a production-based economy to one that is oriented to services.* As such, we are, for example, becoming less involved with producing steel and its many by-products and more involved with computers and related information services that computers make possible.

With this new focus in mind, several questions important to your future career might well be asked. They are:

1. What effects are the rapid changes in the world economy having on the records management field?
2. What specific jobs in records management and allied fields are being created (or maintained) in the new service-oriented economy?

316

3. How can you keep up-to-date on career opportunities in records management in order to take advantage of opportunities as they occur?

As you seek answers to such questions, keep in mind that in a service-oriented world, *information is a* (and in most cases, *the*) *key resource*. All successful organizations, successful workers, and successful citizens accept this viewpoint. Further, they recognize that in order for information to be used repeatedly, it must be recorded. Time and time again as you worked your way through this textbook, you were reminded of the vital role that records play in operating business organizations.

Records and their relationship to information systems are briefly discussed next. (Even though some of these concepts have been discussed in one or more of the twelve chapters in this textbook, they are discussed here in the context of careers so you can understand the relationship of such careers to the business firm and the world economy of which it is a part.)

Information Resource Management

As Chapters 5, 10, and 11 pointed out, many new information technologies are rapidly being employed in the operation of businesses. Consider how important to the operation of a business are computers, microimage systems, telecommunications, and many other hardware and software systems. (Notice, for example, the almost universal presence of computers and computer terminals in offices of all sizes.)

Because of the importance of information to the large firm, a new concept of information management has emerged. **Information resource management (IRM)** is dedicated to establishing company-wide controls over the staff, equipment, and services that generate information. These controls include the traditional records management responsibilities for creating, processing, storing, retrieving, and using information. IRM is therefore concerned with not only the necessary paper records systems, but also the growing number of technological developments being applied to handle a firm's information needs. Because information is such an expensive and vital resource, it must be represented at the top levels of management. For this reason, many forward-looking firms have created the position of **chief information officer (CIO)** as the top-level manager in charge of all information services including computers and records management. Such an approach recognizes the importance of information as a costly, important resource. With the expanded processing and use of information, many new jobs in information-related fields are created. Thus, we can see that records management as a part of IRM continues its rapid growth as the need for information increases.

Records Management—A Growing Area

A few years ago records management was known as the efficient storage and retrieval of paper records. With the passage of time and the increase in information technology, however, organizations are growing larger and more complex. As a result, the records management field has expanded to include many diversified areas dealing with information resource management. Examples of such areas include:

- forms and reports management
- correspondence management
- records center operations
- records and information retention
- vital records
- archival records preservation
- integrated technology records applications as discussed in Chapters 10 and 11
- an understanding of the business world's dependence on records in the global community

As more records are produced, more jobs are opened to qualified people. As we see in this section, job opportunities in records management exist in many new as well as in many continuing "scenes."

The Small-Business "Scene". Small businesses require generalists—employees who can handle a variety of office tasks. Take the secretary as an example. The typical secretary in a small firm takes dictation or transcribes dictated messages, answers routine correspondence, screens calls, makes appointments, handles travel arrangements, and *maintains filing systems*. Thus, if you expect to work for a small business, you will be the "files specialist" responsible for paper and automated records along with your other duties.

The Large-Business "Scene". In large firms, much more specialization can be practiced. Within departments, secretaries and general support personnel, such as file/records clerks, may be responsible for all records activities. If the firm has a records management program, these responsibilities may be centralized under a records manager with a specialized staff. The nature of such specialized staff positions is discussed later.

The Professional-Office "Scene". In an increasingly specialized world, we find many professional offices that require the management of their specialized records (see Figure A-1). Brief examples of such office settings are discussed next.

Figure A-1 ■ Staff Members Generating Specialized Records at a Meeting
FPG International/Telegraph Colour Library

Law Office Jobs. As legislation and its enforcement grows and as greater controls are applied to our world, the number of attorneys and law offices grows. Large law firms—some with hundreds of attorneys on their staff—employ records personnel at the three levels (managerial, supervisory, and operating). All three levels require an understanding of general records management principles and practices. Further, such staff members must have specialized knowledge of how attorneys think and work and of the unique characteristics of storing legal records.

Medical Office Jobs. One- and two-physician offices still domi-
nate the medical field although the number of multiple-physician
clinics is increasing. As the number and size of hospitals and medical
clinics expand, their recordkeeping requirements multiply. The
relationship of records to the health insurance field also creates many
new records jobs. Note, for example, these common medical records.
Patient charts are used not only for histories, diagnoses, treatment,
and research, but also as information needed for bill collections. Other
typical records include discharge summaries, operative and pathol-
ogy reports, X-ray information, and health-insurance correspondence. A knowledge of medical terminology and records functions is
especially important to handle such records.

Other Professional Office Jobs. In other professional offices, such
as the government offices at the city, county, state, and federal levels
and offices primarily responsible for technical computer processing,
special records job opportunities exist. Records personnel in city and
county government offices keep track of registrations, licenses, cases,
taxes, and citizen protection. At the federal and state levels, these
same types of records are maintained with additional information—
and additional records—required at each succeeding level. In all four
levels of government, more and more records are computerized and
many are microfilmed. Centralized records management positions
are available in most state and federal offices, which provides a longer
career path for the student to consider. Information on such career
opportunities is available from the administrative services or archives
division in the state capital and from each of the main offices responsible for administering federal agencies.

Students with career interests that combine the computer and
records management must understand basic computer concepts,
especially how automated records are created, stored, and retrieved.
At the same time, they should know the fundamentals of records
control as outlined in this textbook. Armed with such information,
students can gain entry-level positions in large organizations in
which the computer tracks records through the records life cycle and
provides appropriate reports about the records' uses as needed.
Similar information on careers in the library records field can be
obtained from the American Library Association (ALA), 50 East
Huron Street, Chicago, IL 60611.

RECORDS MANAGEMENT CAREER OPPORTUNITIES AND JOB DESCRIPTIONS

The three job levels and position titles typically found in records management are shown in Figure A-2. By advancing from the operating level to the supervisory level and finally to the managerial level over a period of time, a career path for the employee is provided. Thus, a **career path** outlines a typical route of advancement for workers on the job. Knowing that there is opportunity for advancement motivates the worker toward more effective performance; at the same time, a career path piques the interests of students seeking opportunities for professional growth and advancement.

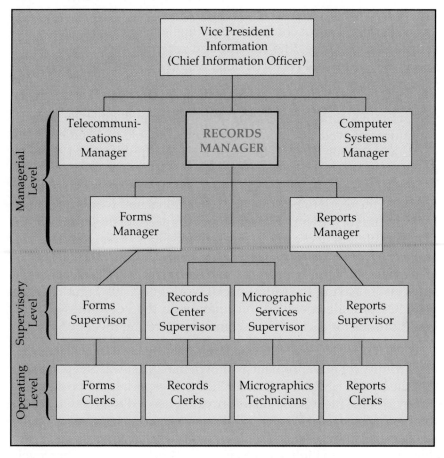

Figure A-2 ■ Records Management Organization Chart

In this section, job descriptions for common records positions shown in Figure A-2 are discussed, and job opportunities including career paths for each of the job levels are explored. However, we give primary attention to the operating level because it is at this level that you will likely enter the work force.

Operating Level

At the *operating level*, as shown in Figure A-2, workers are generally responsible for routine filing and retrieving tasks, and assisting with vital records and records retention. In large organizations, however, other more specialized jobs are found, as explained below.

Job Opportunities. Figure A-3 (on the next page) illustrates a job description for the *records clerk* (sometimes called a *records and information clerk*), the most common operating level position. (A **job description** summarizes the content and essential requirements of a specific job. Similar job descriptions would be available for all positions in the records department.) A *records center clerk* is another typical operating level position in a centralized records management program. Generally, operating level personnel must be able to communicate well orally and in writing, be able to handle details (such as working frequently with names, numbers, and titles of documents), and handle and process records.

Other operating duties assigned will depend on the specific nature of the work to be done, the educational and work experience backgrounds of the worker, and the records needs of the organization. For example, some organizations provide *forms clerks*, *reports clerks*, and *micrographic technicians* at this level to handle technical duties of an elementary nature. Each of these employees works closely with supervisors having the same special work interests. Figure A-4 on page 324 provides detailed information on the key duties and job qualifications for each of these common operating-level positions.

Career Path. Each of the personnel at this work level has the opportunity for advancement as shown in Figure A-2. Keep in mind that the lowest rung on the career ladder is especially important, for it provides the most basic job information needed to understand the total records system. Workers with the motivation to advance up the ranks usually appreciate most their operating-level experience after their promotion to higher levels of work. Workers with higher levels

---

JOB TITLE: Records Clerk   Job Code: 482.10

Date: March 1, 19—

<u>Duties</u>

1. Sort and classify documents and other material for filing.
2. File materials.
3. Retrieve material from files.
4. Maintain charge-out system for records removed from files.
5. Assist in accession, reference, and disposal activities of the department/records center.
6. Assist with vital records.
7. Maintain logs and indexes to provide status of information.
8. Follow-up on materials charged out to users.
9. Set up new file categories.
10. Perform other clerical duties as assigned by supervisor.

<u>Job Requirements</u>

1. Ability to maintain pleasant working relationships with all levels of personnel.
2. Must have good oral and written communication skills.
3. Must have analytical mind in order to analyze data for answers to questions concerning stored information.
4. Must have mechanical aptitude and be able to operate office equipment including typewriters and keyboard data-entry equipment.
5. Some lifting (up to 40 pounds) is required.
6. Ability to handle confidential information.

<u>Education/Work Experience</u>

This is an entry-level position requiring:

1. High school diploma or equivalent; or demonstrated skill to perform the job.
   OR
2. Work experience as file clerk, office trainee, or clerk-typist in lieu of high school graduation.

<u>Career Path</u>

Advancement to Records Center Supervisor

Figure A-3 ■ Job Description for Records Clerk

of education but without work experience at the operating level may, therefore, possess certain limitations that restrict their full understanding of records management programs.

Supervisory Level

Supervisory-level personnel oversee the work of operating-level workers and are responsible for other administrative duties as well.

Job Title	Duties	Personal Characteristics	Education/ Work Experience	Advance To
Forms Clerk	Analyze forms requirements; design forms; revise existing forms; maintain forms; control records	Ability to analyze data; provide answers to questions; work well with all levels of personnel; be accurate in working with detailed infor-mation	High school diploma; some experience in working with records preferred	Forms Analyst (if job is avail-able); Forms Super-visor
Micro-graphics Techni-cian/ Clerk	Prepare documents for microfilming; operate microfilm-ing equipment; develop and main-tain index and retrieval aids	Ability to work well with people; have mechanical aptitude; understand office procedures	High school diploma or equivalent; technical training in microfilming; two years business ex-perience required; records experience preferred	Micro-graphic Services Super-visor
Reports Clerk	Review firm's reports; design report formats; assist forms and records clerks	Ability to work well with people; good writing skills; creativity; self-motivation	High school diploma; some experience in working with records and reports	Reports Analyst (if job is avail-able); Reports Super-visor

Figure A-4 ■ Job Duties, Personal Characteristics, and Education/Work Experience Required of Three Common Operating-Level Records Personnel

Supervisors must work with budgets, motivate and train workers, delegate responsibilities, and evaluate the workers' performance. These duties require the ability to write instructional materials and procedures, to give and follow up on instructions, and to plan and organize work.

Job Opportunities. Supervisory positions in records management will only be found in large organizations with records management programs because such organizations can afford work specialization. As shown on Figure A-2, supervisory positions include *records center supervisor, forms supervisor, reports supervisor,* and *micrographic services supervisor.* Figure A-5 shows a job description for records center

---

JOB TITLE: Records Center Supervisor   Job Code: 1482.00

Date: March 1, 19—

Duties

1. Supervise the work of the other supervisory personnel and of the operating-level staff.
2. Arrange for pickup and transportation of records.
3. Coordinate the creation, receipt, storage, retrieval, and disposition of records.
4. Develop procedures for controlling all aspects of the records life cycle (from creation through disposition).
5. Coordinate the transfer of records from active to inactive storage.
6. Select and supervise staff.
7. Make salary recommendations for records personnel.
8. Review performance of records personnel.
9. Plan, schedule, and assign work tasks.
10. Recommend budget for the areas of assigned responsibility.
11. Perform other supervisory-level duties as requested by the records manager.

Job Requirements

1. Strong oral and written communication skills.
2. Ability to supervise effectively and coordinate the use of resources assigned to the program.
3. Ability to plan and organize work, motivate personnel, and make sound decisions regarding work assignments.
4. Ability to recognize, analyze, and solve problems.
5. Thorough knowledge of records management principles and practices.

Education/Work Experience

1. Minimum of 2 years of college, or equivalent level of related work experience.
2. Knowledge of automated records systems principles and practices.

Career Path

1. Records Manager or Records Administrator
2. Other staff positions

Figure A-5 ■ Job Description for Records Center Supervisor

supervisor, the most common position at this work level. Figure A-6 on the next page outlines key duties and job qualifications for other common supervisory personnel in records management programs. Note that the work of such supervisors requires some college-level education or from 3 to 5 years of closely related work experience. Many times this work experience is obtained as the worker advances from operating levels to supervisory levels of work within a business. Such workers, by the time of promotion, know their organizations

Job Title	Duties	Characteristics	Education/ Work Experience	Advance To
Forms Super-visor	Supervise work of forms clerks; analyze forms and coordinate forms control program; provide forms assistance to departments; select forms clerks.	Ability to work well with and motivate people; good communication skills; broad background in manual and automated forms control practices.	Minimum of two years of college; at least five years experience in business and in records systems work.	Forms Manager or Assistant Records Manager
Micro-graphic Services Super-visor	Plan, organize, and coordinate micro-image systems program; select staff; work closely with department heads and other records supervisors.	Ability to work well with and motivate people; good communication skills; organizational and analytical skills; and mechanical aptitude to maintain equipment.	High school diploma plus two years micro-graphics work experience and four years related work experience.	Records Analyst (if available) or Assistant Records Manager
Reports Super-visor	Supervise work of reports clerks; analyze reports and coordinate reports control program; develop and train reports clerks.	Ability to work well with and motivate people; maintain confidentiality of data; good writer, planner, and creative reports organizer.	Minimum of two years of college; at least five years experience in business and in records systems work.	Reports Manager or Assistant Records Manager

Figure A-6 ■ Job Duties, Personal Characteristics, and Education/Work Experience Required of Three Common Supervisory-Level Records Personnel

well and usually can become more productive sooner than persons hired from outside the organization.

Career Path. The typical promotion route for supervisors in business, industry, and government is to advance to manager. This same principle applies to supervisors in records management programs. In Figure A-2, the career path for each of the supervisors discussed earlier is identified by those positions appearing immediately above on the organization chart.

Managerial Level

The records management program is directed by a *records manager* (sometimes called a *records administrator*), a middle management position. As a rule, both a college degree and considerable work experience in records systems are required for this top position;

however, motivated persons often move up through the "experience" ranks to such a position without the degree. A job description for a records manager is provided in Figure A-7. It shows responsibilities

---

JOB TITLE: Records Manager   Job Code: 2482.01

Date: March 1, 19—

Duties

1. Report, as instructed, to Vice President, Information (Chief Information Officer).
2. Establish company-wide procedures for creating, classifying, storing, retrieving, and disposing of company records.
3. Assist departments to plan, develop, improve, and modernize records availability and maximize service to records users.
4. Coordinate the preparation of records management manuals.
5. Use effectively automated storage and retrieval systems to the extent possible.
6. Coordinate the use of microimage systems throughout the organization.
7. Select methods for safeguarding records.
8. Coordinate the supervision and evaluation of all records personnel, equipment, and procedures with supervisors.
9. Report regularly to top management to justify, publicize, and support the records management program.
10. Plan and develop a budget and cost control system for the records management program.

Job Requirements

1. Excellent oral and written communication skills.
2. Strong organization, planning, and evaluation skills.
3. Ability to lead and motivate people and to work effectively with all levels of personnel in the organization.
4. Professional appearance as evidenced by active participation in professional organizations and up-to-date knowledge of information technology.
5. Sound problem-solving capability.
6. Excellent overall knowledge of records management and its relationship to information resource management.

Education/Work Experience

1. College degree, with MBA degree and five years experience in records management preferred. Must demonstrate that course work has been completed in computer systems, business law, and human relations and have a working knowledge of automated records systems.
2. Work experience may, in some cases, be substituted for college course work.

Career Path

1. Vice President, Information Services (Administrative Services)
2. Vice President, Information Resources

Figure A-7 ■ Job Description for a Records Manager

for (1) many administrative duties (organizing resources, staff pro-curement, motivation, and evaluation; and establishing effective systems), (2) many technical areas (microimage systems, forms control, and records protection), and (3) a growing body of knowledge of computers and other information technology.

Very large firms may also have other managerial-level personnel reporting to the records manager. These positions include *reports manager* and *forms manager*. Candidates for such positions may "come up through the ranks," that is, advance from one or more lower levels in the program; or they may be hired from outside the organization. Typical duties and job qualifications for these managers are shown in Figure A-8. (In some progressive firms with strong information services orientation, records and information analysts as well as an assistant records manager may also be provided at this same work level.) Depending on the breadth of experience and education, a successful records manager may advance to higher levels of information systems, such as director of administrative services, or chief information officer.

Students interested in learning more about such positions should complete more advanced courses in records management and corre-spond with ARMA, 4200 Somerset, Suite 215, Prairie Village, KS 66208.

Job Title	Duties	Personal Characteristics	Education/ Work Experience	Advance To
Forms Manager	Plan, organize, and implement a forms control program throughout the firm; evaluate the work of forms supervisor; select forms staff.	Ability to work well with and motivate people; excellent communication skills; understanding of manual and automated forms systems; good problem solver.	College degree and five years experience in forms work.	Assistant Records Manager (if available) or to Records Manager
Reports Manager	Plan, organize, and implement a reports control program throughout the firm; evaluate the work of reports supervisor; select reports staff.	Excellent communica-tion skills; high level of creativity in designing and analyzing reports in the organization; ability to work well with people.	College degree and five years experience in reports work.	Assistant Records Manager (if available) or to Records Manager

Figure A-8 ■ Job Duties, Personal Characteristics, and Education/Work Experience Required of Two Common Managerial-Level Records Personnel

PROFESSIONAL DEVELOPMENT IN RECORDS MANAGEMENT

A wise business executive once said to a college student, "Once you graduate from school, your *real* education begins." What this statement means is simply this: Each new "hire" must learn all phases of the new job; and once experience on that job is gained, the worker must maintain a continuous program of learning through self-development courses as well as participate in the programs offered—some voluntary, some required—by the employer. Further, this self-development should continue throughout the employee's career. Several types of professional development approaches are available.

Taking Professional Development Courses

At the operating level, in-house courses may be taught by the records manager or supervisor. Courses in forms design, reports management, and records automation may be offered free to the employee on the job as a means of increasing the employee's skills level. With such skills the doors to better work performance and more advanced opportunities open. Similar programs are offered by outside professional groups such as ARMA, the American Management Association, or by consultants with expertise in areas relating to the firm's records program. Educational institutions, such as a local college or community college, offer credit and noncredit courses, often at night, that not only add to the skills level of the employee but also help to accumulate college credit toward a college degree. With a degree, a records management employee may be eligible for positions in management sooner than without the degree.

Participating in Professional Organizations

Many forward-looking employees seeking to advance in the business world belong to professional organizations in their fields.

However, membership alone is not enough; you must take an active part, that is, participate on a continuing basis in such organizations to get the maximum benefit from them. Such organizations provide you with the opportunity:

- to meet professional-minded persons in positions similar to yours.
- to exchange ideas on making your records system more efficient.
- to become acquainted with performance standards recommended by the organization.

- to become aware of, and participate in, the research conducted to improve your records systems operations.
- to keep up-to-date on management thinking and technology affecting the records management field.

Professional organizations of special interest to records personnel include (1) the *Association of Records Managers and Administrators, Inc.* (ARMA), for general records management coverage; (2) the *Association for Information and Image Management* (AIIM), which specializes in microimage systems; and (3) for records personnel in the government, the *National Association of Government Archives and Records Administrators* (NAGARA). Organizations having closely related interests are the *Administrative Management Society* (AMS), the *Association for Systems Management* (ASM), the *Society of American Archivists* (SAA), the *American Library Association* (ALA), the *American Medical Records Association* (AMRA), and the *National Business Forms Association* (NBFA). Information on these professional organizations is available in city, college, and university libraries.

Of all these organizations, ARMA is the most active and most relevant to business records management; it continues to grow in numbers and importance to the records management profession. Typical of ARMA's professional developments are the guidelines for various filing methods discussed in this textbook, job description guidelines for the various records management positions, and the certification program discussed below. ARMA also sponsors technical publications and a series of seminars as well as an annual conference. Locate the ARMA chapter nearest you and attend one or more of its meetings. Guests—as prospective members—are always welcome!

Becoming Professionally Certified

Certification programs are designed to test and verify that candidates successfully meeting the program's requirements have the qualifications for managerial work in the area. Typically, such certification is attained when the member passes qualifying examinations that test the knowledge, skill, and other relevant information pertaining to the professional field.

The certification program in records management is administered by the Institute of Certified Records Managers (ICRM). The CRM examination consists of the following six parts:

1. Management principles and the records management program
2. Records creation and use
3. Records systems, storage, and retrieval
4. Records appraisal, retention, protection, and disposition
5. Equipment, supplies, and technology
6. Case studies

These six parts can be taken in any sequence; each part can be taken over separately, but all must be passed within five years for the individual to be CRM-certified. Candidates for certification must have a minimum of three years' full-time or equivalent professional experience in records management in at least three of the areas covered in the CRM examination. In addition, the candidate must have been awarded a bachelor's degree from an accredited institution before certification can be achieved. In some cases, the ICRM permits the substitution of additional qualifying experience for some of the required education. By meeting these educational, experience, and test requirements, the candidate is given the designation Certified Records Manager, which indicates a high degree of professional competence in records management.

To promote a similar degree of competence in the medical records profession, the American Medical Records Association (AMRA) sponsors its own certification programs. Information on education programs, certification examinations, and career opportunities in the medical records field is available from AMRA, 875 North Michigan Avenue, Suite 1850, Chicago, IL 60611.

Other records-related associations also offer certification programs. ASM, mentioned earlier, sponsors the *Certified Systems Professional* (CSP) program covering systems environments, project management, systems analysis, systems design and implementation, and systems tools and technology. The NBFA sponsors the *Certified Forms Consultant* (CFC) program, which covers such topics as business forms production and materials, forms design, construction and control, business systems and procedures, products, and processing and handling equipment. Other office-related certification includes the *Certified Administrative Manager* (CAM) program sponsored by AMS, and several computer-based certification programs, such as the *Certified Data Processor* (CDP) program developed by the *Data Processing Management Association* (DPMA).

Professional-minded persons proudly display their certification, which sends a strong message to the business public. CRMs, for example, have met high professional standards and are recognized internationally by their profession. Such attainment leads not only to professional advancement but also to respect from their subordinates, peers, and superiors on the job.

SOME FINAL THOUGHTS ABOUT A CAREER IN RECORDS MANAGEMENT

Career choices that affect your future involve one of the most important decisions you'll ever make. Make your decision carefully after considerable study and thought, but in the process don't let the growing number of professional associations and detailed information about careers set your head spinning!

As you prepare for full-time employment (or if you are now employed full time or part time and are seeking other employment), keep in mind these final thoughts about a career in records management:

1. *Information processing is now our biggest industry, nationally,* and records—in whatever form—are storehouses of information.
2. *The persons in control of records are actually controllers of information;* and that means power, for using information leads to knowledge, and knowledge leads to power in society as well as in the workplace. More important, however, is that your career should lead to personal satisfaction. Visit one or more records installations in your area and talk to persons with experience in the field before making your career decision.
3. *The days of full-time, often monotonous, manual filing operations are numbered.* In their place will be greater numbers of automated records systems that are integrated with the information systems by which the organization is managed. The "bottom line," then, is that in records management you can become a member of the information systems team and along with it, enjoy a rewarding and even exciting career. You need not have a business major to pursue such a career. Students with majors in liberal arts, library science, and other nonbusiness fields can find satisfying positions in records management.

4. *Keep up-to-date.* Information on career opportunities as well as new developments in the field can be found in ARMA's publication, *The Records Management Quarterly*, in the *Dictionary of Occupational Titles*, and in the *Occupational Outlook Handbook*. The other professional associations cited earlier also publish valuable periodicals that contain similar information about records management careers. Copies of such publications are commonly found in college, university, and city libraries.

As always, the final decision is up to you, your interests, and your aspirations. Regardless of whether or not you are employed full time in records management, you will still be using records to a significant degree in whatever field you enter. Good luck to you in making your career decision!

APPENDIX B

CARD AND SPECIAL RECORDS

Two types of records are emphasized in this textbook: (1) *paper records* and (2) *nonpaper records*, such as microimage records and the many types of automated records created in computer systems. Along with these two record types, we find a large number of other records that are frequently used in business. In Appendix B, we discuss card and special records that you will use in your personal and professional lives.

CARD RECORDS

If you were to look behind the record "scenes" in every company, you would find much information stored on cards for internal and external uses. (The definition of "card record" and a discussion of its advantages and disadvantages are presented in Chapter 2.) Card records are usually stored in special filing equipment rather than in the folders used in storing correspondence. Usually, we find that card records are smaller in size than correspondence.

To familiarize yourself with a very common card record, go to the card file drawers maintained by your college library. (Even if your library uses automated records, the manual card catalog file probably will be in place for some time.) Select a card record at random; notice that it lists related information on one reference stored in the library and tells where that reference is stored. Notice, too, that the cards are arranged in alphabetic order and grouped by title, by author, and by subject. Figure B-4B on page 339 shows a typical card record for the third edition of this textbook. A group of such library cards—each related to the other—makes up a *card catalog file.*

Card records are described in three ways: (1) by physical characteristics, (2) by use, and (3) by the filing equipment used.

Physical Characteristics

As a rule, paper companies manufacture card records in standard sizes. The most common card sizes are 5" x 3", 6" x 4", 8" x 5", and 9" x 6", with the horizontal measurement of the card listed first. Each of these sizes has been standardized so that the card fits the commonly used storage equipment discussed later.

Cards may be blank or have horizontal and/or vertical rulings, such as those used in accounting journals, sales department quotation forms, and medical patient histories. Cards may also be of single thickness, folded, or hinged to provide additional sides for recording information, as shown in Figure B-1. Other cards are designed as special records and discussed later in this appendix.

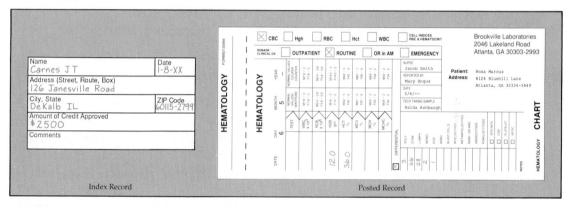

Figure B-1 ■ Two Types of Card Records

Use

Card records that contain information used for reference only are called **index records** (see Figure B-1 for an example). Index records are found in most offices and contain the following kinds of information:

1. Names and addresses of customers, clients, or patients
2. Employee or membership lists
3. Names and addresses of suppliers or vendors
4. Locations of furniture and equipment within the organization
5. Prospective customer lists
6. Most frequently used telephone numbers
7. Subscription lists

For example, an alphabetic card file of names and addresses of customers would be consulted in order to answer such questions as: What is the telephone number of the Baker Insurance Company? What is the customer number of the Kendall Tool and Die Company? and What is the address of Leff and Favor law firm?

A second type of record classified by use is the posted record. A **posted record**, sometimes called a *secondary record*, contains information that is continually updated (see Figure B-1 for an example). This means that the information on the record is added to, deleted, or changed in some other way to reflect the current status. New information is posted on the card record either by hand or by machine. Examples posted records are:

Credit and collection cards	Medical and dental record cards
Department ledger cards	Payroll cards
Hospital records	Stock control cards
Inventory cards	

Filing Equipment

The type of filing equipment used determines how card records are filed. Many card records are filed *vertically*; that is, on edge or in an upright position. A collection of such records is called a **vertical card file**, or simply a *vertical file*. This is the most popular way to file card records—it is commonly used in filing papers as well—and is discussed in a later section of this appendix. A second way to file cards is to store such records *horizontally* in an overlapping arrangement. When the cards overlap, one margin of each card—usually the bottom margin—is visible when the tray in which the card is held is pulled out from the file cabinet. For this reason, a collection of this type of card record is called a **visible card file**, or simply, a *visible file*. A horizontally filed card record need not be—and usually isn't—removed from the file to be used.

The information on the visible margin of the card summarizes the detailed information entered on the other areas of the card. In a lumberyard inventory file, for example, the visible margin of the card may show "2 x 4 Grade A pine," while the remaining areas of the card show a history of the receipts and withdrawals of such lumber from inventory over a period of time. Figure B-2 on the next page shows a vertical card file and a visible card file with one record tray pulled out for retrieving information from or posting information to the record card.

Figure B-2A ■ Vertical Card File

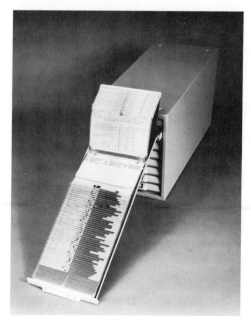

Figure B-2B ■ Visible Card File
Acme Visible Records

A third type of filing equipment used to store such records is **rotary (wheel) equipment**. In rotary equipment, card records are attached to a frame that rotates on an axis like a wheel. (See Figure B-3 for a small, compact desktop unit.) Larger rotary card files are available, as discussed later in this appendix.

Figure B-3 ■ Rotary Card File

In addition to cards, many visible record systems use one-line strips of card stock. The information on the strips may identify a customer name, address, or telephone number or some other readily used item of information from a list.

EQUIPMENT AND SUPPLIES FOR CARD FILES

The equipment and supplies required for card record files depend solely on the type of filing equipment—vertical, visible, or rotary—used. The equipment and supplies used in each type of card record files are discussed in this section.

Vertical Card Files

Remember that vertical card files store records *"on end,"* as compared with the type of storage used in visible systems. Card records stored in rotary wheel files appear in a modified version of both vertical and horizontal files.

To operate an effective vertical card file, manufacturers provide special equipment and supplies, the most important of which are explained here.

Equipment. Cards may be filed vertically in two types of filing equipment: (1) manual equipment that includes drawers housed in cabinets, boxes, trays, and rotating wheel equipment; and (2) motorized or power-driven equipment.

Drawer Cabinets. Perhaps the most widely used housing for vertical card records is the *drawer cabinet*, which has drawers similar to, but smaller than, correspondence file cabinet drawers (see Figure B-4). Filed records rest on their longest edge in these files; thus, the 8"

Figure B-4A ■ Two-Drawer Vertical Card File Cabinet
ATAPCO OFFICE PRODUCTS GROUP

Figure B-4B ■ Multidrawer Vertical Card File Cabinet Showing a Library Card for the 3rd Edition of This Text.

edge of an 8" x 5" card rests on the bottom of the drawer. In cases where card records are used in conjunction with other types of records, such as correspondence, a file cabinet is selected that provides drawers for vertical card record storage and other drawers that accommodate business forms or correspondence. Such cabinets may be purchased in many heights, ranging from two to six or more drawers.

Boxes. Boxes of heavy cardboard are sometimes used to store card records, which are most often found in 5" x 3", 6" x 4", and 8" x 5" card sizes. Box files are commonly used for home and small-office record storage (See Figure B-5).

Figure B-5 ■ Box File

Trays. Card records may be stored on trays, either individually as shown in Figure B-6 on the next page, or as a set of multiple trays placed side by side. Such an arrangement makes the trays portable. Individual trays may be removed from the multiple group of trays for use on the desktop for storage in a desk drawer, or for distribution of trays to various departments in the firm. By mixing card and tray sizes, a variety of card records may be stored in a mechanized unit.

Supplies. In the typical correspondence system, records are stored in folders that act as separators between the many records stored. In vertical card files, because no folders are required, cards are filed

Figure B-6 ■ Card Records Tray Unit

upright and separated by guides into the desired sections. Guides and signals are the main supplies used in vertical card files.

Guides. Guides used in vertical card files are much the same as those used in correspondence files, varying only in size. To separate card files into sections, guides are available for cards filed in drawer cabinets, boxes, trays, and rotary files. Guides also help the filer to file the cards in an orderly fashion and, when needed, to locate quickly the section of the file in which the requested record is stored. In vertical card files, the guide tab is visible, protruding above the height of the card.

The most important consideration in selecting guides is durability, which in turn depends on the type and weight of the guide material. Guides are made from various materials. However, bristol board or pressboard is usually used for guides in vertical card record files. The thickness of the stock used for guides is referred to in terms of points, a point being 1/1000 of an inch. The greater the number of points, the thicker and more durable the paper. Common thicknesses of paper stated in terms of points are shown as follows:

11 points = heavyweight paper
14 points = extra heavyweight paper
17 points = bristol board
25 points = pressboard
35 points = fiberboard

Vinyl guides in bright colors are also available for vertical and rotary files. Vinyl guides are washable and will not warp, crack, or become dog-eared from extensive use—problems that may develop if paper-based guides, such as bristol board or pressboard products, are used.

Signals. **Signals** are special markers used for drawing immediate attention to specific records. Two types of signals are used in vertical card files to convey to the filer special information about the cards. (See Figures B-2B and B-9 for illustrations of signals). Special add-on or clip-on markers of movable transparent or opaque materials are frequently attached to the top of selected cards. In other cases, a distinctive color is placed on the signal, on the tab, or on the cards themselves. Different colors may be used to show different types of information on the marked cards. For example, the names of customers in a certain geographic area may be indicated by green cards.

Visible Record Files

The kinds of equipment and supplies used for visible records depend on the following factors: (1) the requirements of the organization as reflected by the number of cards or strips to be filed; (2) the importance of their location to their use; (3) whether the files must be portable, that is, able to be carried from one location to another for use; (4) the frequency of use; and (5) whether the visible records are to be used for reference or for posting purposes.

Equipment.   The main types of visible card equipment are (1) card visible files and (2) reference visible files. Each type of equipment is discussed in this section.

Visible Card Files.   A number of different forms of card visible files, often called *posting visible files*, are available. The most frequently used visible equipment is the cabinet with shallow drawers or trays, each one labeled to show the contents. Each drawer contains a number of overlapping cards held horizontally by hangers or hinges or in slots called *pocket holders*. Figure B-7A shows such equipment with drawers that can be pulled out and down but that remain attached to the cabinet by a hinge. Card holders are attached to the trays by wires that snap in and out of the drawer. Cards are held in by slots in the holders, and both sides of the card may be used.

By raising the set of cards preceding the card that requires posting, the filer can quickly post the desired information on the card. Note

Figure B-7B that shows an example of the contents of the visible margin on such a card. In this case, the name identifies a customer in the credit department of a manufacturing company.

Figure B-7A ■ Visible Record Cabinet
Acme Visible Records

Customer Name	Customer No.
WELTE SHOE CO	03-30-24

Figure B-7B ■ Contents of Visible Margin on a Card

Cards are inserted into the holders so that one or two lines of each card are visible. Pocket holders are slotted to accommodate cards of various sizes. Some holders have transparent edge protectors, while some have the complete pocket made of transparent material. This see-through covering protects the edge or the entire card from wear, tear, moisture, and dirt.

When portability of cards is a factor and the volume of cards to be filed is small, or when many employees need to post simultaneously, hinged pocket books may be used instead of other methods of storage. These card books may have fastenings at the top of the cards for ease in posting, or the cards may be snapped in and out at any point. Loose-leaf books with removable panels of cards provide portability and contain much data in a small space. Labeling of the contents of the book is done on the back binding.

Racks and cabinets are used to house card books. On the racks, books stand in an upright, closed position with the aid of bookends. Cabinets have compartments, and the books are stored in an upright position. The cabinet may revolve so that several persons can refer to the information.

Reference Visible Files. If only one line or a few lines of information are needed for reference purposes, using an entire card to record a small amount of information is unnecessary and wasteful. In such cases, *reference visible files* are used, and information is placed on narrow strips of card stock that are inserted into holders attached to panels, trays, or frames. Figure B-8 shows one-line strips of information on panels attached to a revolving center post.

Figure B-8 ■ Visible Strip File Desk Stand
Kardex Systems, Inc.

Supplies. Visible records housed in horizontal trays do not need guides. When the trays are pushed into their cabinets, labels on the front of the trays indicate the range of the tray contents. Thus, the only guides used for visible records are those found on strip file panels in vertical equipment such as that shown in Figure B-8. Guide tabs at the sides of the panels are the primary dividers that indicate the range of the names on each panel.

Visible card files also use signals or markers that call attention to some specific condition or content of the card. Signals (also called *flags*) that may be used with visible equipment include colored card stock, special printed edges that may be cut in various ways, and removable metal or plastic tabs of various colors and shapes (see Figure B-9).

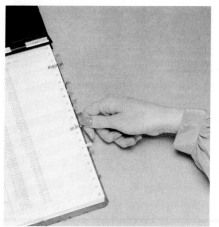

Figure B-9 ■ Flags (Signals) Used in Visible Cards Systems
Photos courtesy of Ames Color-Files, division of Ames Safety Envelope Company, Somerville, Massachusetts

Rotary (Wheel) Files

Two types of rotary files are used for storing card records: (1) manual rotary files and (2) motorized rotary files. Each is discussed in this section.

Manual Rotary Files. *Manual rotary files* provide an arrangement in which the card records are attached directly to the equipment frame. Such equipment provides storage for card records and guides that are snapped into place over a center rod, and the records are kept within bounds by the outer rims of the wheel. Wheel files may contain one or more rows of card records side by side as shown in the compact desktop rotary card file in Figure B-3 on page 338. The entire file is rotated by hand to the position of the desired record.

Larger versions of manual rotary files, called *rotary file cabinets*, are also available. These cabinets rotate horizontally around a hub, as shown in Figure B-10, an arrangement that permits several persons to access the file at the same time. Records kept in such files require less floor space than would be needed to house the same number of records in drawer cabinets. Such files, placed between workstations, eliminate walking because the cards can be rotated to the persons who use them. Fewer misfilings occur because fatigue, discomfort, and poor visibility (often found when using drawer cabinets) are reduced. Also, records need not be duplicated because one set of records can serve several departments; and sliding covers with locks are available on some models for making the records more secure. Because rotary files actually store records in a vertical fashion, they use the same kinds of vertical file supplies (cards, guides, signals) that have been specially designed for the equipment in which they will be stored.

Figure B-10 ■ Multitiered Rotary File with Shelf for Cards
Delco Assoc., Inc.

Motorized Rotary Files. *Motorized* or *power-driven rotary files* provide shallow trays on movable shelves for the storage of card records. Such shelves are powered by an electric motor and mounted on a frame inside the cabinet using a revolving motion similar to the operation of a Ferris wheel. Any shelf can be brought to the front of the machine by pressing one or more of a series of buttons mounted on a control panel. Figure B-11 illustrates such a motorized unit with trays of cards appearing in a horizontal side-by-side arrangement. The trays can, if desired, be removed from the shelves; or the operator may consult the card records without removing any of the trays from the unit.

Figure B-11 ■ Motorized Card Record Storage Unit
Kardex Systems, Inc.

SPECIAL RECORDS

The two most common types of records discussed earlier in this book are correspondence and business forms. As a rule, these records appear in paper form, frequently in 8-1/2" x 11" size for letters and many business forms, or as heavier card stock as discussed earlier.

Special records are records of unconventional size, shape, or weight commonly used in business and professional offices. Such records often cause difficulty for the filer who does not have an effective procedure for storing these items so that they can be found quickly and also preserved for later use. Therefore, efficient storage procedures for each type of special record are needed and are discussed in the first part of this section. The second part briefly reviews storage and retrieval procedures for special records.

METHODS OF STORING SPECIAL RECORDS

Many of the special records discussed in this section have been created because of the advances made by technology in the office. Thus, automated offices produce large volumes of computer output that require special types of files, and microfilm technology has created its own types of special records. These records and their storage systems are discussed in Chapters 10 and 11 respectively.

In traditional offices, special records continue to be produced and used in large numbers. These records are *special* because they differ in size, shape, and construction from the regular office records and are stored in specialized equipment. The nature of the information, especially the manner by which the information is retrieved, tells us how these records should be stored.

Accounting Records

Noncomputerized offices in small firms continue to use large numbers of records that are prepared by hand or by relatively simple machines, such as typewriters and accounting machines. Of special importance are those records, such as cash receipts journals and ledgers, that store administrative information about the accounting system—a system that is vital to the survival of the organization.

Although automated operations in banks and other financial institutions are changing the check-handling procedures, the typical method of handling canceled checks still requires many manual operations. Many banks still return canceled checks to their customers along with a list of all deposits and withdrawals.

Business firms usually store returned checks in small drawers housed in vertical records storage equipment. Usually checks are stored according to the number on the check, which is typically chronologic. Lightweight portable boxes can be used for storing a small volume of checks. Figure B-12 shows typical equipment for storing checks.

Figure B-12 ■ Check Storage Equipment
Kardex Systems, Inc.

Another common accounting record—the **voucher**—is used to confirm that a business transaction has occurred. Vouchers are usually larger than checks but smaller than correspondence and are stored alphabetically or numerically in special equipment in keeping with the size of the vouchers. For example, vouchers 8" x 5" in size would be stored in drawers of a corresponding size near the workstation.

Drawings

Large organizations with highly specialized departments require a wide variety of nonstandard records. For example, art and advertising departments store posters, art prints, tracings, and other types of graphic art. Also, engineering departments commonly use blueprints, charts, maps, and other types of drawings, some of which are very large and bulky. Maps and engineering drawings are often rolled and stored in pigeon-holes for convenience. However, this practice is not recommended because rolled records are difficult to use after they have been rolled for any length of time.

For storing large flat items, two alternatives are recommended: (1) placing the records in flat shallow drawers in cabinets made for this purpose, or (2) hanging the items vertically using hooks or clamps. Figure B-13 shows a type of flat-file cabinet commonly used for storing bulky records. The labels on the drawers show the range of the contents, arranged either by alphabet or number.

Figure B-13 ■ Large Records Flat-File Cabinet

Legal Documents

Many of the records maintained in the offices of attorneys are different in size from those found in nonlegal offices. In fact, 8-1/2" x 14" paper continues to be called "legal size" and is widely used for legal records, such as abstracts, affidavits, certificates of incorporation, contracts, insurance policies, leases, and mortgages. In addition to the use of legal-size vertical file cabinets, frequently legal-size records are stored in document boxes on open shelves. Numbers are assigned to the boxes, and an alphabetic card file and accession book are required as discussed in Chapter 9. These boxes are labeled appropriately to show their contents.

Magnetic Records

In addition to the special records stored on paper, many offices store information on magnetic records. Perhaps the most commonly used magnetic records are the cassettes and other media used for storing dictation. A growing number of records stored on tape, disks, and diskettes are used in data processing and text/word processing systems. Chapter 10 addresses these automated systems records in detail.

Cassettes. **Magnetic tape cassettes** are small containers in which magnetic tape is stored for the convenience of the dictator (word originator) and transcriptionist. Such tape provides immediate playback for the word originator to review. It also allows the transcriptionist to key the dictation to produce acceptable hard copy. Also, cassettes protect magnetic records against dirt and destruction. Several equipment options for storing cassettes may be used:

1. Albums or binders with molded plastic page forms that can hold six or eight cassettes on each side of a page are available (see Figure B-14A on the next page). Cassette albums and binders are stored on shelves.
2. A hanging panel may be used that fits into conventional desk drawers. Each panel holds six or eight cassettes.
3. Carousels (rotary storage devices) may be chosen. Carousels are often placed on desk tops for easy reference (see Figure B-14B on the next page).
4. Small shelves into which cassettes will slide are also popular. Cassettes are housed in their own plastic holders.
5. Desk or table drawers or cabinets are also used for cassette storage. Drawers having dividers are available to separate cassettes (see Figure B-14C on the next page).

Each of the pieces of equipment discussed in this section must have labels affixed to an outer surface to show the contents of the cassettes being stored. Labeling may be by subject, name of the person dictating, name of the person transcribing, date of the dictation, or the cassette number. Cassettes are usually labeled on their flat, broad surfaces; however, the edges of the plastic containers holding cassettes may be correspondingly labeled so that each cassette can be quickly retrieved and later returned to its proper place in the file.

Other Dictating Machine Records. In addition to cassettes, plastic belts and disks are used to record and store dictation. After these magnetic records have been transcribed by the word processing operator or typist, they are usually retained for a specified period of time. Temporary storage is usually provided in boxes, drawers, or folders and arranged chronologically by date of dictation or by record number. Sometimes, too, these "used" records are arranged alphabetically by the names of the dictators.

Figure B-14A ■ Cassette Storage Album

Figure B-14B ■ Cassette Storage Carousel

Luxor Corporation

Figure B-14C ■ Cassette Storage Drawer

Luxor Corporation

Photographic Records

Cameras are used to photograph many types of records, some of which are highly specialized. However, only the most common photographic records are discussed here.

Films and Filmstrips. Motion-picture films are commonly placed in canisters that are stored vertically in open wire racks. These photographic records may be stored alphabetically by subject or film title or numerically by film number. Thus, when a numeric storage system is used, an alphabetic card file is required for reference to titles or subjects; and an accession book is necessary for assigning numbers. The equipment used for storing motion-picture films is similar to that used for storing computer magnetic tapes shown in Figure 10-7, page 242.

Usually filmstrips are kept in cabinets with shallow drawers to hold the small metal containers. The drawers may have compartments formed by adjustable or fixed dividers. The top of the small container is labeled for identification of the contents in much the same way the large motion-picture film canisters are labeled. Like films, filmstrips are stored using subject, alphabetic title, or filmstrip number; and each drawer is labeled to show the range of its contents.

Slides. Slides are usually stored in boxes with compartments, or in ring binders. Oblong or rotary slide trays that fit into a projector may store in sequence all slides relating to one subject, with the tray being labeled to indicate the subject. Numbered slots in drawers in which slides may be stored correspond to numbers written on the slides. In addition, a master list of numbers with slide identification is kept either on cards, on separate sheets of paper, or on the computer.

Published Materials

Large organizations maintain extensive libraries related to the special interests and needs of their personnel. Small offices, too, store many types of published materials. The most common methods of storing published materials, such as books, catalogs, periodicals, and pamphlets, are discussed briefly in this section.

Books. To save office space and still provide convenient access, books should be stored in bookcases or on other types of shelves. Books may be arranged alphabetically by book titles or by the names of their authors, or numerically by the decimal method. As a rule, books are labeled on the back binding or spine. Frequently used reference books, such as dictionaries and secretarial office manuals, are kept at the workstations where the reference books are used. Charge-out procedures, similar to the procedures used for other types of records discussed in Chapter 6, should be developed to ensure proper control over these important and expensive records.

Catalogs. Catalogs are highly useful references and need to be carefully stored in the office. Office equipment catalogs, educational program catalogs, and catalogs representing a growing number of mail-order firms are examples of the types of printed publications that require storage in the office.

Catalogs are best housed on shelves or in bookcases. The following procedures have proved effective for storing catalogs:

1. *Place the catalogs in alphabetic order* by the names of the firms issuing the catalogs. Also, prepare a separate subject card file listing the names of all firms issuing catalogs on each specific subject.
2. *Assign numbers to the catalogs* according to the order of their receipt and store them numerically. An accession book to use when assigning numbers and a card file are necessary. Such a file contains (a) cards showing the names of the firms in alphabetic order with their assigned numbers and (b) subject cards listing by number all catalogs on a given subject.

Frequently the publishers of catalogs send supplements to their catalogs rather than publish an entirely new catalog, which saves much publishing and mailing expense. Because these supplements often contain only a few pages and therefore are quite flimsy, file folders are used for storage to provide the needed rigidity. When this practice is used, the folders are labeled according to the storage system used (alphabetic, numeric, etc.) and stored next to the respective catalogs.

Periodicals. Current issues of magazines are usually kept in stacks and arranged in chronologic order by date of publication, with the most recent issue on top. The order of the stacks on the shelves is usually alphabetic by magazine name. Sturdy fiberboard or metal boxes with open backs may also be used to house current issues to keep them from becoming worn and dusty. Some publishers sell boxes with the names of their magazines already printed on them, in which case only date information need be added to the label on the back of the box. These boxes are stored chronologically by date of publication.

Pamphlets. Because they lack rigidity, pamphlets cannot be stored satisfactorily side by side on shelves or in drawers. Therefore, storing pamphlets in folders according to subject is recommended. Pamphlet folders are stored in alphabetic order by subject.

PROCEDURES FOR STORING AND RETRIEVING CARD AND SPECIAL RECORDS

Steps required to store and retrieve special records are the same steps needed to store and retrieve other manually processed records. However, special records have certain unusual features that more traditional records do not possess. These special features affect the procedures for storage and retrieval. In this section, an abbreviated discussion of storage and retrieval procedures is presented.

Inspecting

Inspecting special records requires much more time than does the inspection of regular paper records. This is the case because many special records are used with mechanized equipment that will not function properly with damaged records. Inspection of a special record means checking to see if the record is in good condition or damaged as well as determining if it is complete in all respects. Also, such a record should be inspected to be sure that it is clean, properly encased (if a protective cover is required), and that the record bears a cross-reference to its source if it is a partial copy or excerpt of an original.

Indexing

The indexing step requires carrying out the same procedures that are used to index and classify regular paper records. The filer analyzes the contents of the record to determine under what category the record should be classified and stored.

Coding

Because of the wide variety of special records, coding procedures will vary. For example, coding could involve affixing a number on a film canister, labeling envelopes containing photographs by subject, or affixing labels to the backs of books. The purpose of coding, however, is always the same—to make the task of storing records easy as well as to speed up the task of replacing in storage a record that has been charged out and returned.

Cross-Referencing

In some cases, special records do not require cross-references. Such records are unique, and there may be only one place for them to be stored. If, however, a record is requested by an alternate name, by a subject, or by number, a cross-reference should be prepared and inserted in the alphabetic card file or the subject listing in the usual manner. Chapters 2 and 3 contain detailed information on cross-referencing procedures.

Sorting

If a number of special records of the same type must be stored, a separate sorting procedure will save time when the filer takes the records to the equipment to be stored. For instance, if 15 numbered filmstrip boxes need to be stored, arranging such boxes in sequential order in a carrying tray would save time at the storage cabinet.

Storing

Special records should be stored as soon as possible after they are approved for storage. Because they are unusual and often bulky, special records may be unsightly and give a cluttered, inefficient appearance to the office if they are allowed to accumulate over long periods of time. Care must be taken to turn all special records of the same type in the same direction (covers of books facing forward and spines of magazines readable from the same direction, and so on). Because of the varying sizes of special records, as discussed earlier, large records frequently must be stored alongside small records. Thus, the filer needs to be alert to see that the smaller records do not get crushed among the larger ones.

Retrieving

The efficient retrieval of special records will follow these steps:

1. Whenever a special record is removed from storage to be used by someone other than the filer, a requisition form should be presented.
2. After the record is found and removed from storage, an OUT or IN USE indicator is inserted in place of the borrowed item.

With this information on hand, the office manager or records manager knows where every record can be located, when it was taken from storage, and when it is due to be returned.

SELECTING EQUIPMENT AND SUPPLIES FOR CARD AND SPECIAL RECORD FILES

Before equipment and supplies can be properly selected for *any* record file, the system in which the records are used, stored, and retrieved must be carefully studied. In such a study the records manager must ask questions, such as the following, in order to obtain information needed in decision making:

1. What kind of information is needed, and why is this information stored on cards (or special records)? Is there a better type of record form to use?
2. Who uses these records and how frequently?
3. How are the records used, stored, and retrieved?
4. What volume of records are used?
5. How much time will the equipment and supplies be used?
6. What type of records protection is required?
7. How much space is available for the equipment and supplies?

The same sources of information needed to select equipment and supplies, in general, can be used for selecting card and special record files.

GLOSSARY

accession log — A serial listing of numbers assigned in a numeric system.

accuracy ratio — A measure of the ability of records personnel to find requested records.

active record — A record that is used three or more times a month.

activity ratio — A measure of the frequency of records use.

alphabetic file — An alphabetic list or file containing names of correspondents and any subjects used in a numeric file with the assigned numbers indicated.

alphanumeric — A coding system that is a combination of alphabetic and numeric characters.

aperture card — A standard data processing punched card with a precut opening (aperture) for mounting microfilm.

archive record — An historical record preserved permanently by the organization.

archives — A permanent storage place for records.

ARMA (Association of Records Managers and Administrators, Inc.) — The professional organization for the records management field.

ASCII — An acronym for the American Standard Code for Information Interchange. The code assigns specific numeric values to the first 128 characters of the 256 possible byte combinations.

audio-response system — A form of computer input that uses a computer-activated voice to answer questions using a vocabulary stored in the system.

automated records system — An information system in which all or most of the records functions are controlled by the computer or related equipment.

automation — A process that operates automatically and regulates or controls itself.

bar coding — A type of binary code used on roll film and microfilm that is used to retrieve microrecords.

bellows (expansion) folder — A folder that is made with creases along its bottom and sides so that it can expand like an accordion.

binary digit (bit) — The coding unit used to record information in the computer. A binary number system allows the computer to perform mathematical operations.

blip — A rectangular mark placed below or above each microimage and used for retrieving microrecords in a fully automated system.

block numeric storage — A numeric storage method based on the assignment of groups of numbers to represent primary and secondary subjects.

business form — A paper record used to record and transmit information in a standardized manner.

byte — The smallest addressable unit of information a computer can process. A byte is composed of eight bits.

caption — The content identifying information on a label.

card record — A piece of card stock used for storing information that is referenced often.

career path — A typical route of advancement for workers on the job.

charge-out — A procedure used to account for records that are removed from storage.

charge-out log — A form for recording what record was taken, when it was taken, who took it, the date borrowed, the due date, the date actually returned, and the date an overdue notice was sent.

chief information officer (CIO) — The top-level manager in charge of all information services including computers and records management.

chronologic storage — A method for filing records by calendar date. The most recent date is *always* on top.

coding — The physical marking of the record to indicate by what name, number, or subject it is to be stored. The key unit is underlined, and each succeeding unit is numbered.

color accenting — A method by which different colors are used for the different supplies in the storage system.

color coding — A method by which different colors are used to divide the alphabetic sections in the storage system.

communicating word processor — A form of electronic mail in which the processor is capable of keyboarding, editing, and transmitting its output over telephone lines.

computer input microfilm (CIM) — The process of taking plain language (uncoded) data on microrecords for translation into computer-language code for storage on magnetic tape as input to a computer.

computer output microfilm (COM) — The process of photographing and reducing to microimage form the information stored in digital (binary) form within the computer or on magnetic tape.

computer record — The total collection of fields or specific pieces of information about one person or item.

computer-assisted retrieval (CAR) — The process of merging the computer (for great speed in storing and searching data) with microimage systems.

computer-based message system (CBMS) — A form of electronic mail in which a computer sends and receives voice messages electronically.

consecutive numbering method — Numeric storage in which consecutively numbered records are arranged in ascending number order—from the lowest to highest number.

constant data — Data on a form that are printed on the form and thus do not require rewriting each time the form is filled in.

control — The managerial function that measures how well one's goals have been met.

cross-reference — An aid used to find a record stored by a filing segment other than the one selected for storing.

database — A collection of facts or information organized especially for rapid search and retrieval. A database has common terms and processes.

database structure — The database structure defines the categories of information that make up the database.

decimal-numeric — A system for coding records in units of ten. An unlimited number of subdivisions is permitted through the use of digits to the right of the decimal point.

densitometer — A device that measures the contrast between the dark and light areas on microfilm.

density — A numeric measure of the contrast between the dark and light areas on microfilm.

desktop publishing (DTP) — A word processing software package that provides for writing, assembling, and designing publications through the use of microcomputers.

direct access — Reference to a record is made by going directly to the file—an index is not necessary.

duplex-numeric — A coding system using numbers with two or more parts separated by a dash, space, or comma. An unlimited number of items may be included under any one division or subdivision.

efficiency ratio — A guideline for measuring several aspects of records operations.

electronic funds transfer system (EFTS) — A form of bank automation in which customers request information about their checking and savings accounts as well as withdraw money and make deposits.

electronic mail — A means of transmitting records over telephone lines or relaying messages via satellite network.

electronic mailbox — The storage location for messages received and transmitted in a computer-based message system.

encyclopedic arrangement — A subject filing arrangement in which the main subjects are arranged in alphabetic order with their subdivisions also arranged alphabetically.

external record — A record that is created for use outside the firm.

facsimile — The most popular form of electronic mail in which a machine is attached to the telephone line to send a message to its destination (a second facsimile machine); also known as *fax*.

field — A combination of characters to form words, numbers, or a meaningful code.

file — A collection of related records in a database.

file management database — A simple database used to keep track of one or two relevant facts, such as names and addresses in a customer mailing list.

filename — A unique name given to a file stored for computer use; it must follow the computer's operating system rules.

filing method — The way records are stored in a container. The four major methods are alphabetic, subject, numeric, and geographic.

filing segment — The name by which the record is stored and requested.

fine sorting — Arranging records in exact sequence prior to storage.

flash card — A kind of tab or guide for a microfilm record file with identifying information to aid in retrieving microrecords.

flash indexing — The process of dividing into sections of records on roll film by using a flash card as a divider tab to assist in the retrieval of microrecords.

folder — A container used to hold stored records in an orderly manner.

follow-up — Checking on the return of borrowed records within a reasonable (or specified) time.

follower block (compressor) — A device placed at the back of a file drawer that may be moved to allow for contraction or expansion of the drawer contents.

general folder — A folder that contains records to and from correspondents with a small volume so that an individual folder is not necessary.

geographic storage method — An alphabetic records storage system arranged by the locations or addresses of the correspondents, followed by their names.

guide — A rigid divider in the storage equipment that guides the eye to the location of the folder being sought.

important records — The records that assist in performing a firm's business operations and are replaceable only at great cost.

inactive record — A record that is referred to less than 15 times a year.

index record — A card record that contains information used for reference only.

indexing — The mental process of determining the filing segment by which the record is to be stored.

indexing order — The order in which units of a filing segment are considered when a record is stored.

indexing rules — Written procedures that describe how the filing segments are ordered.

indexing units — The various words that make up the filing segment.

indirect access — The procedure for storing and retrieving (accessing) a record in which an index must be referenced before a record can be stored/retrieved.

individual folder — A folder containing records of an individual correspondent.

information management database — A more complex type of database that deals with keeping track of the data in full documents.

information resource management (IRM) — A management process dedicated to establishing controls over the staff, equipment, and services that generate information.

inspecting — Checking a record for its readiness to be filed.

internal record — A record used to store information needed to operate the firm.

jacket — A transparent plastic carrier with single or multiple horizontal channels into which strips of 16mm or 35mm microfilm can be inserted; also known as a *microfilm jacket*.

job description — A summary of the content and essential requirements of a specific job.

key unit — The first unit of the filing segment.

keyword — A word or phrase that identifies a specified topic for the business.

label — A device by which the contents of a drawer, shelf, folder, or a section of records is identified.

lateral file cabinet — A cabinet with drawers that open from the long side and looks like a chest of drawers or a set of bookshelves with doors.

leading zero — A zero that is added to the front of a number so that all numbers align on the right and the computer will sort the numbers in numeric order.

lettered guide plan — A geographic storage method using guides printed with alphabetic letters—sometimes with letters and numbers—in additon to guides with location names printed on them as main divisions.

light pen — An electrical device resembling a pen that is used for writing or sketching on the display screen to provide input to the computer.

local area network (LAN) — An automated system within a firm that transmits computerized records of business operations over telephone lines within a firm under the direction of the computer and its software.

location name guide plan — A geographic storage method using location names (such as names of countries, provinces, states, counties, or cities) as the filing segments that make up the main divisions.

magnetic tape cassettes — Small containers in which magnetic tape is stored for the convenience of the dictator (word originator) and transcriptionist.

magnification ratio — The relationship between the size of a microrecord and the enlarged record on a microfilm reader screen.

mainframe — The largest type of computer, which is capable of controlling hundreds of terminals and storage devices and is commonly used in large organizations.

management — The process of using an organization's resources to achieve specific goals through the functions of planning, organizing, leading, and control.

master index — A printed alphabetic listing or a card file of all subjects used as categories for storage.

microcomputer — The computer that is smallest in size and capability and is the least expensive; also known as *personal computer (PC)*.

microfacsimile — A system that takes microfilmed records, digitizes them, and transmits them over telecommunication lines to a hard-copy fax machine; also known as *microfax*.

microfiche — A sheet of film containing a series of microrecords arranged in rows and columns; usually shortened to *fiche*.

microfilm cartridges — Convenient packages for rolls of microfilm that permit automatic threading of the film into the viewer.

microfilm cassettes — Microfilm containers that include two film reels (the feed and the take-up) that eliminate the need for rewinding the cassette when it is removed from the viewer.

microfilming — The process of photographing documents and reducing them in size to create microimages of records.

microforms — The manner in which microfilmed records are packaged, such as roll film, microfiche, microfilm jackets, and aperture cards.

micrographics — The full range of services for creating, storing, retrieving, using, and protecting microrecords.

microimage system — A combination of key elements that form an efficient unit for using records in microform.

microimages — Very small records stored on microfilm; also known as *microrecords*.

micropublishing — The process of substituting microfilm for paper publications.

middle-digit storage — A numeric storage method in which the middle numbers are considered first.

minicomputer — A computer that provides less processing and operating power than a mainframe and is used in smaller firms or within departments of large organizations.

mnemonic code — A code that assists memory. The code may be alphabetic, numeric, or a combination. The placement of the letters and/or digits are consistent and have specific meanings.

mobile aisle system — Electrically powered mobile shelving that can be moved to create an aisle between any two shelf units.

mobile shelving — Records storage shelves that move on tracks attached to the floor.

motorized rotary storage — A motorized file unit that rotates around a central hub.

name index — A special listing of correspondents' names used with subject filing.

networking — The process of linking together a series of varied information systems activities including the transmission of records.

nonconsecutive numbering — A system of numbers that either has no logical sequence or has a logical sequence from which blocks of numbers have been omitted.

nonessential records — The least valuable records that should be destroyed after use.

numeric index — A current list of all files by the file number.

numeric storage method — A numeric storage method wherein records are assigned numbers and then stored in one of various numeric sequences.

offline storage — The storage equipment that is not directly connected to the computer.

on-call (wanted) form — A written request for a record that is out of the file.

one-period transfer method — A method of transferring records at the end of one period of time, usually once or twice a year.

online storage — The storage equipment that is directly connected to the computer.

operating system — The link between the computer hardware, the user, and the application software.

optical digital data disk — An information storage medium in which a laser beam burns or etches holes to form a dot pattern of the letters, numbers, lines, and drawings as it copies from the original onto the disk; usually shortened to *optical disk*.

optical-character recognition (OCR) equipment— A type of scanning device that eliminates the need for human operators to manually keyboard data into a computer.

OUT folder — A special folder that replaces a folder that has been removed from storage.

OUT guide — A special guide that replaces records that have been removed from storage.

OUT sheet — A form that is inserted in place of a record or records removed from a folder.

parity bit — A binary digit used to check the accuracy of the completed electrical circuits.

periodic transfer method — A method of transferring active records at the end of a stated period, usually one year, to inactive storage.

permanent cross-reference — A guide that is put in place of an individual folder to direct the filer to the correct storage place.

perpetual transfer method — A method of transferring records continuously from active to inactive storage areas whenever they are no longer needed for reference.

planetary camera— A camera using 35mm film to microfilm oversize engineering drawings and other large documents placed upon a plane (flat) surface.

pocket folder — A folder with more expansion along its bottom edge than that of an ordinary folder.

position — The location of the tab on the edge of a guide or folder.

posted record — A record containing information that is continually updated; also known as a *secondary record*.

primary guide — A main division of the storage method that precedes all the other material in a section of a file.

quality standard — A measure of how good or how bad the work or the worker's performance is.

quantity standard — A measure that involves counting the number of resources used in factory and office operations and comparing them with standards of resource use.

reader — A device that displays the enlarged microimage on a screen so that the record can be read; also called a *viewer*.

record — Recorded information, regardless of media or characteristics, made or received by, and used in the operation of, an organization.

record life cycle— The life span of a record with five functional phases that occur from the creation of a record to its final disposition.

recorder— A special tape-to-film photographic device used to convert computer output stored in digital form to a microimage on 105mm roll film or microfiche.

records audit — A regular examination of the records management program to determine how well the program is functioning.

records inventory — A survey used to find the types and volumes of records on file as well as their location and frequency of use.

records management — The systematic control of all records from their creation, or receipt, through their processing, distribution, organization, storage, and retrieval to their ultimate disposition.

records management database — An index of stored records.

records management manual — The official handbook of approved policies and procedures for operating the records management programs.

records retention schedule — A listing of an organization's records along with the stated length of time the records must be kept.

records system — A group of interrelated resources—people, equipment and supplies, space, procedures, and information—acting according to a plan to accomplish the goals of the records management program.

records transfer — The physical movement of active records to inactive storage areas.

reduction ratio — The size of a microimage as compared to the original document.

reference documents — Records that contain information needed to carry on the operations of the firm over long periods of time.

relative index — A dictionary-type listing of all words and combinations of words by which records may be requested.

release mark — An agreed-upon mark placed on a record showing that the record is ready for storage.

reprographics — The personnel, equipment, and procedures involved in copymaking.

requisition — A written request for a record or for information from a record.

resolution — A microfilm term that refers to the sharpness of lines or fine detail on a microrecord.

retrieval — The process of searching for and finding records and/or information.

retrieval efficiency ratio — A measure of the speed with which records are found and a verification of how files personnel spend their time.

roll film — A length of microfilm containing a series of images much like movie film.

rotary (wheel) equipment — Filing equipment in which the card records are attached to a frame that rotates on an axis like a wheel.

rotary camera — A microfilming camera using rotating belts to carry documents through the camera and make images on 16mm film.

rough sorting — Arranging records according to sections but in random order within the sections.

service bureau — A private firm that specializes in the storage and preservation of microrecords.

shelf files — Shelves arranged horizontally for storing records.

signals — Special markers used for drawing immediate attention to specific records.

sorter — A device used to hold records temporarily which serves to separate the records into alphabetic or numeric categories to be stored later.

sorting — The act of arranging records in a predetermined sequence according to the storage method used as an aid to final filing.

special (auxiliary) guide — A guide that leads the eye to a specific place in the file.

special folder — A folder that follows special or auxiliary guides in an alphabetic arrangement.

special records — Records of unconventional size, shape, or weight commonly used in business and professional offices.

standard — A measure or yardstick by which the performance of a system is rated.

step and repeat camera — A camera used to film microfiche in which images are directly photographed onto 4-inch film.

storage (filing) method — A systematic way of storing records according to an alphabetic, subject, numeric, geographic, or chronologic arrangement.

storage — The actual placement of materials into a folder, on a section of magnetic disk, or on a shelf, according to a plan.

storage procedures — A series of steps for the orderly arrangement of records as required by a specific storage method. The steps are: inspecting, indexing, coding, cross-referencing, sorting, and storing.

storing — The actual placement of records in containers.

straight dictionary arrangement — A method of storing subject folders in correct A to Z order.

subject records storage method — A method of storing records by subject matter or by topic.

subsystem — A lower level of system.

suspension (hanging) folder — A folder with built-in hooks that hang from the parallel bars on the sides of the storage equipment.

system — A set of related elements that are combined to achieve a planned objective or goal.

system (as used in records storage) — any storage plan devised by a storage equipment manufacturer.

tab — The portion of a folder or guide that extends above the regular height or beyond the regular width of the folder or guide.

technology — The machines (hardware) and procedures and programs (software) needed to operate records systems.

telecommunication system — A computer connected to a telephone system allowing records to be sent within a firm or to all parts of the world.

terminal-digit storage — A numeric storage method in which groups of numbers are read from right to left.

tickler file — A chronologic arrangement of information that "tickles" the memory by serving as a reminder that specific action must be taken on a specific date.

transaction documents — Records of a firm's day-to-day operations.

turnaround time — The amount of time required to find and deliver a record to the requester after the request for the record has been made.

unit record — A record that stores one main item or piece of information on a card.

unitized microform — A microform containing one unit of information.

updatable microfiche camera — A modification of the step and repeat camera that permits the addition of records to a microfiche.

useful records — Records that are helpful in conducting business operations and that may, if destroyed, be replaced at slight cost.

variable date — Data that change each time a form is filled in.

vertical card file — A collection of card records stored on edge or in an upright position; also known as a *vertical file*.

vertical file cabinet — A conventional storage cabinet in one- to five-drawer sizes.

visible card file — A collection of card records stored in an overlapping arrangement in which the bottom margin of each card is visible when the tray in which the card is held is pulled out from the file cabinet; also known as a *visible file*.

vital records — Records that must be kept permanently because they are needed for continuing the operations of a firm and are usually not replaceable.

voice mail — One-way voice messages stored in the computer mailbox and reconverted to the caller's voice when messages are delivered by means of the computer.

voice-recognition system — A form of computer input that "understands" the human voice as input to the computer.

voucher — An accounting record used to confirm that a business transaction has occurred.

wide-area network (WAN) — A telecommunication network outside the firm for carrying messages all over the world.

word processing system — A combination of people, equipment, and procedures for changing the words originated by a person into a final product and forwarding it to a user.

INDEX